Good-bye, Chunky Rice

CRAIG THOMPSON
TOP SHELF PRODUCTIONS
marietta, Georgia

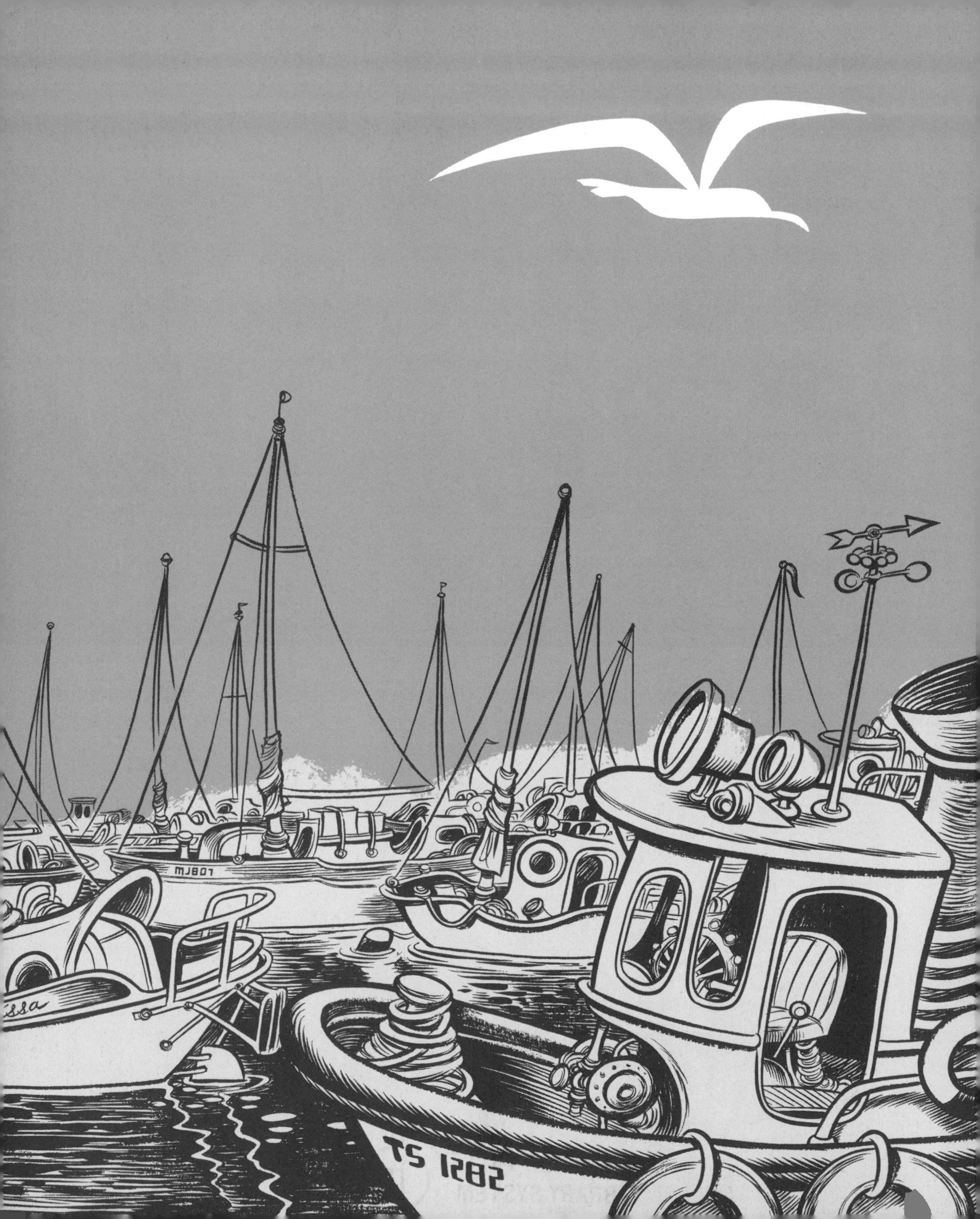
MJ801

1. 2. 3. 4. 5.

— 4th PRINTING —

GOOD-BYE, CHUNKY RICE, May of 2003. Fourth Printing. ©Copyright 2003, 2002, 2001, 1999 Craig Thompson. edited by Chris Staros. Published by Top Shelf Productions Inc., Brett Warnock and Chris Staros, PO BOX 1282, Marietta, GA 30061-1282. Top Shelf Productions and the Top Shelf Logo are TM & ©1999, 2002 Top Shelf Productions Inc. The Stories, characters and incidents featured in this publication are entirely fictional. No part of this book may be reproduced without permission, except small excerpts for purposes of Review. Write for a free catalog or visit <www.topshelfcomix.com>

THOMPSON, CRAIG · GOOD-BYE, CHUNKY RICE / CRAIG THOMPSON · ISBN 1-891830-09-0
1. GRAPHIC NOVELS · 2. CARTOONS · PRINTED IN CANADA

This book is dedicated to all of my friends in Milwaukee, WI.

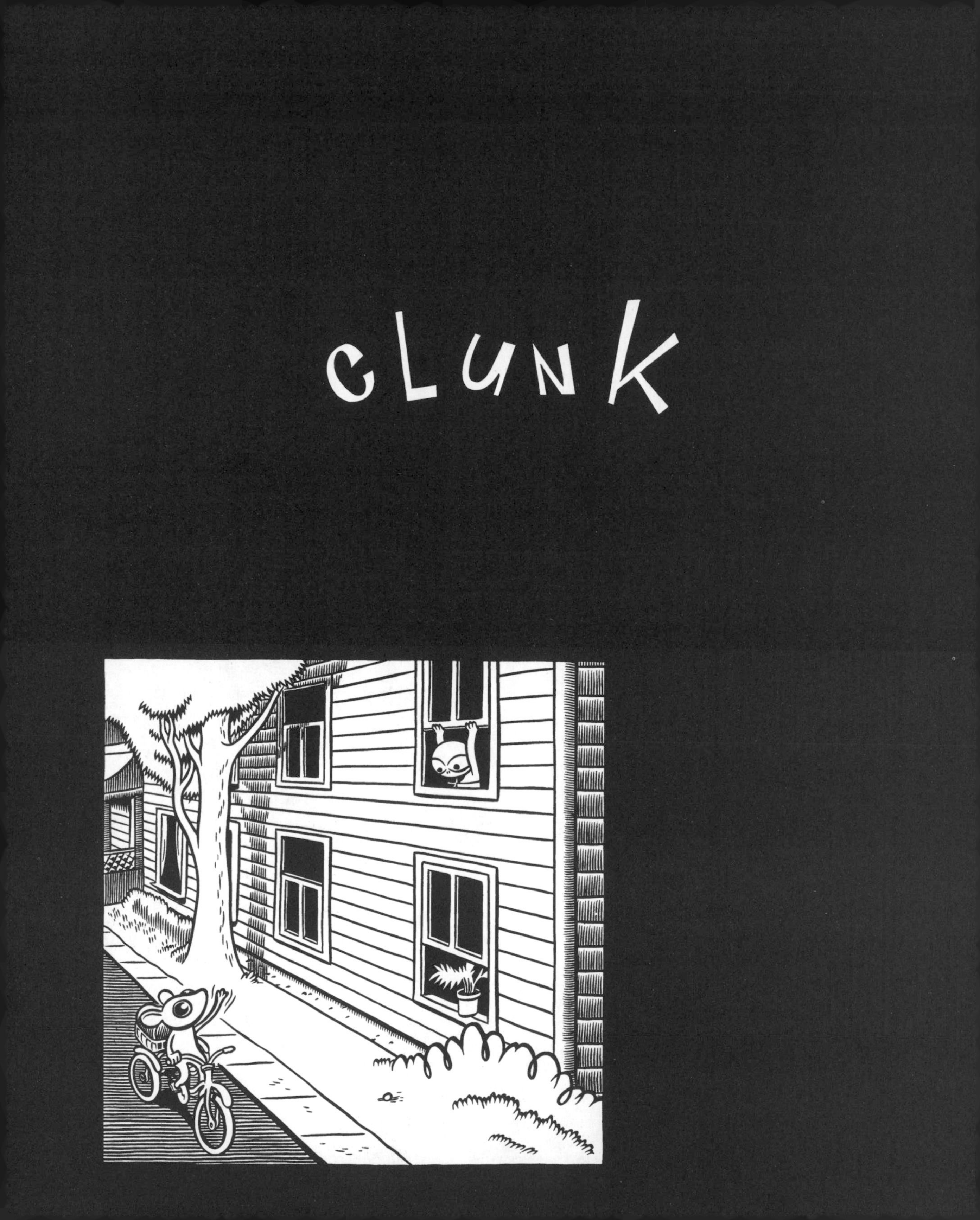
CLUNK

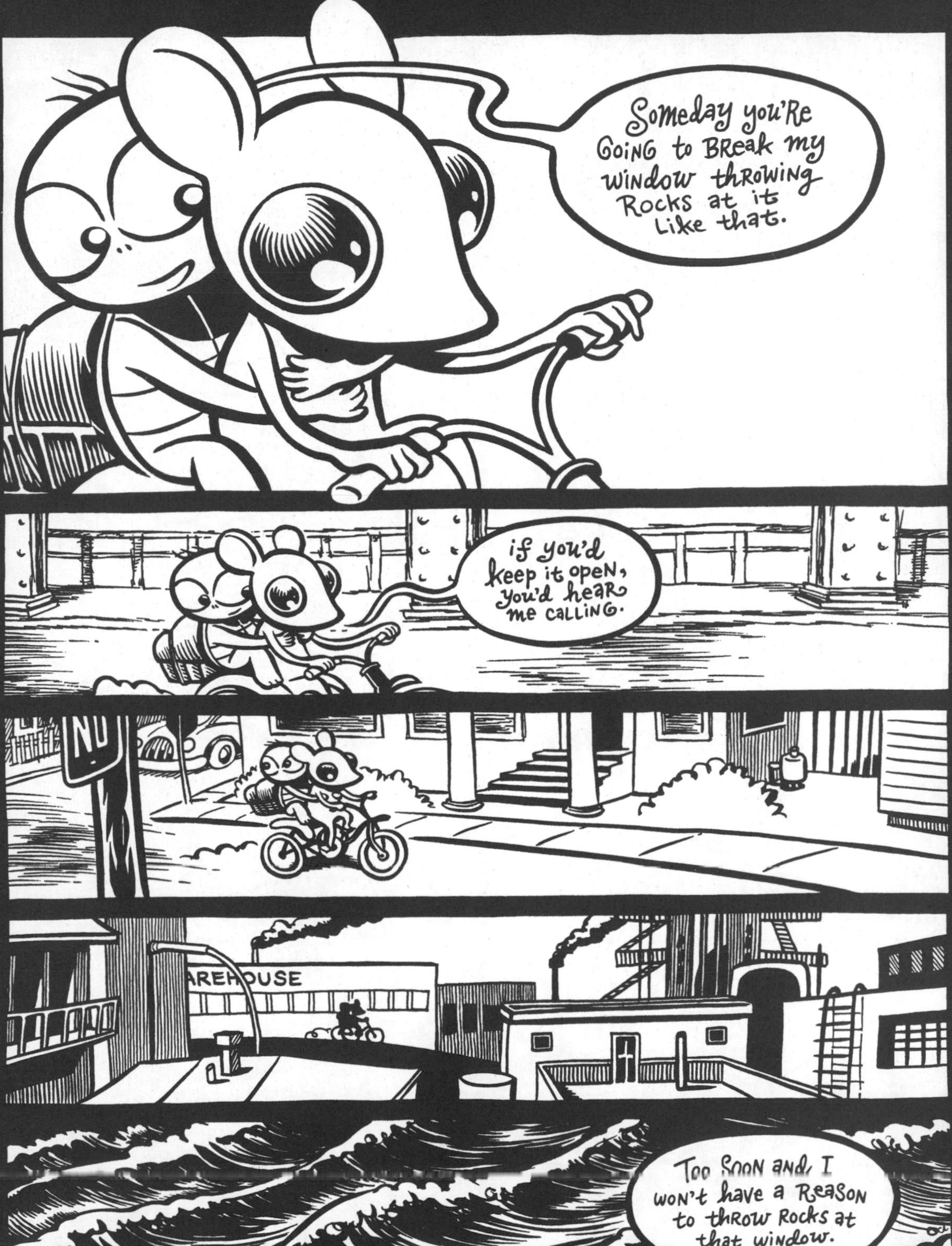
Someday you're going to break my window throwing rocks at it like that.
if you'd keep it open, you'd hear me calling.
Too soon and I won't have a reason to throw rocks at that window.

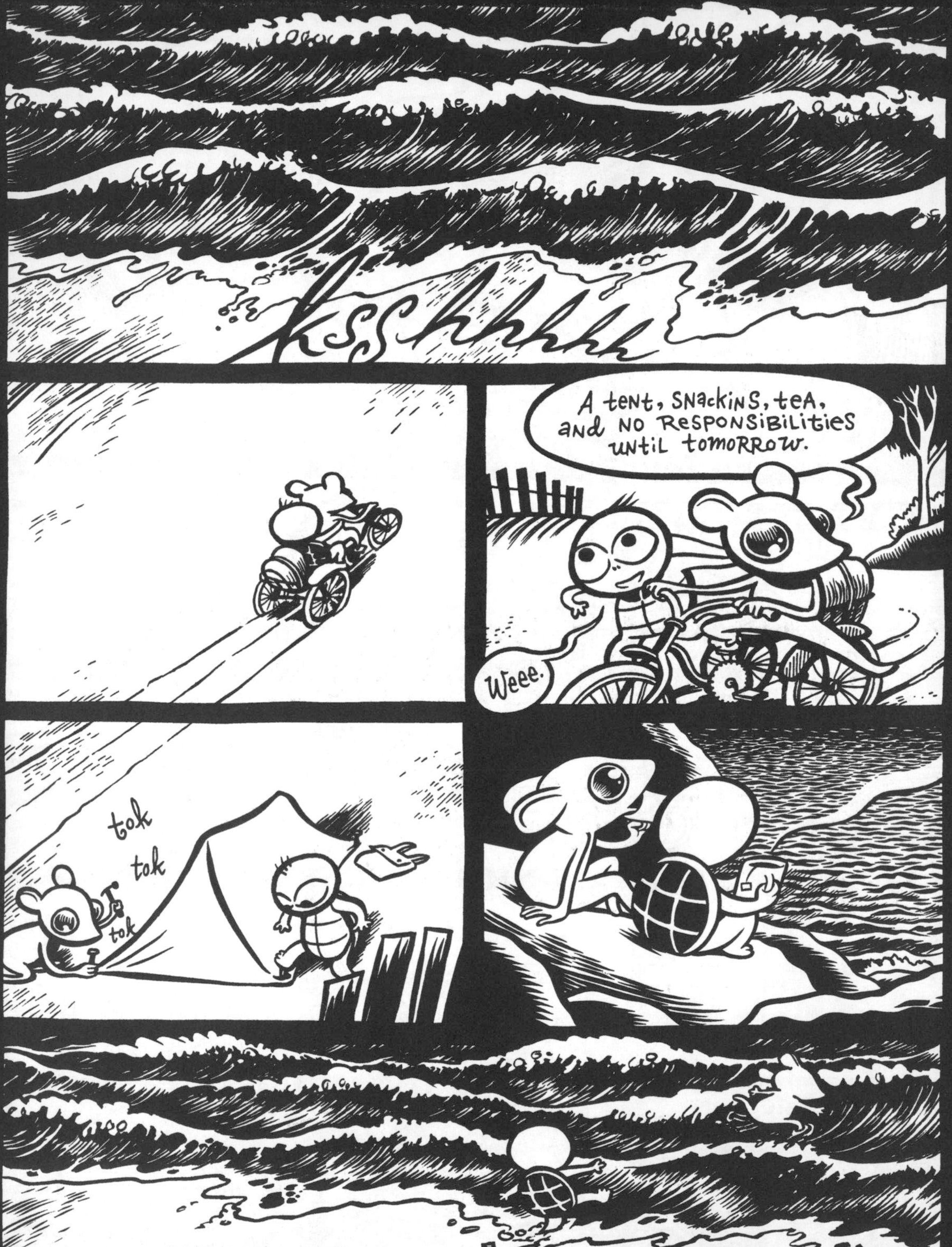
ksshhhhh
A tent, snackins, tea, and no responsibilities until tomorrow.
Weee.
tok tok tok

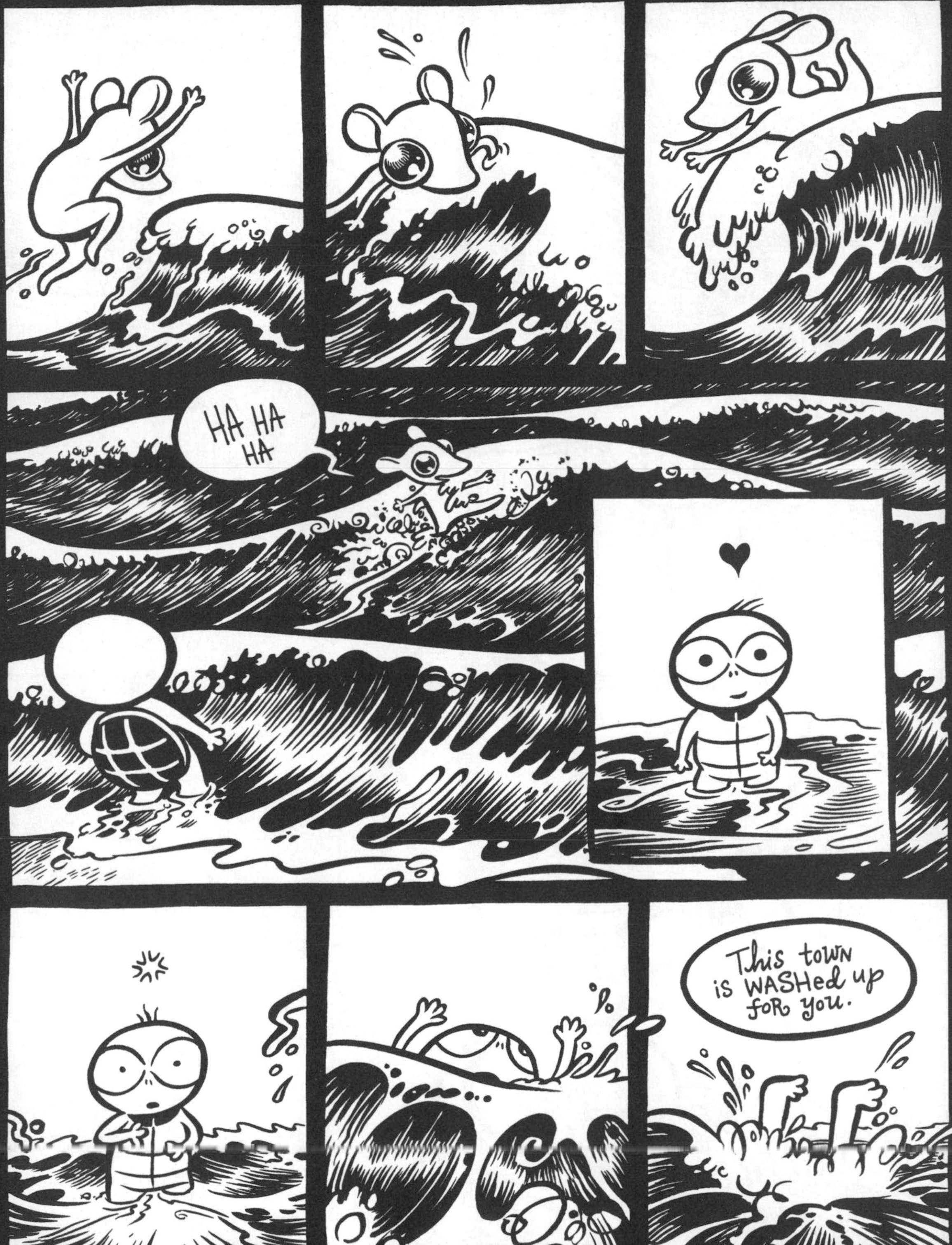
HA HA HA
This town is WASHed up for you.

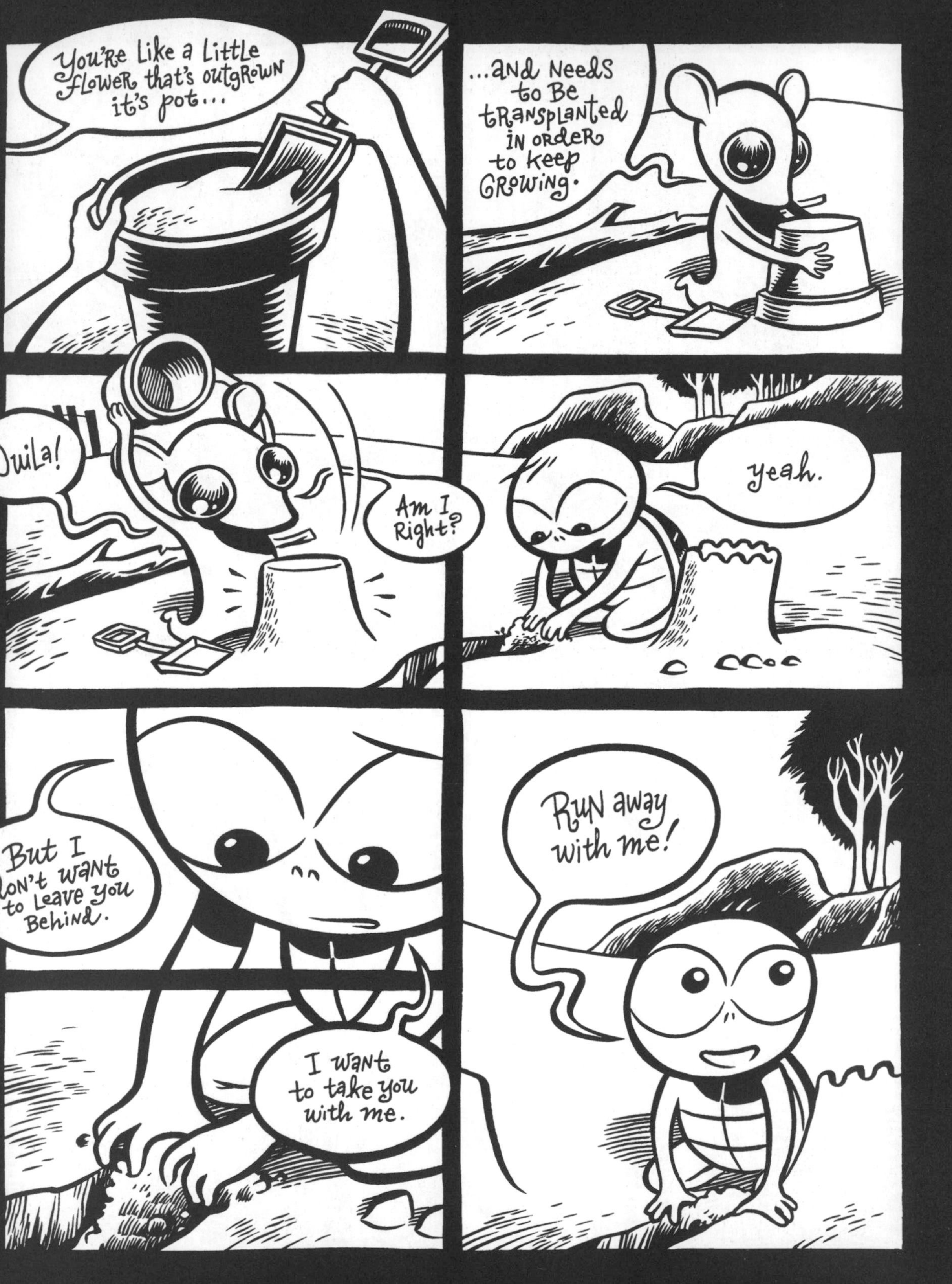
You're like a little flower that's outgrown it's pot...
...and needs to be transplanted in order to keep growing.
Ouila!
Am I Right?
yeah.
But I don't want to leave you behind.
I want to take you with me.
Run away with me!

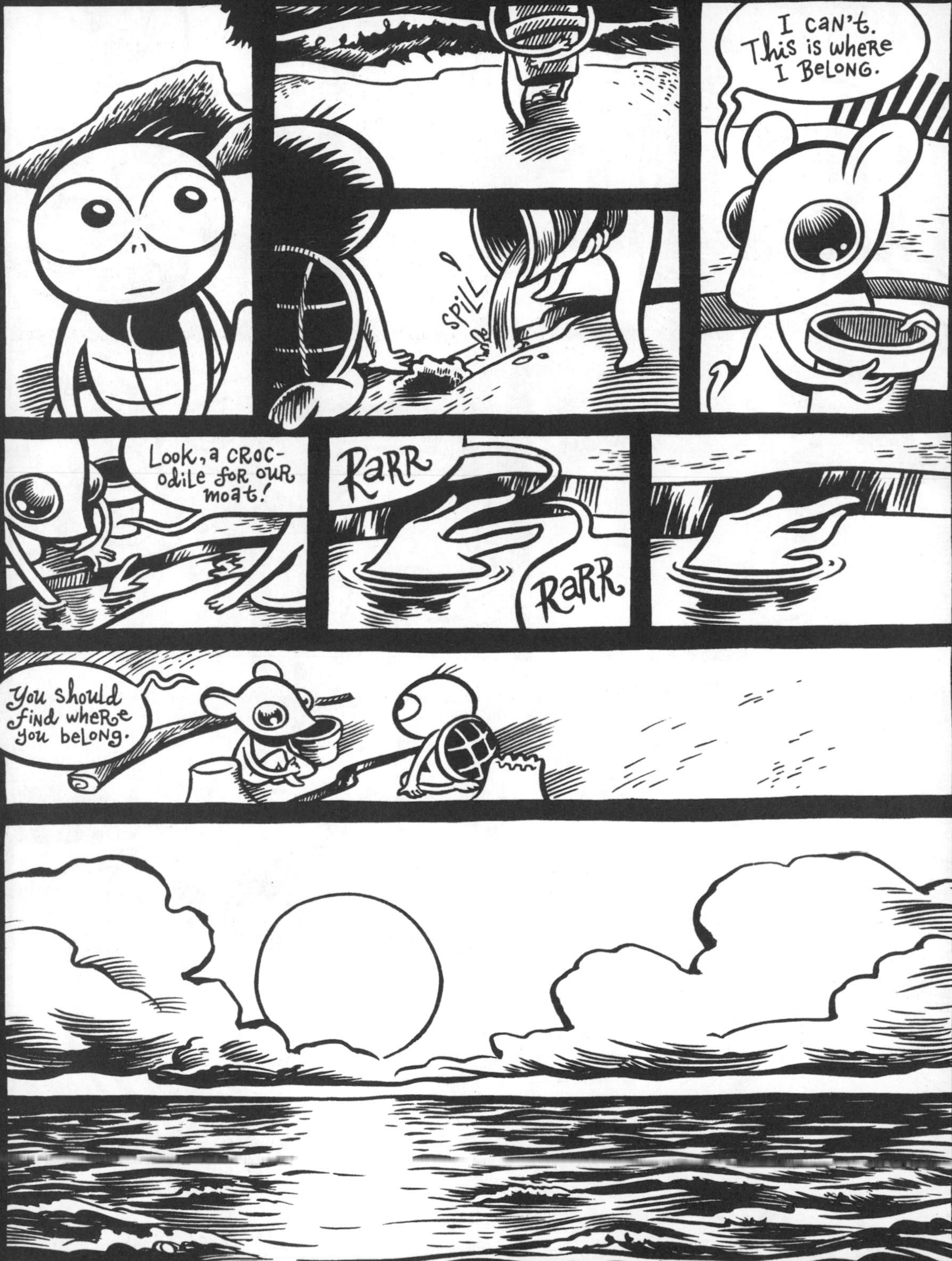
SPILL
I can't. This is where I belong.
Look, a croc-odile for our moat!
RARR
RARR
You should find where you belong.

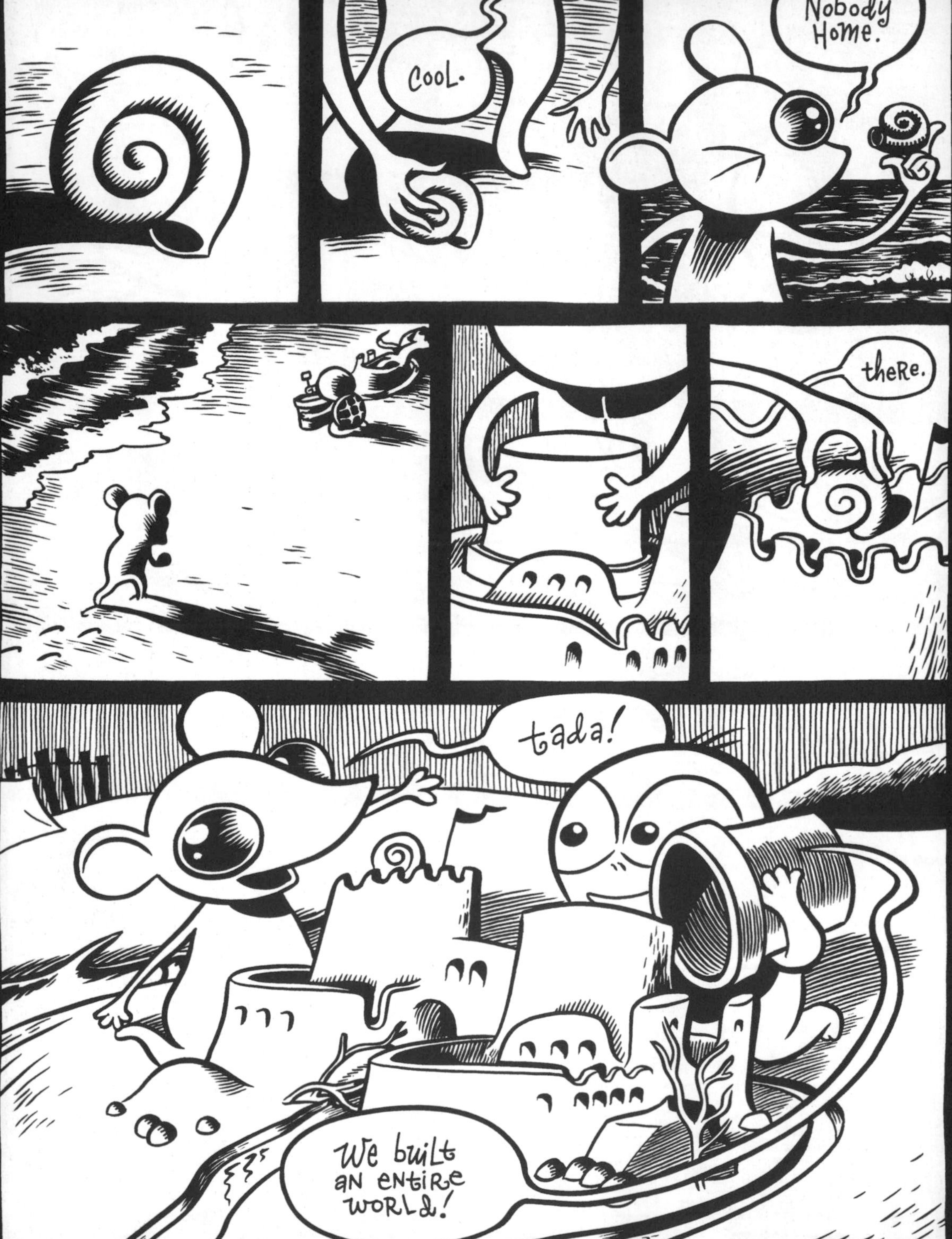
cool.
Nobody Home.
there.
tada!
We built an entire world!

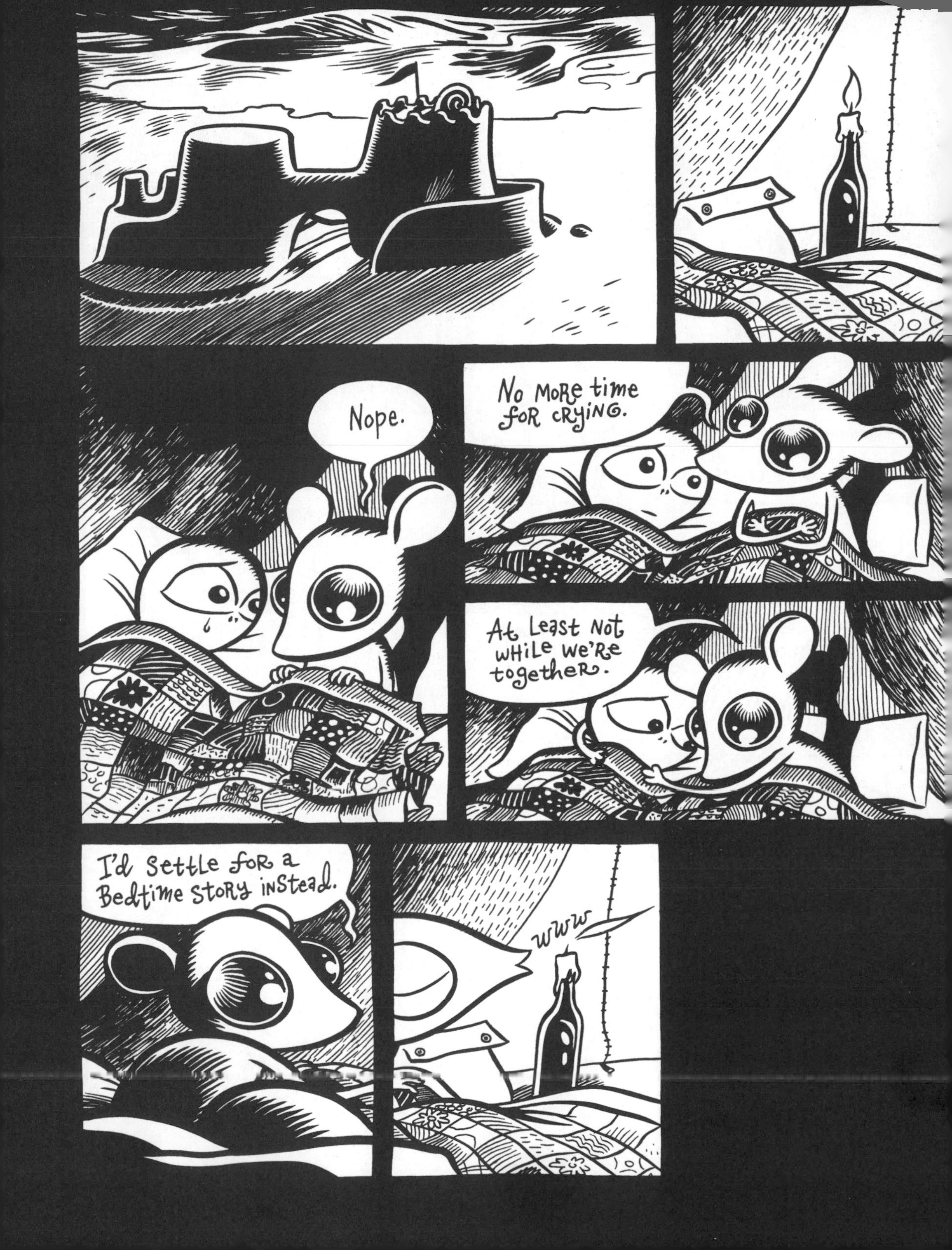
Nope.
No more time for crying.
At least not while we're together.
I'd settle for a bedtime story instead.
WWW

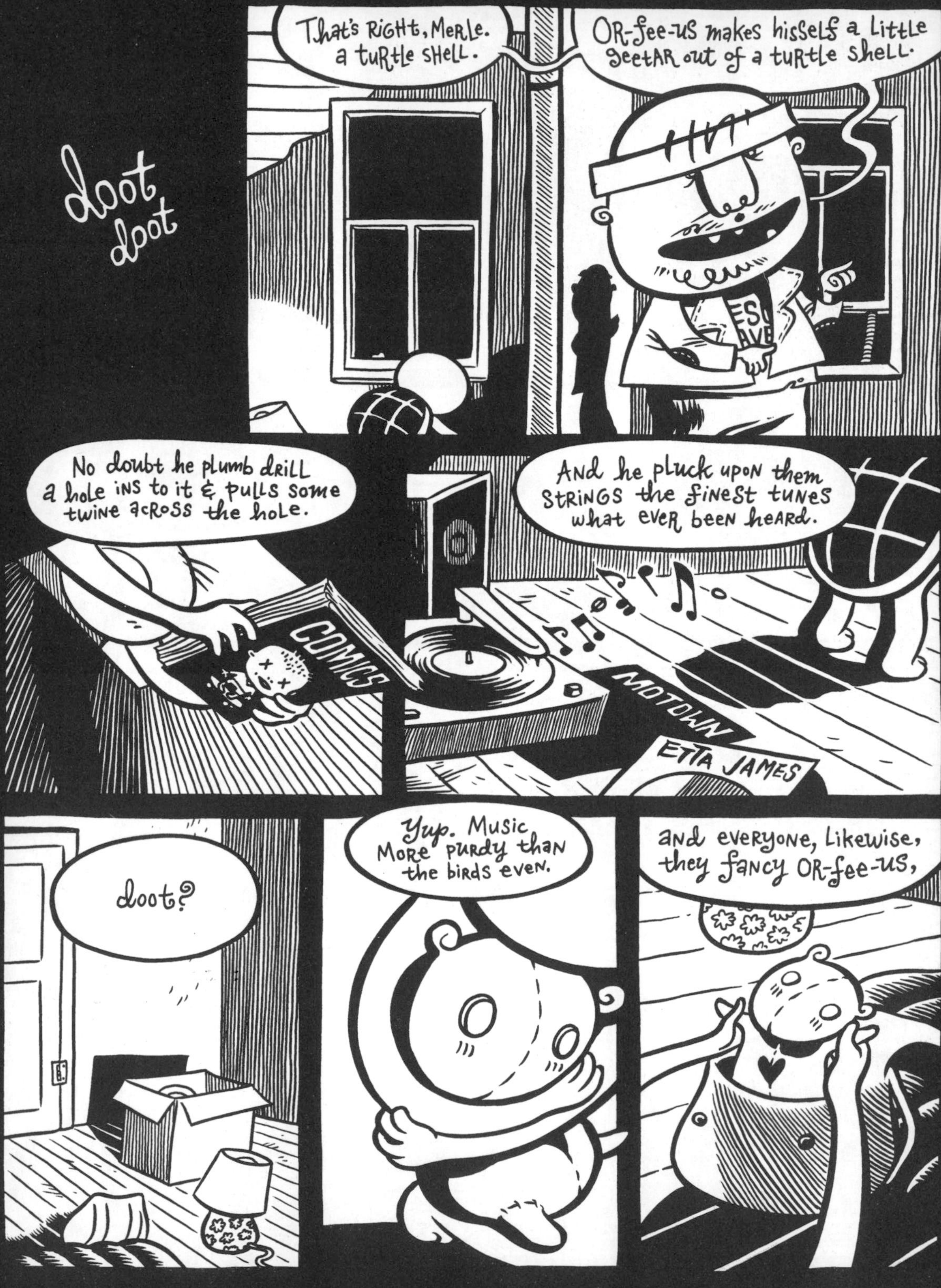
doot doot
That's RIGHT, MeRLe. a tuRtle SHeLL.
OR-fee-us makes hisself a Little geetAR out of a tuRtLe SheLL.
ESQ AVE
No doubt he plumb dRiLL a hole iNS to it & PuLLS some twiNe acRoss the hole.
COMICS
And he pluck upoN them StRiNGS the finest tuNes what eveR been heard.
MOTOWN
ETTA JAMES
doot?
Yup. Music More purdy than the birds even.
and everyone, Likewise, they fancy OR-fee-us,

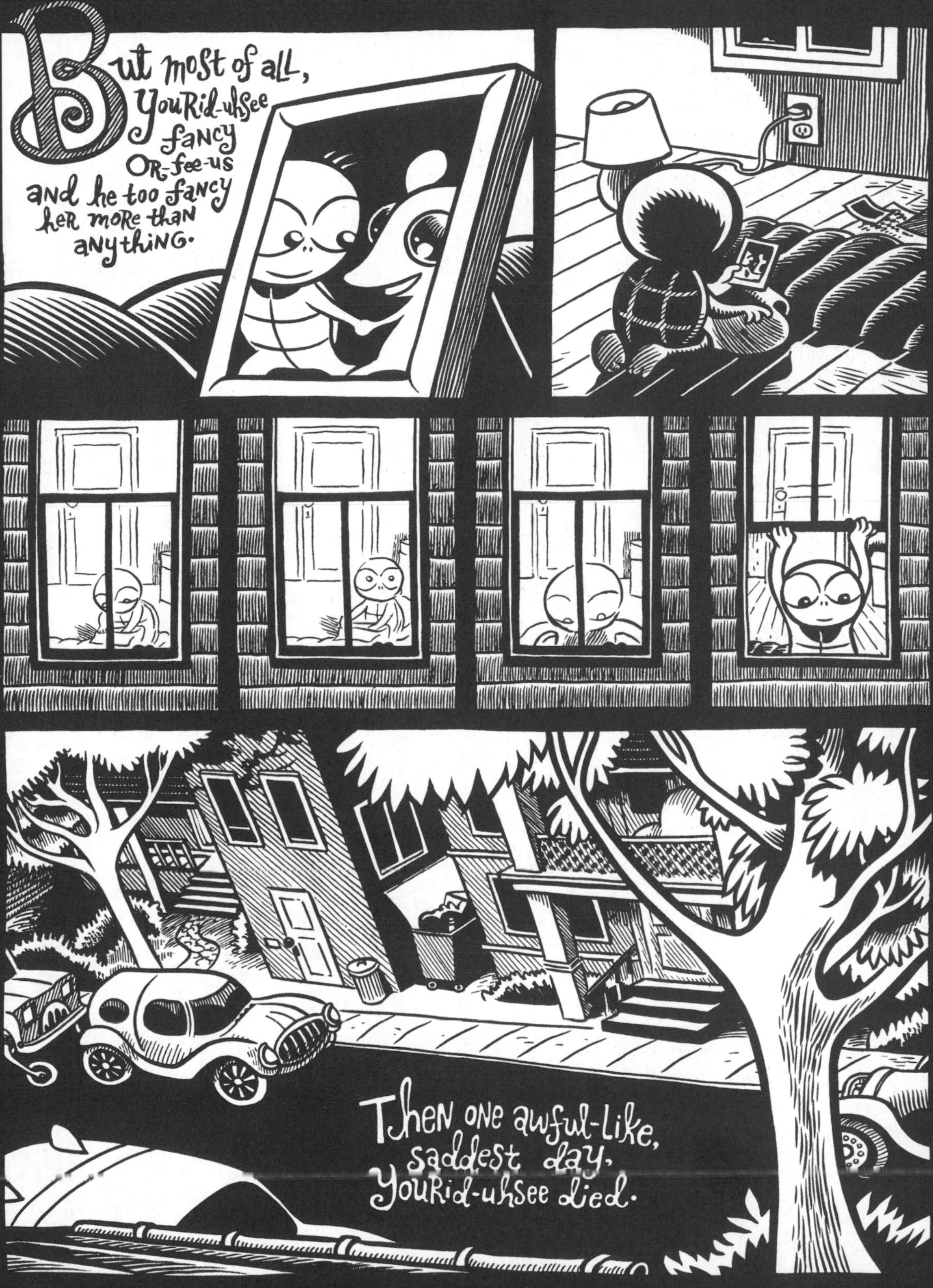
But most of all, YouRid-uhsee fancy OR-fee-us and he too fancy her more than anything.
Then one awful-like, saddest day, YouRid-uhsee died.

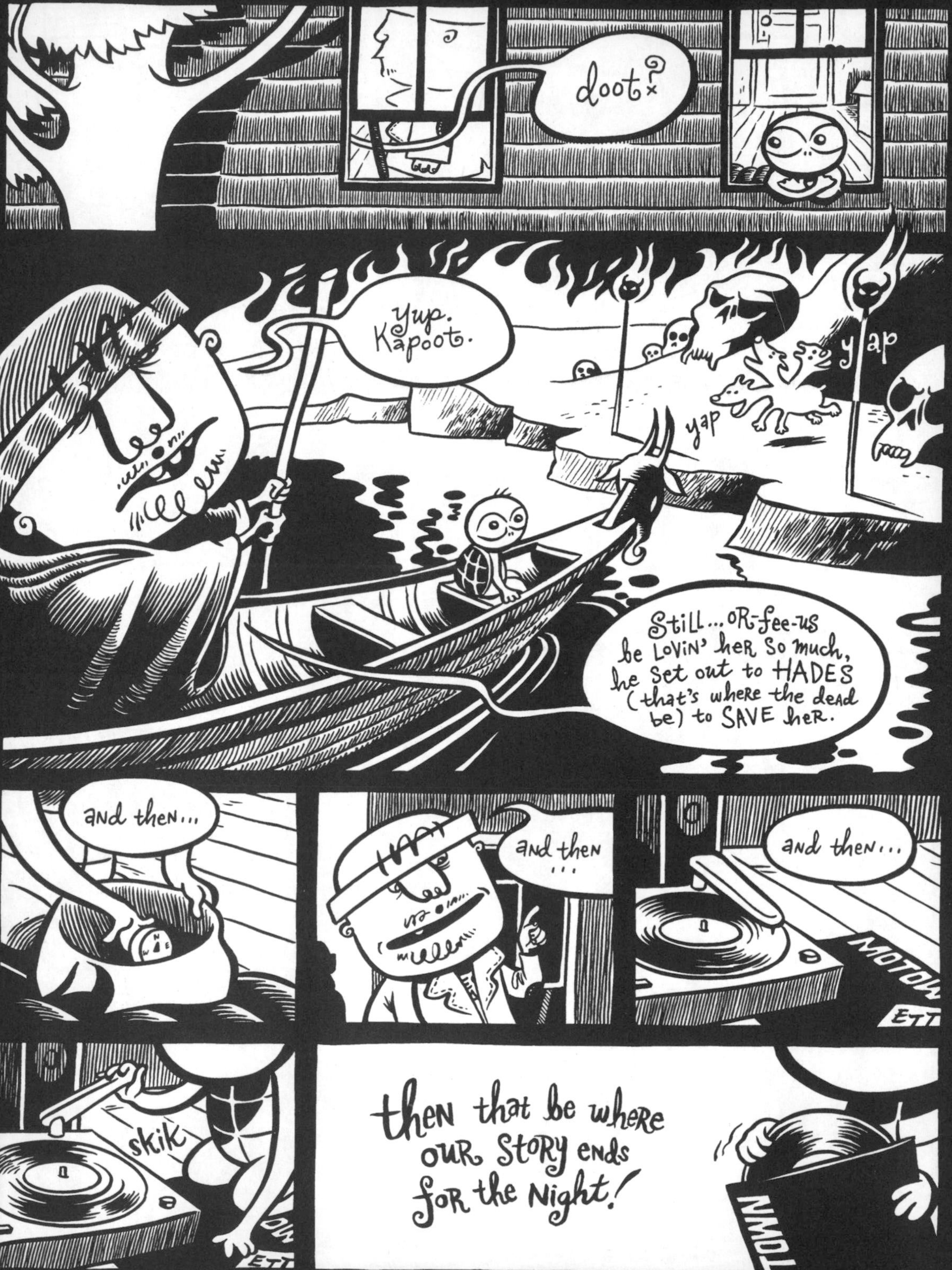
doot?
yup. Kapoot.
yap
yap
Still... OR-fee-us be LOVIN' heR so much, he set out to HADES (that's where the dead be) to SAVE heR.
and then...
and then ...
and then...
MOTOW
skik
then that be where OUR STORY ends for the Night!
TOWN

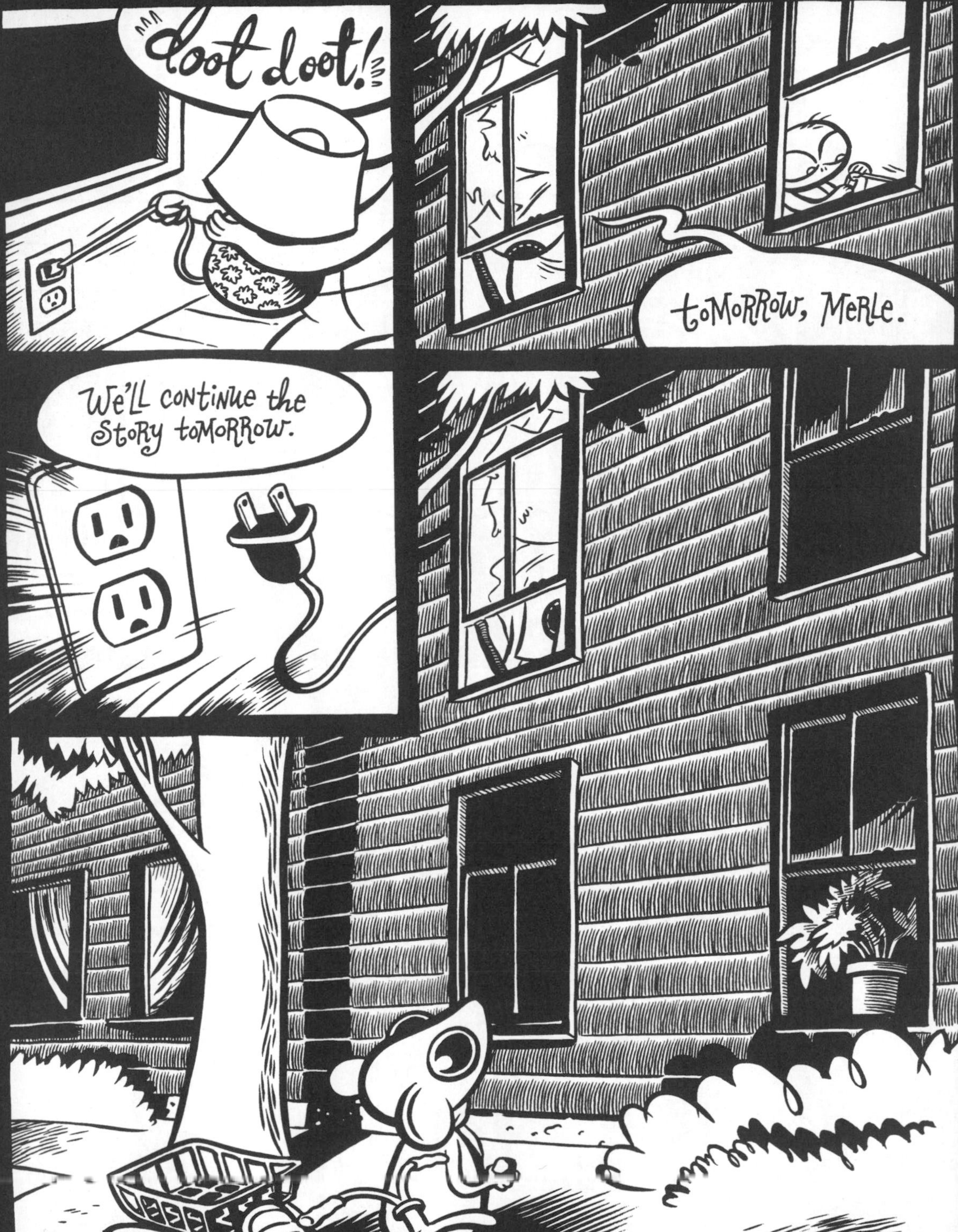
doot doot!
tomorrow, Merle.
We'll continue the story tomorrow.

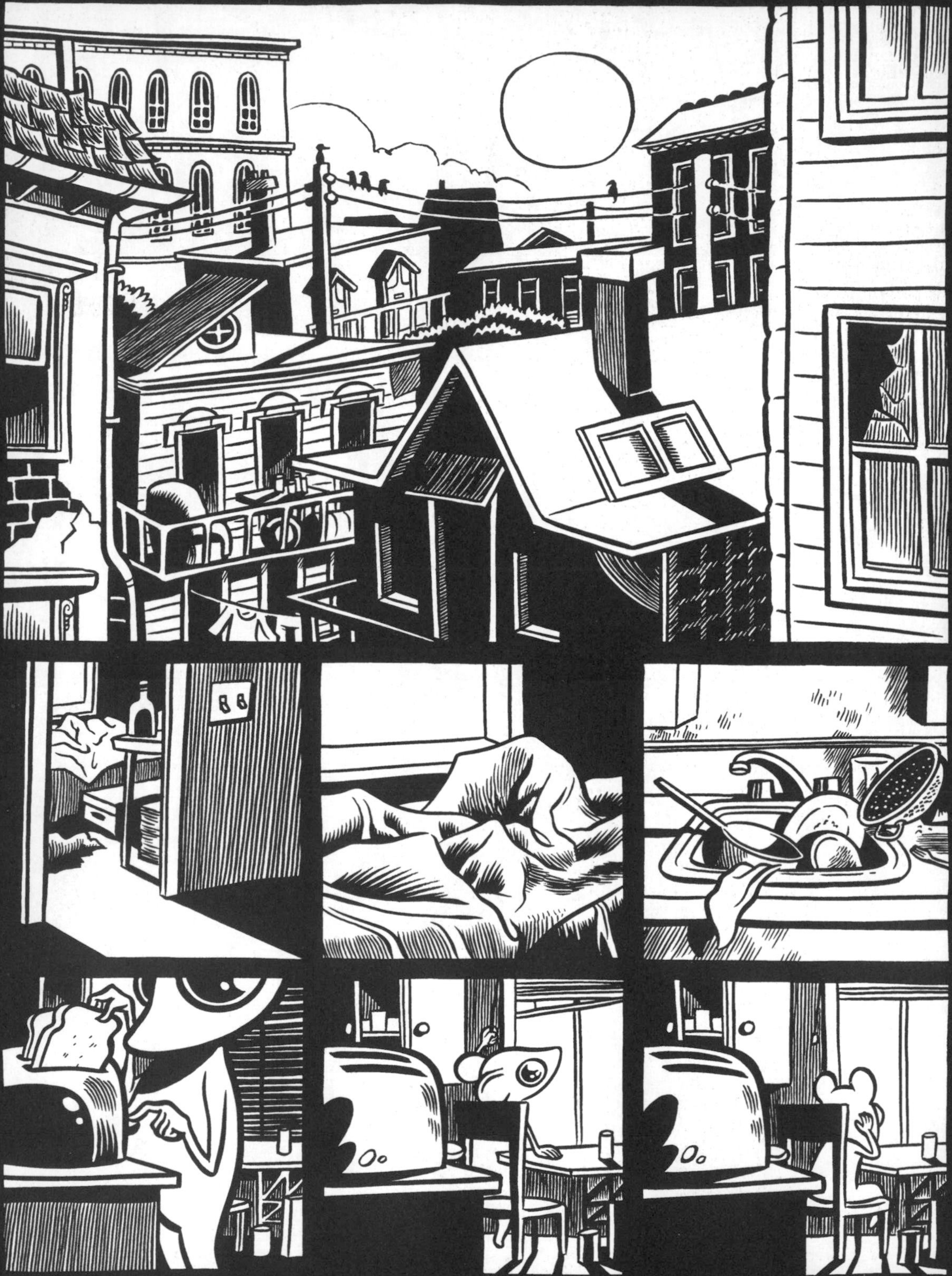

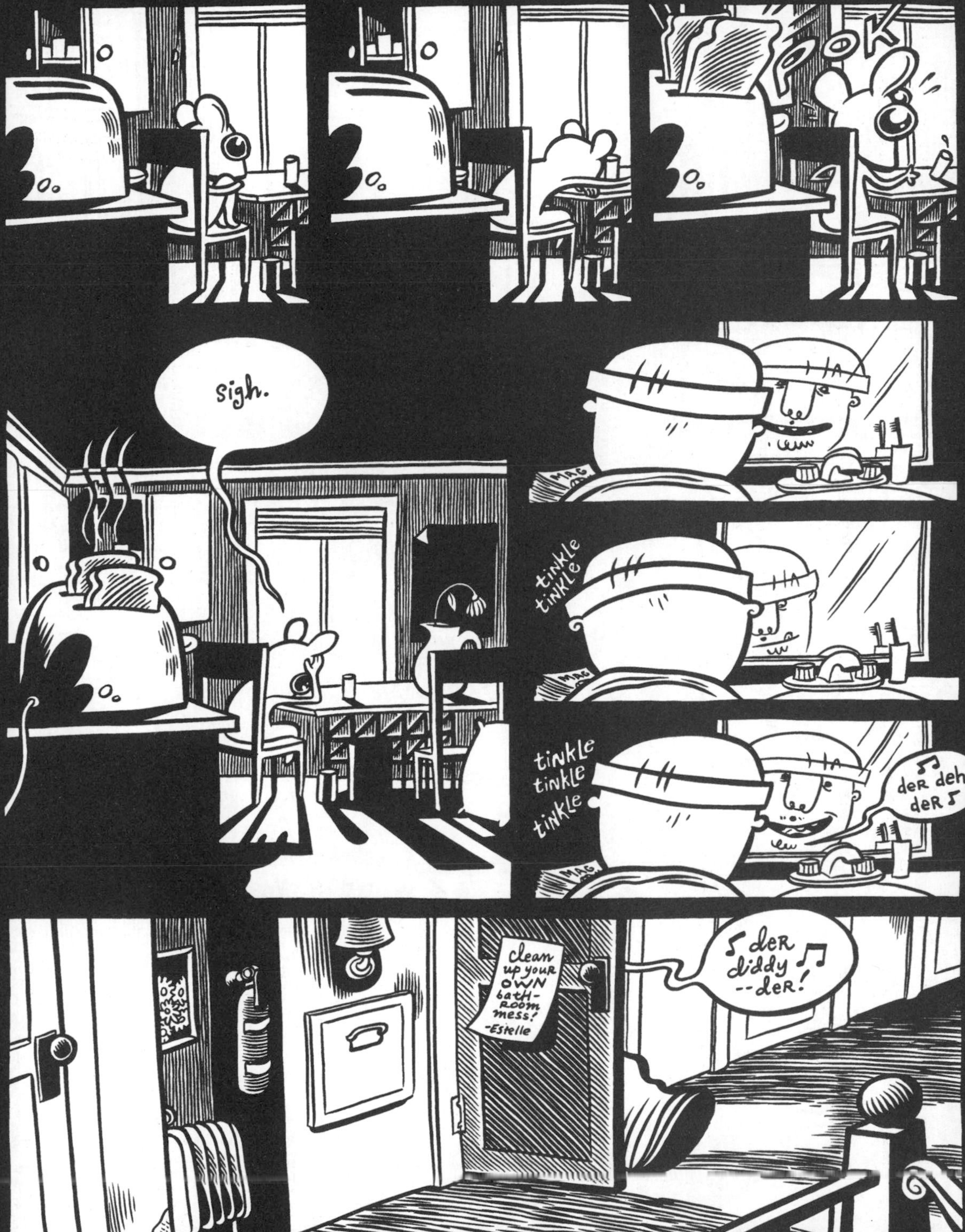
POK
sigh.
tinkle tinkle
tinkle tinkle tinkle
der deh der
clean up your OWN bath-room mess! -Estelle
der diddy --der!

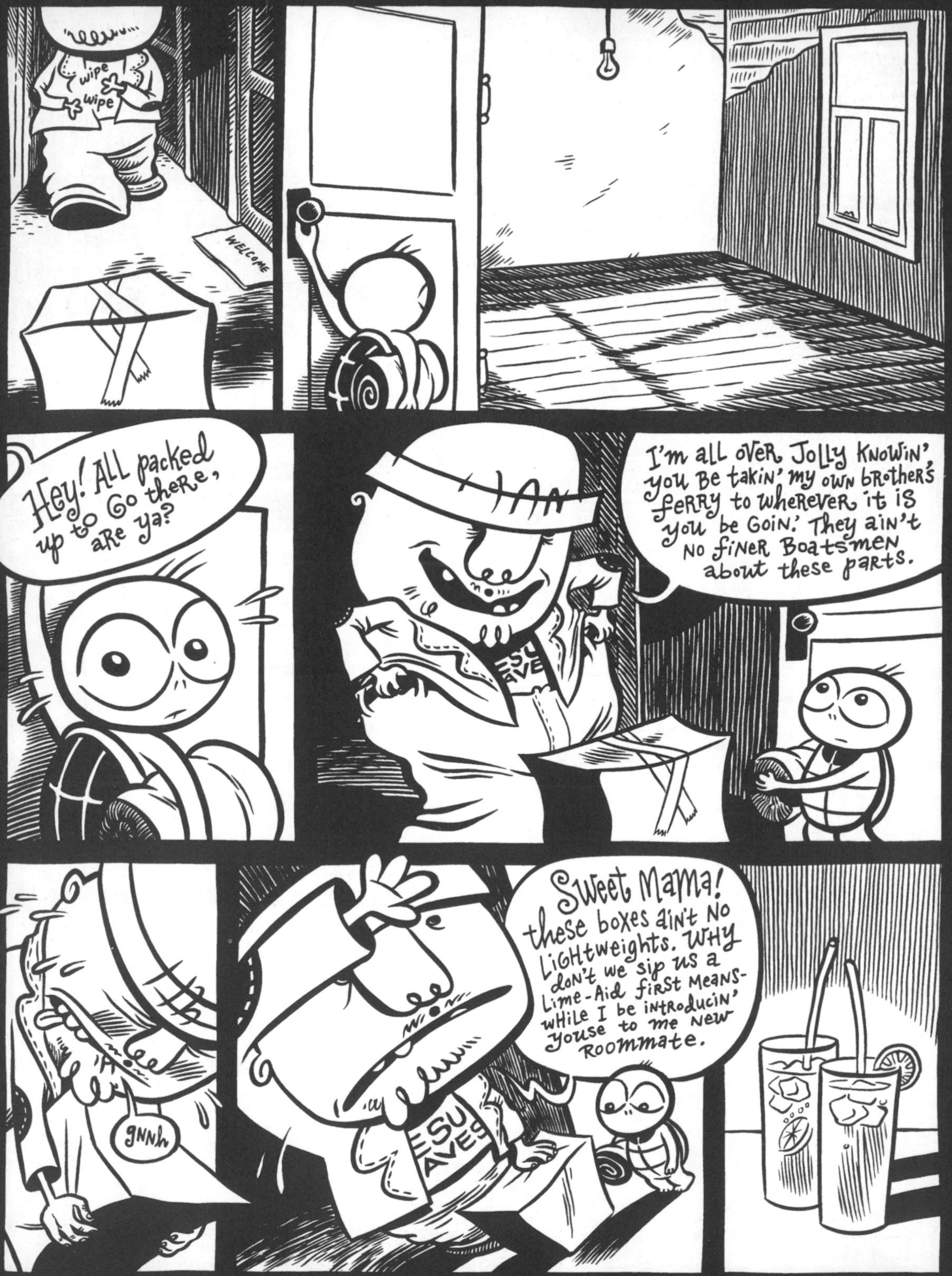
wipe
wipe
WELCOME
Hey! All packed up to Go there, are ya?
I'm all over Jolly knowin' you be takin' my own brother's ferry to wherever it is you be Goin.' They ain't no finer Boatsmen about these parts.
gnnh
Sweet Mama! these boxes ain't No Lightweights. WHY don't we sip us a Lime-Aid first Means-while I be introducin' youse to me New Roommate.

doot doot
MERLE. That's his NAME. I found him.
Li'L Birdie WiNGS PLUMB BeeN CHEWED off by SOMe NASTY PREDATOR NOt UNLiKeLY.
Cute, ain't he?
Go ahead. He AiN't BitiN'
Heh Heh

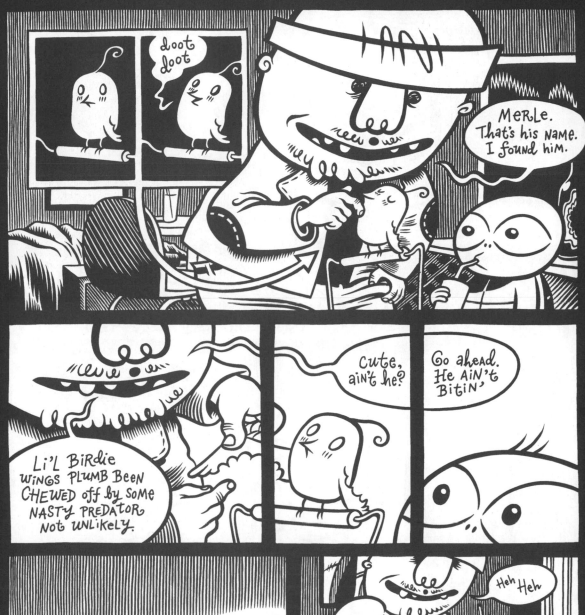

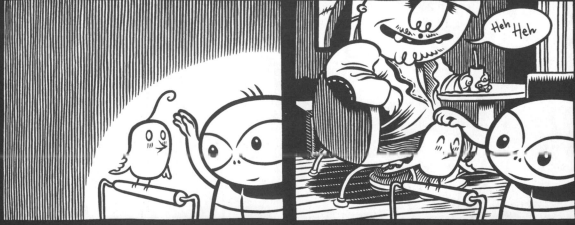

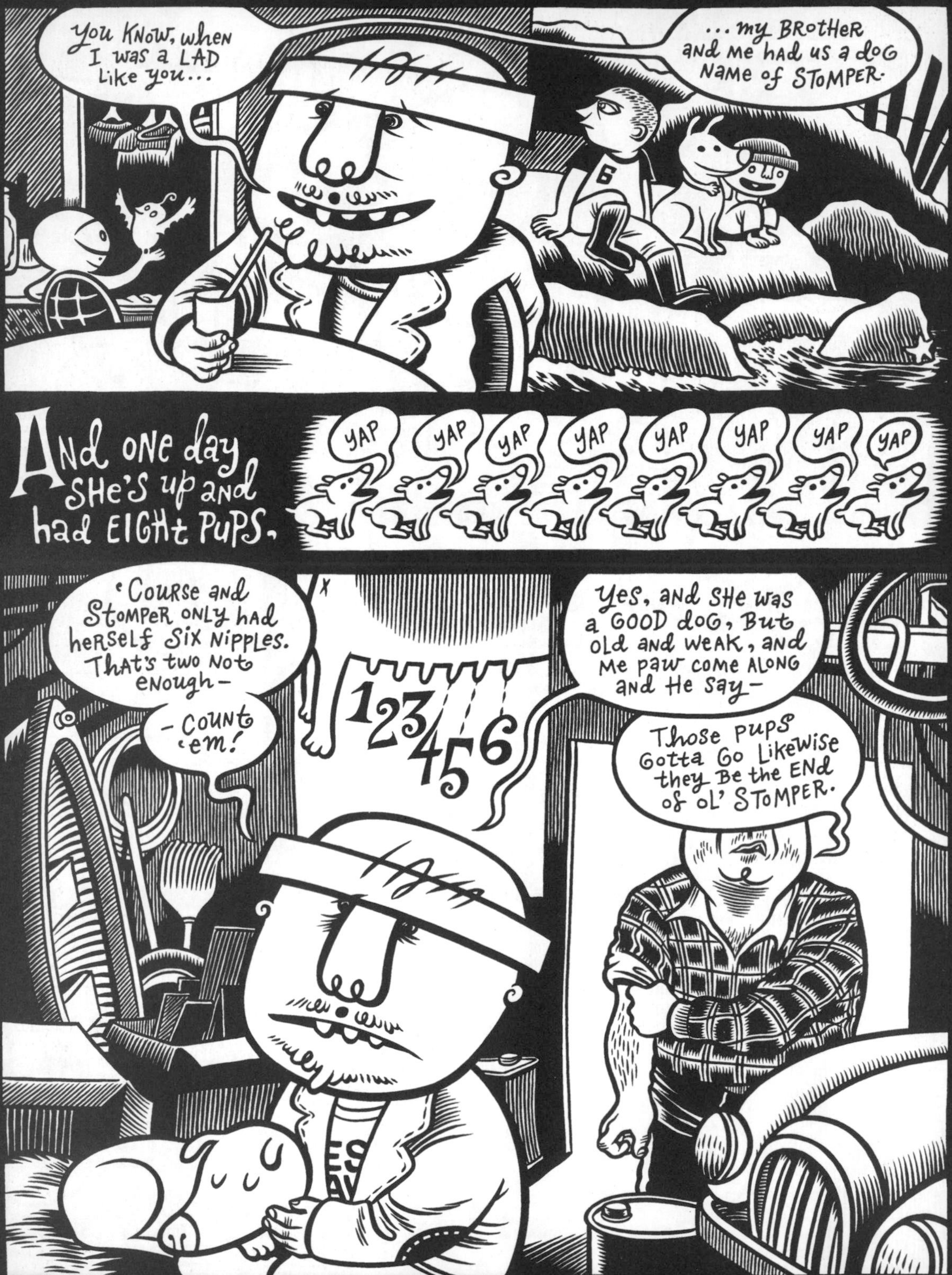

You KNOW, when I was a LAD Like you...
... my BROTHER and me had us a doG Name of STOMPER.
And one day she's up and had EIGHT PUPS.
YAP YAP YAP YAP YAP YAP YAP YAP
'Course and Stomper ONLY had herself Six Nipples. That's two Not enough—
—Count 'em!
1 2 3 4 5 6
Yes, and SHE was a GOOD doG, But old and WEAK, and me paw come ALONG and He say—
Those PUPS Gotta Go Likewise they Be the END of ol' STOMPER.

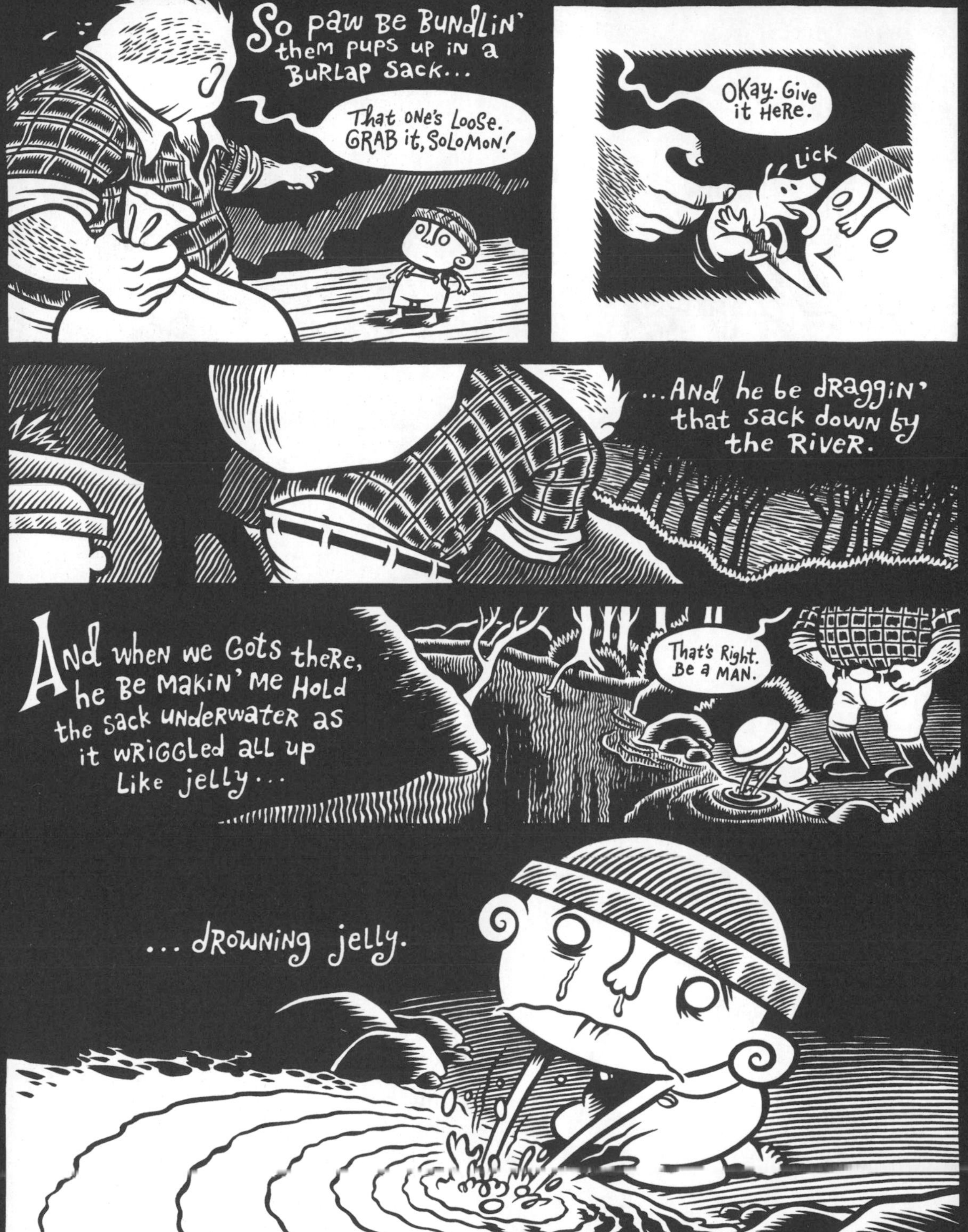
So paw be bundlin' them pups up in a burlap sack...
That one's loose. Grab it, Solomon!
Okay. Give it here.
Lick
...And he be draggin' that sack down by the river.
And when we gots there, he be makin' me hold the sack underwater as it wriggled all up like jelly...
That's right. Be a man.
... drowning jelly.

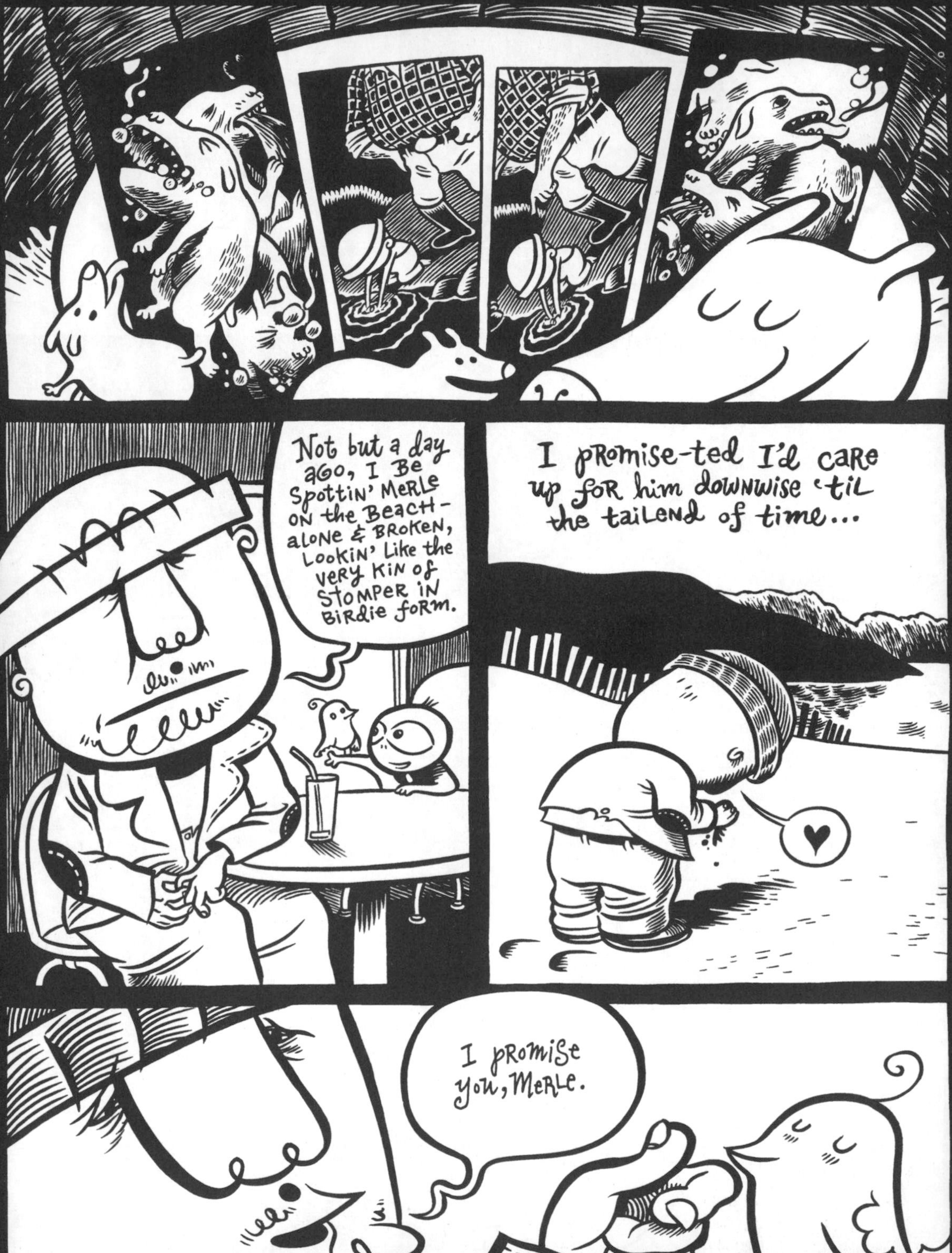
Not but a day ago, I be spottin' Merle on the beach - alone & broken, lookin' like the very kin of Stomper in birdie form.
I promise-ted I'd care up for him downwise 'til the tailend of time...
I promise you, Merle.

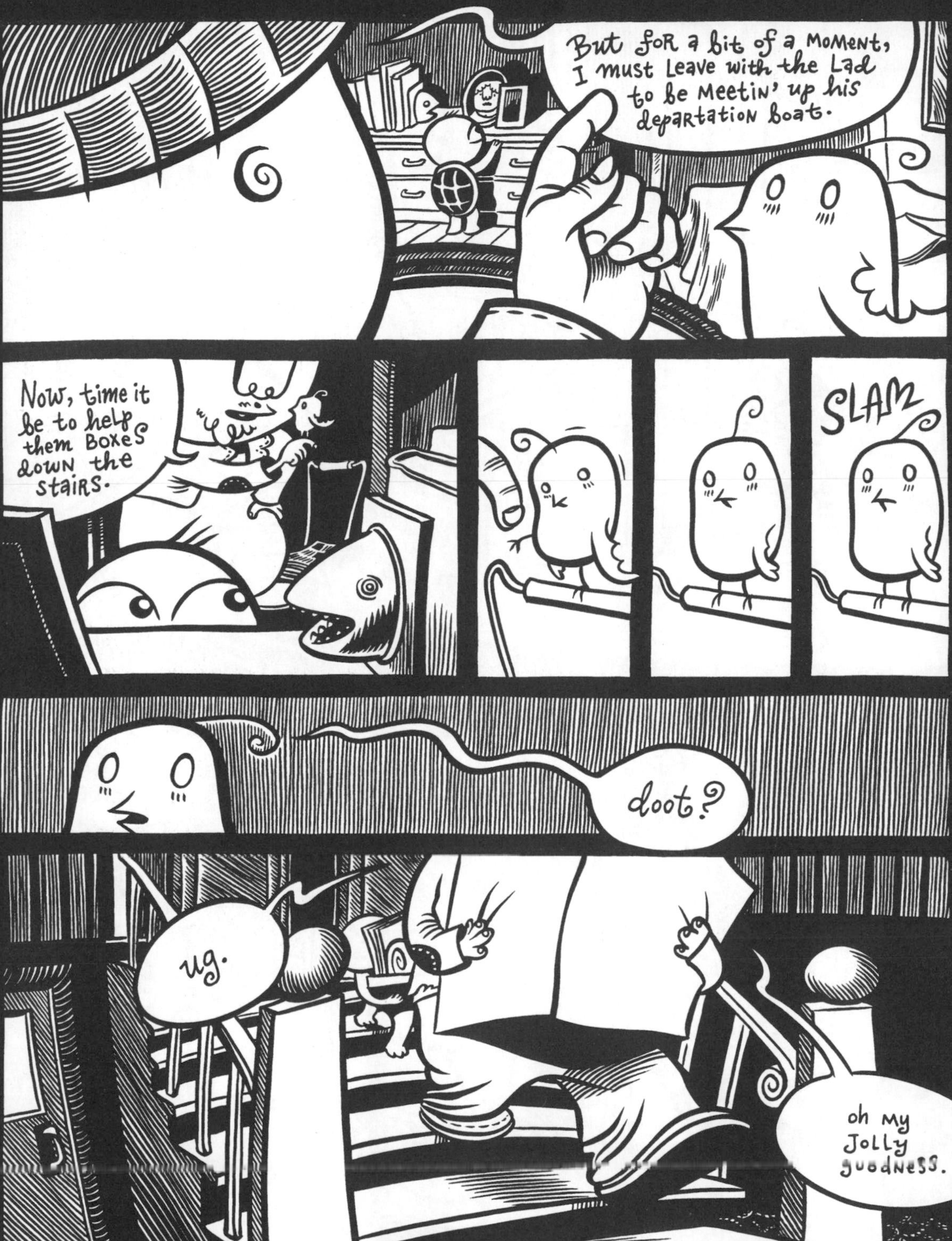
But for a bit of a moment, I must leave with the Lad to be meetin' up his departation boat.
Now, time it be to help them boxes down the stairs.
SLAM
doot?
ug.
oh my jolly goodness.

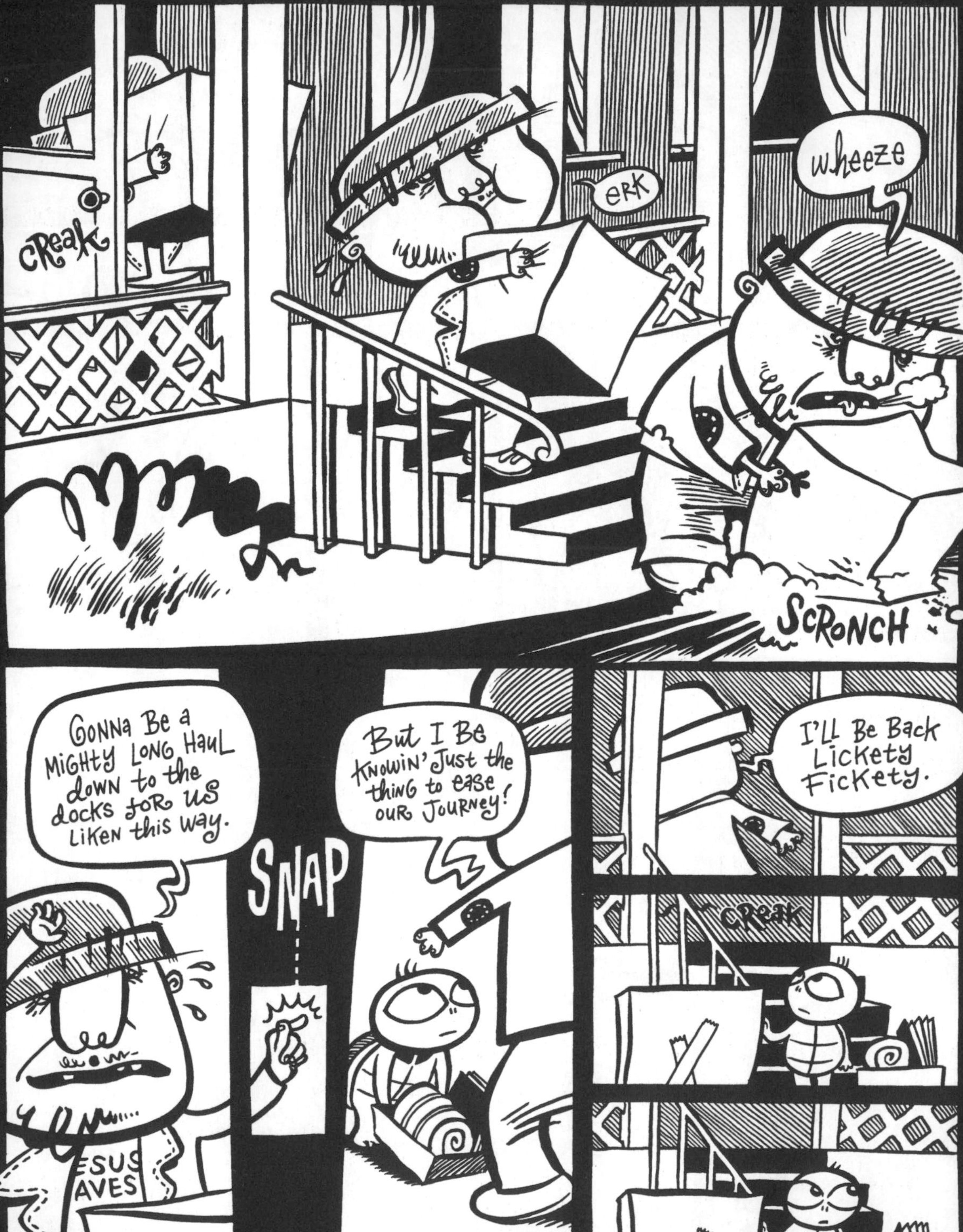

CREAK
ERK
WHEEZE
SCRONCH
GONNA BE A MIGHTY LONG HAUL DOWN TO THE DOCKS FOR US LIKEN THIS WAY.
SNAP
BUT I BE KNOWIN' JUST THE THING TO EASE OUR JOURNEY!
ESUS AVES
I'LL BE BACK LICKETY FICKETY.
CREAK

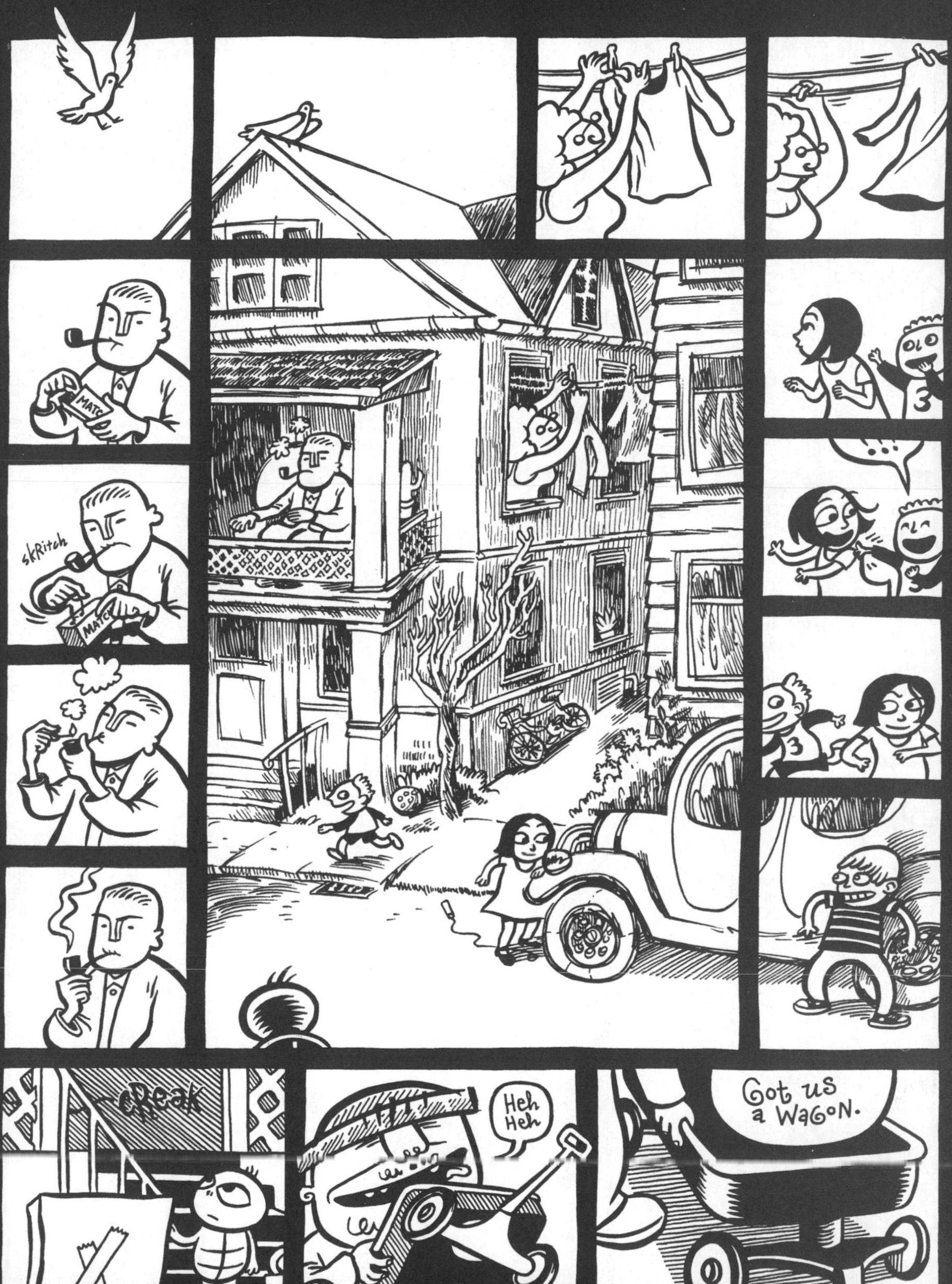
MATC
skRitch
MATC
cReak
Heh Heh
Got us a WaGoN.

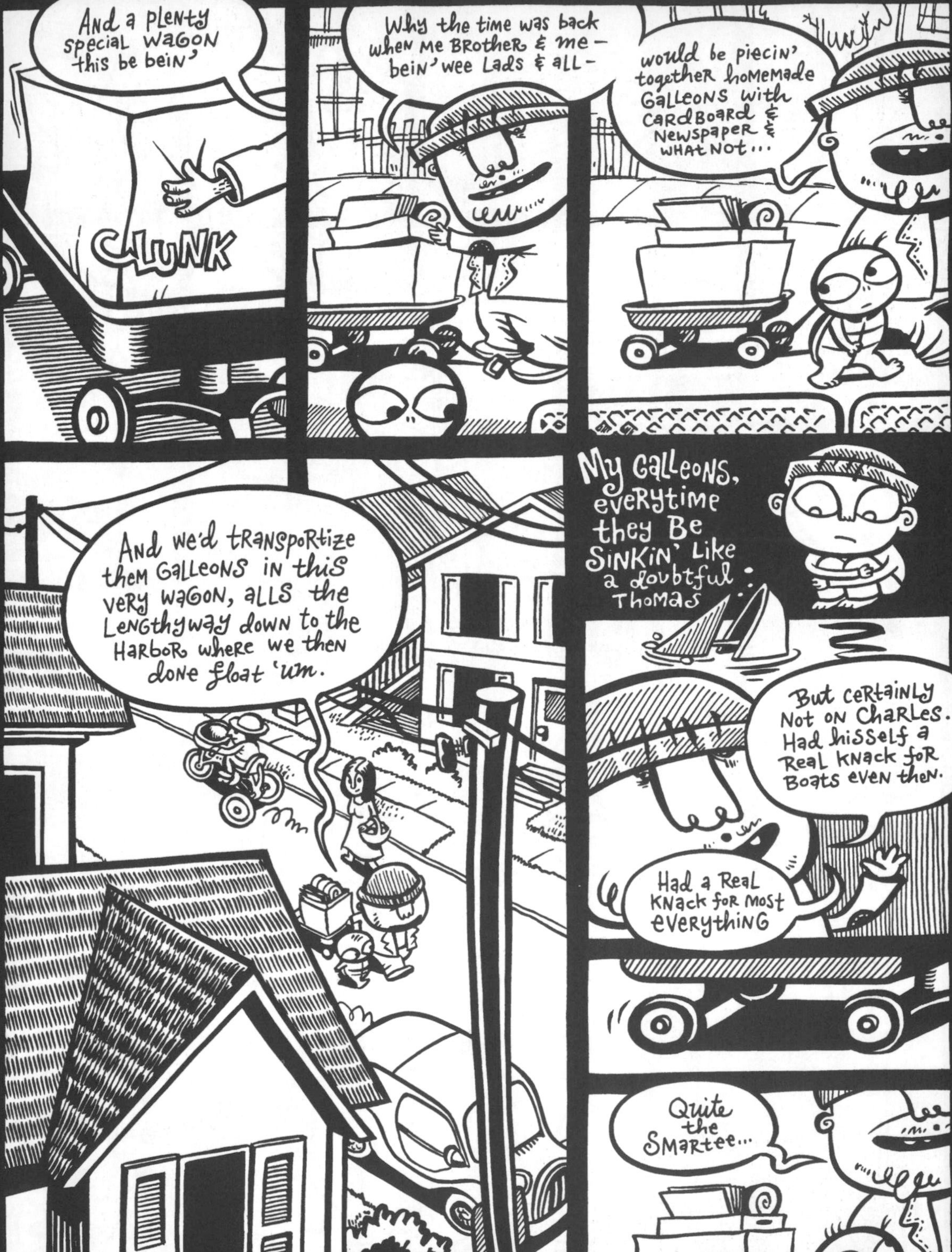
And a plenty special wagon this be bein'
CLUNK
Why the time was back when me brother & me— bein' wee lads & all—
would be piecin' together homemade galleons with cardboard & newspaper & whatnot...
And we'd transportize them galleons in this very wagon, alls the lengthyway down to the harbor where we then done float 'um.
My galleons, everytime they be sinkin' like a doubtful Thomas
But certainly not on Charles. Had hisself a real knack for boats even then.
Had a real knack for most everything
Quite the smartee...

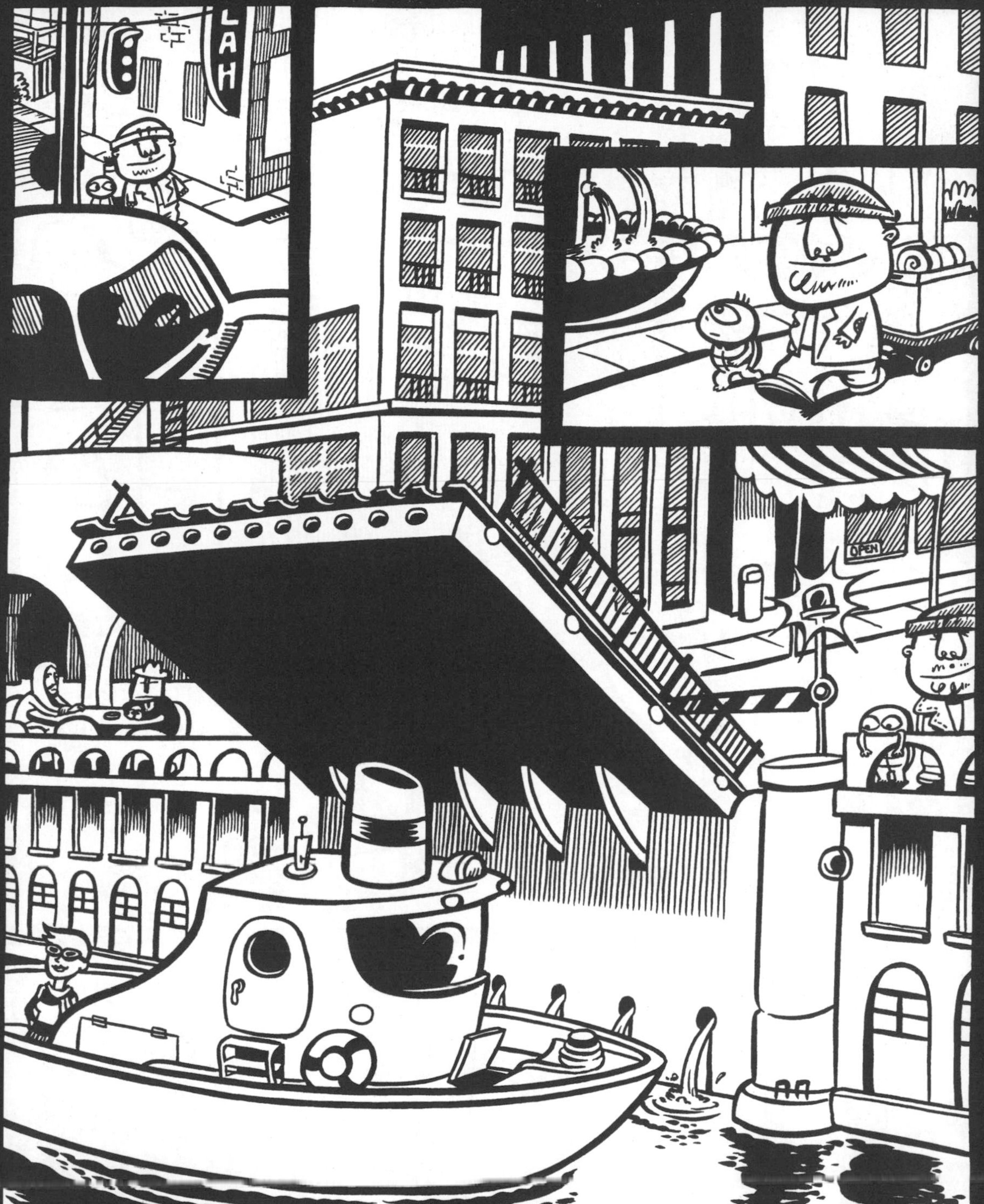
LAH
OPEN

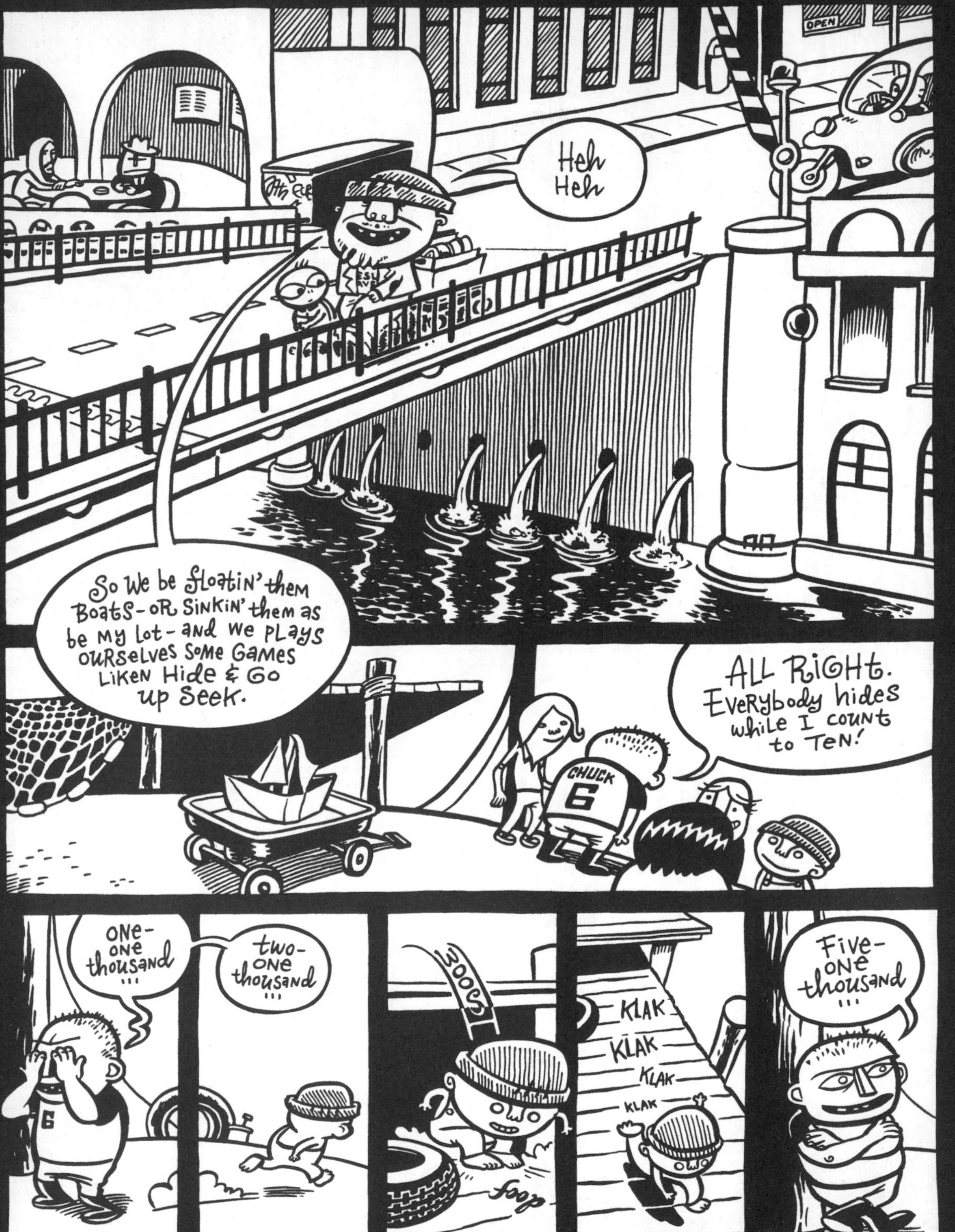
OPEN
Heh Heh
So we be floatin' them Boats- or sinkin' them as be my lot- and we plays ourselves some Games liken Hide & Go up Seek.
ALL RIGHT. Everybody hides while I count to TEN!
CHUCK 6
One- one thousand ...
two- one thousand ...
KLAK
KLAK
KLAK
KLAK
foop
Five- one thousand ...

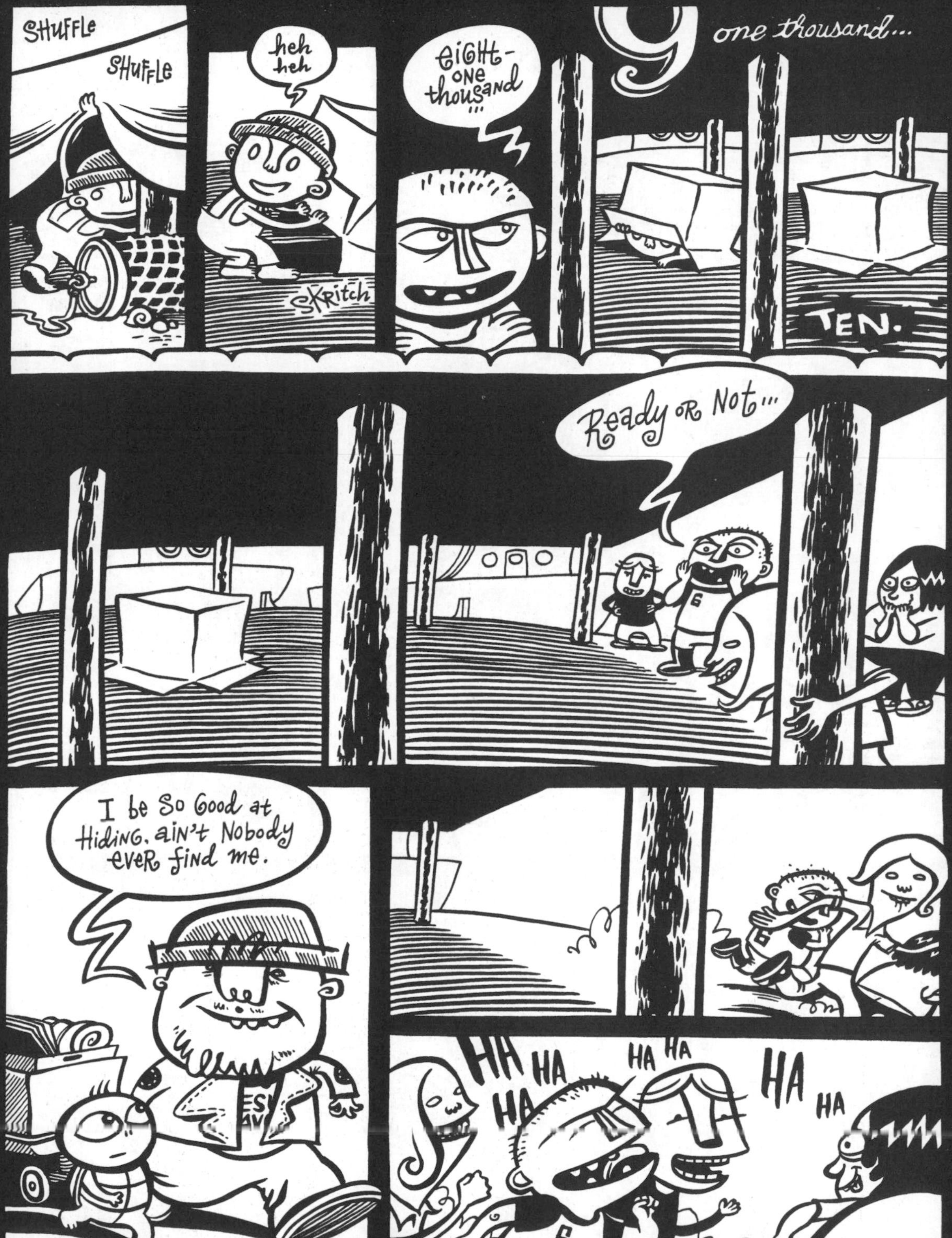
SHUFFLE
SHUFFLE
heh heh
SKRITCH
EIGHT-one thousand...
9 one thousand...
TEN.
Ready or Not...
I be So Good at Hiding, ain't Nobody ever find me.
HA HA HA HA HA HA HA HA

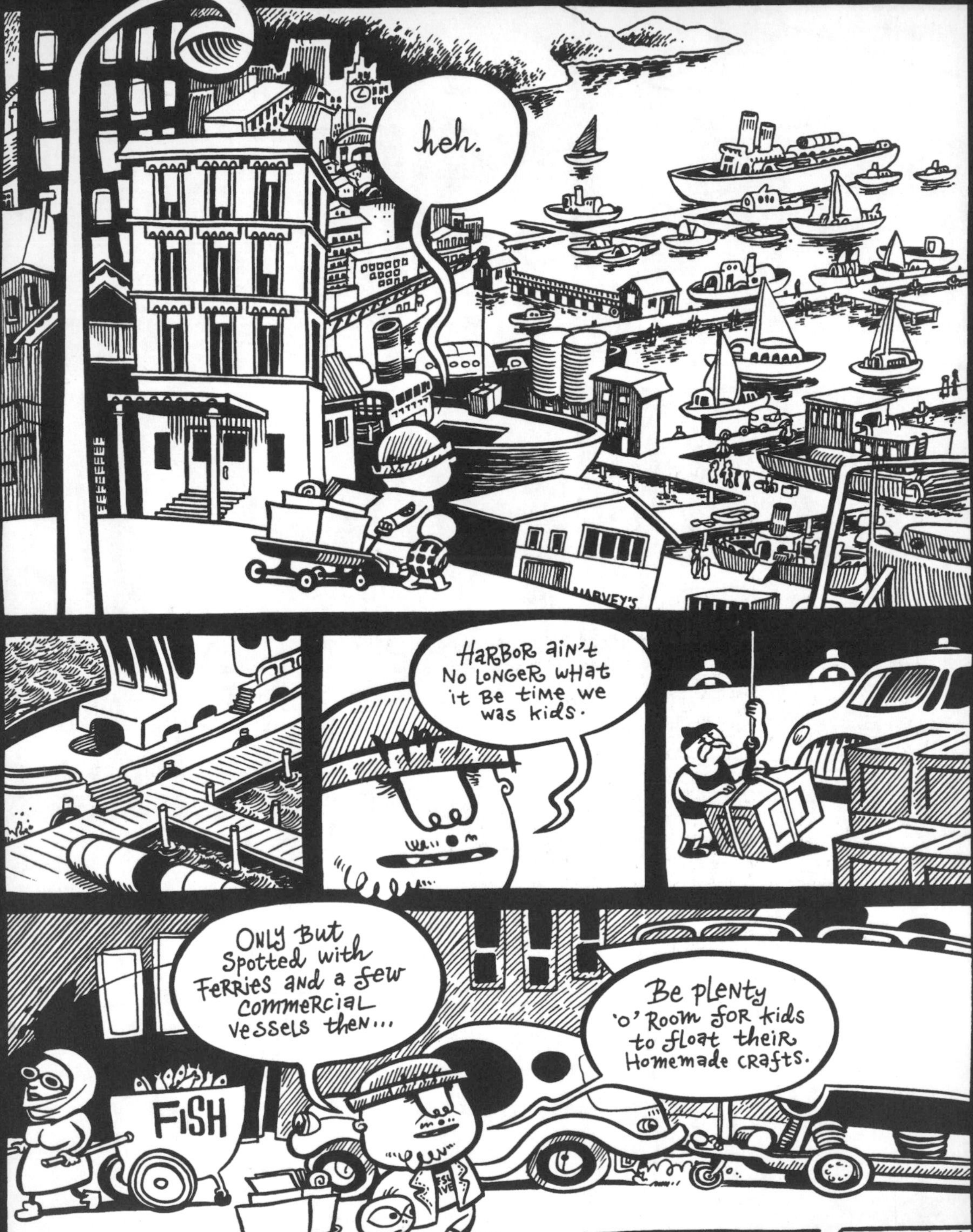
heh.
HARVEY'S
HARBOR ain't No LONGER WHAT it Be time we was kids.
ONLY But Spotted with Ferries and a few commercial vessels then...
Be plenty 'o' Room for kids to float their Homemade crafts.
FISH

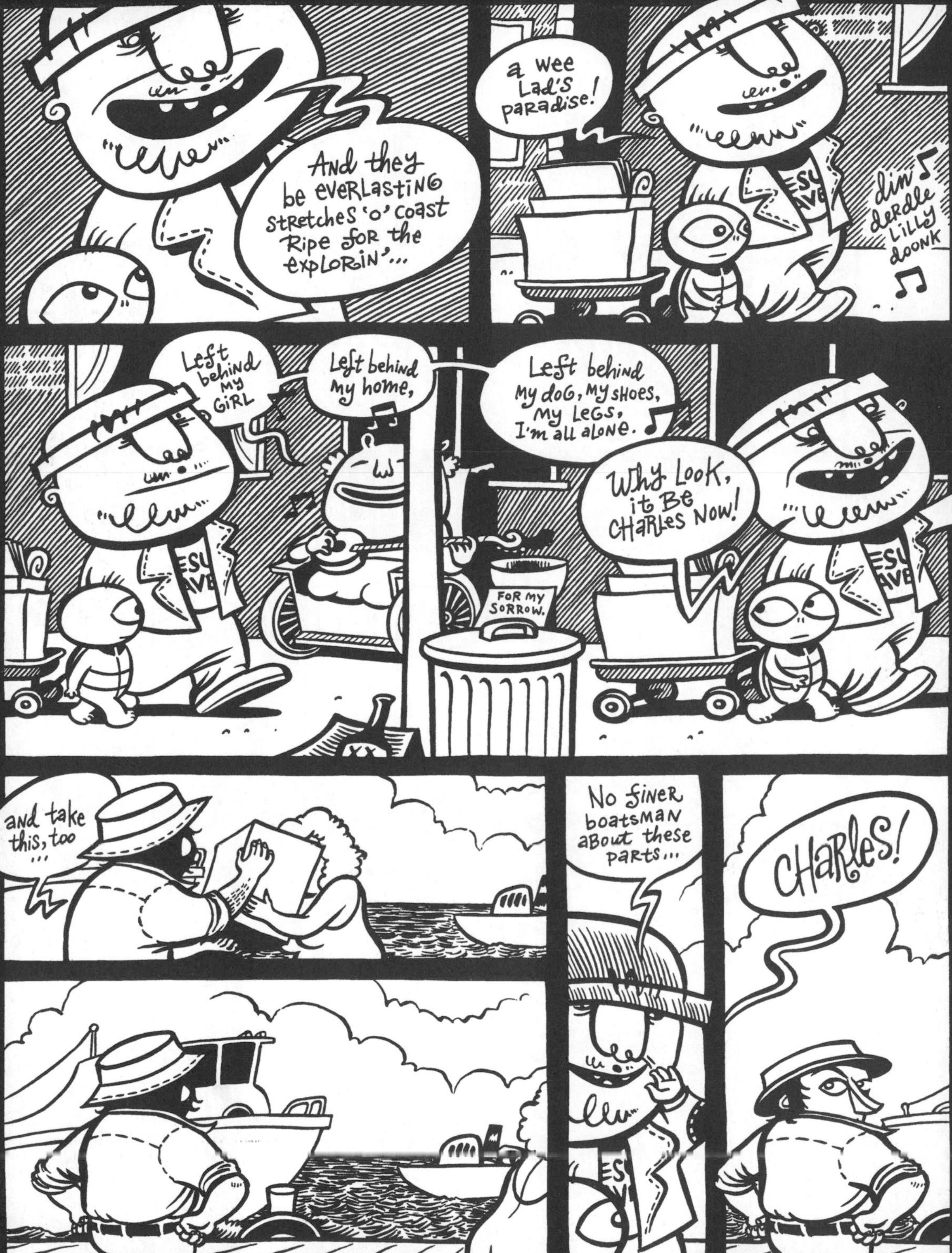
And they be everlasting stretches 'o' coast Ripe for the explorin'...
a wee Lad's paradise!
din derdle Lilly doonk
Left behind my girl
Left behind my home,
Left behind my dog, my shoes, my legs, I'm all alone.
FOR MY SORROW.
Why look, it be Charles now!
and take this, too ...
No finer boatsman about these parts...
CHARLES!

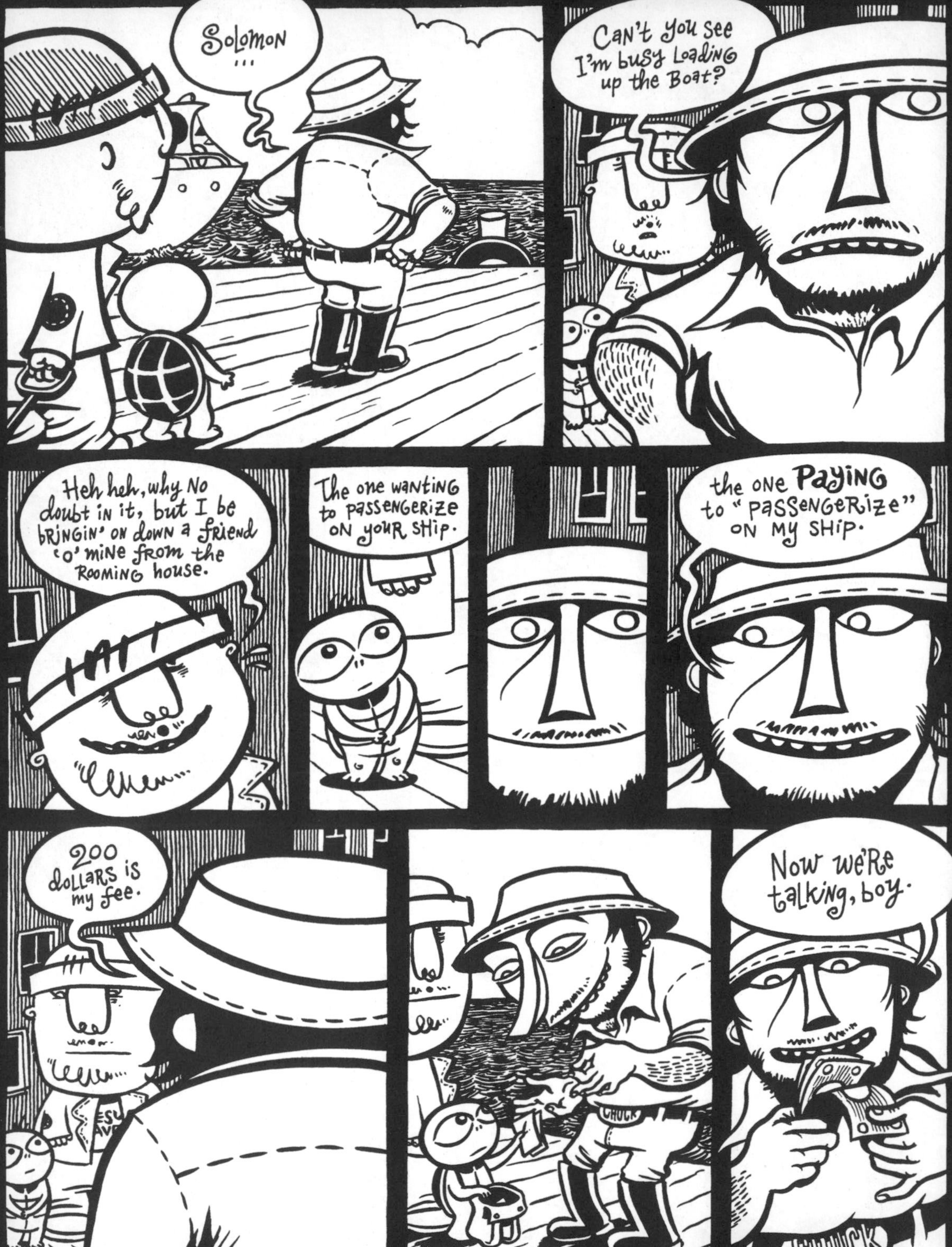

Solomon ...
Can't you see I'm busy loading up the boat?
Heh heh, why no doubt in it, but I be bringin' on down a friend 'o' mine from the rooming house.
The one wanting to passengerize on your ship.
the one PAYING to "passengerize" on my ship.
200 dollars is my fee.
CHUCK
Now we're talking, boy.
CHUCK

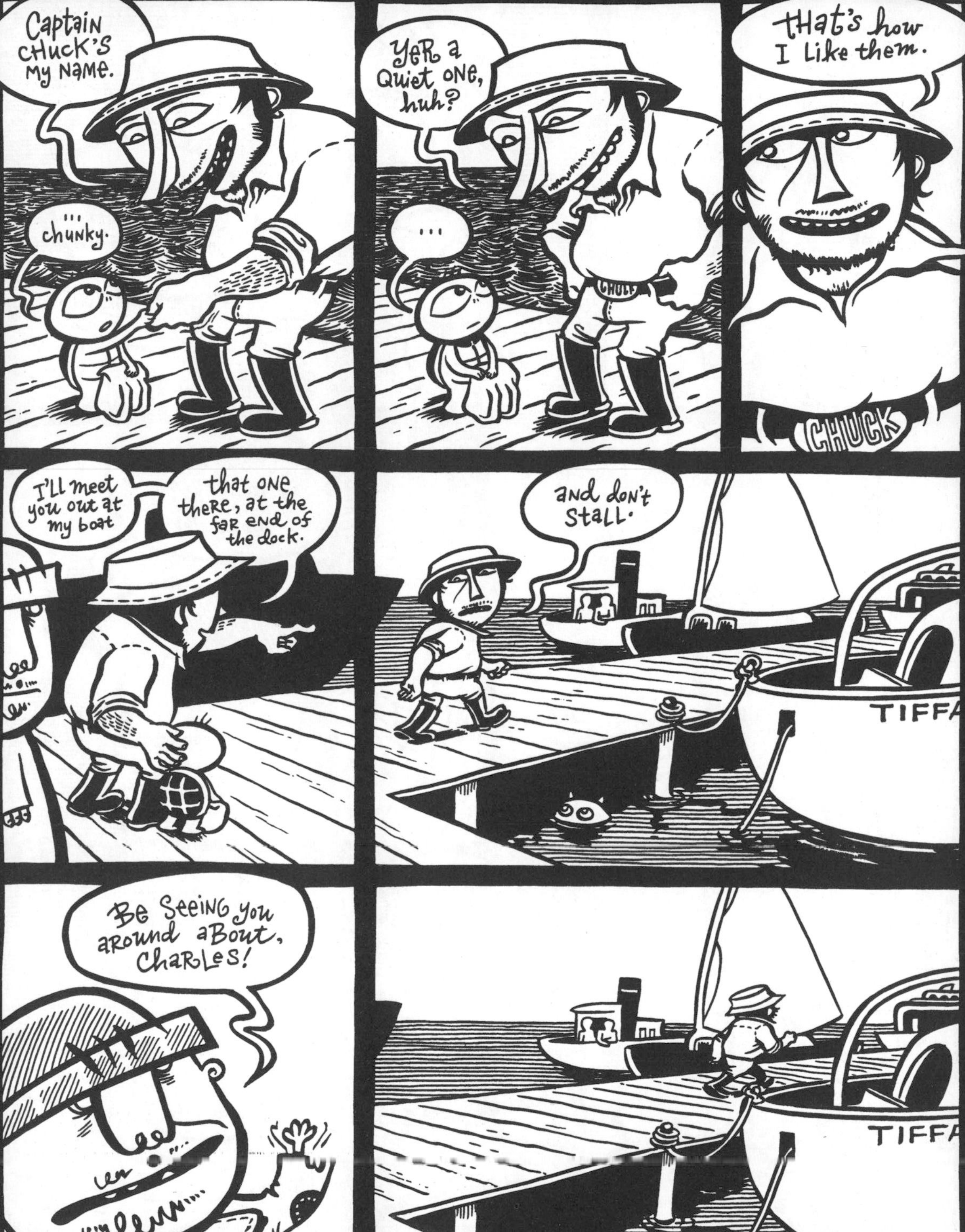
Captain Chuck's my name.
... chunky.
Yer a quiet one, huh?
....
CHUCK
That's how I like them.
CHUCK
I'll meet you out at my boat
that one there, at the far end of the dock.
and don't stall.
TIFFA
Be seeing you around about, Charles!
FSU
TIFFA

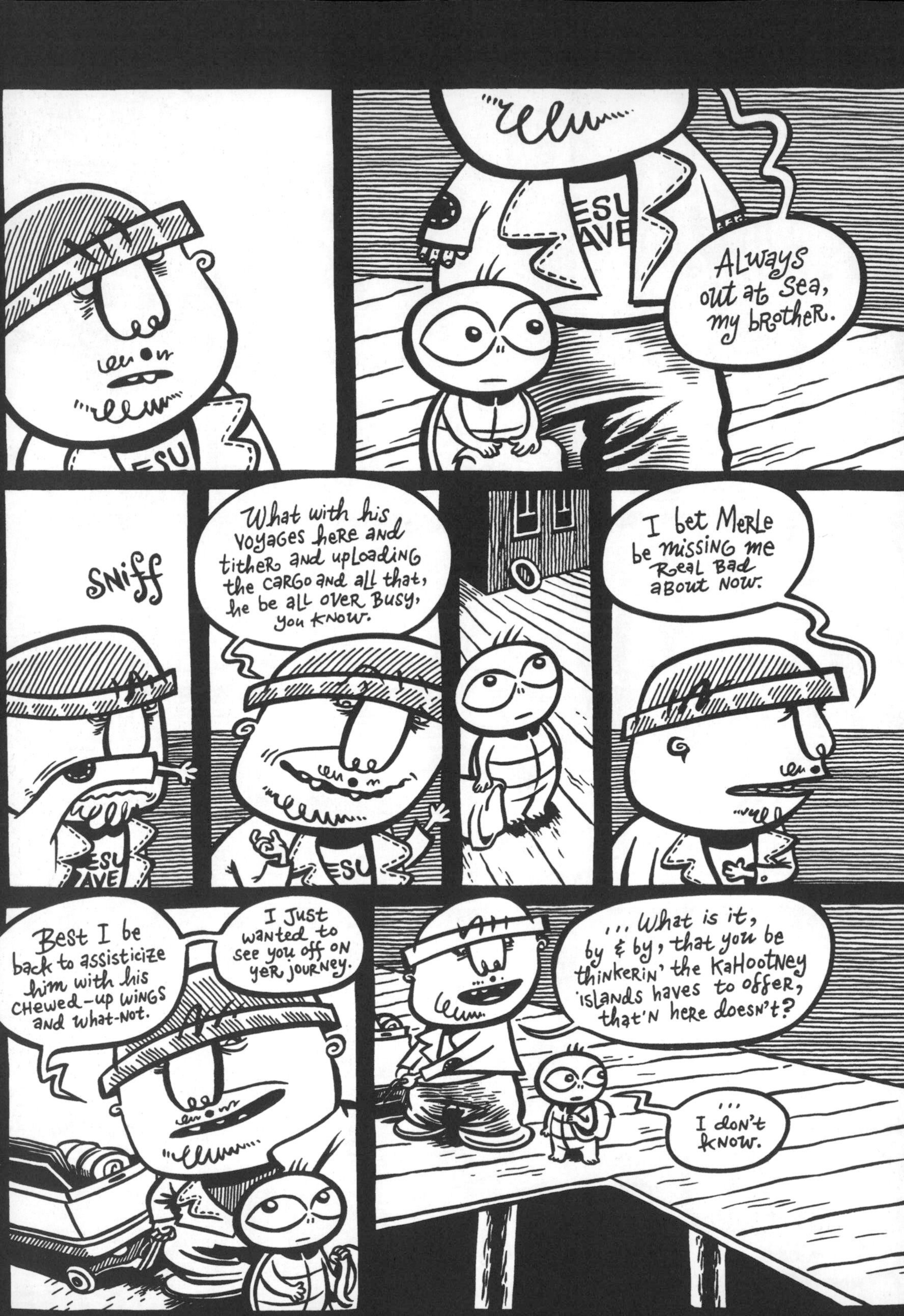
Always out at sea, my brother.
SNIFF
What with his voyages here and tither and uploading the cargo and all that, he be all over busy, you know.
I bet Merle be missing me real bad about now.
Best I be back to assisticize him with his chewed-up wings and what-not.
I just wanted to see you off on yer journey.
... What is it, by & by, that you be thinkerin' the Kahootney islands haves to offer, that'n here doesn't?
... I don't know.

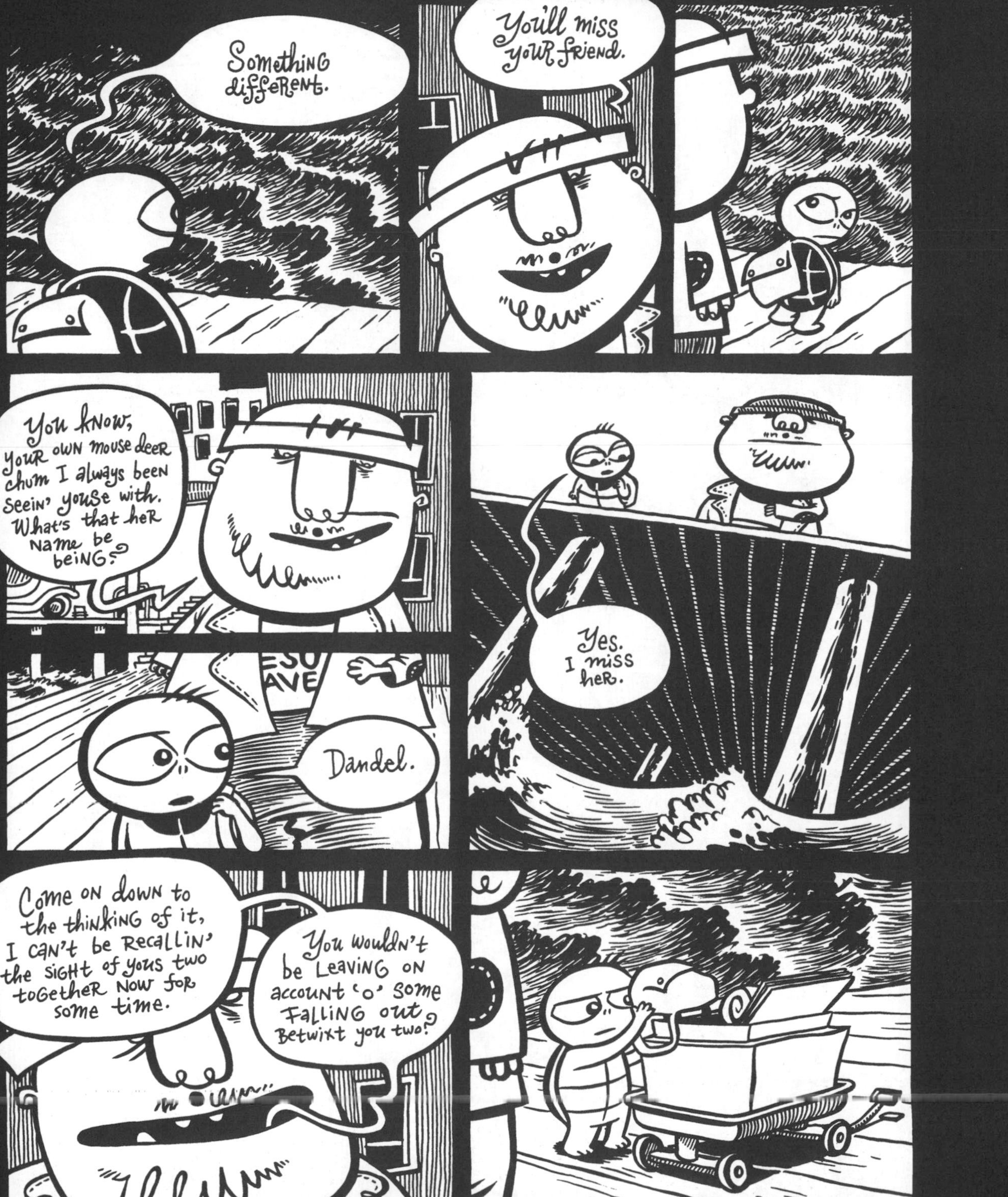
Something different.
You'll miss your friend.
You know, your own mouse deer chum I always been seein' youse with. What's that her name be being?
Dandel.
Yes. I miss her.
Come on down to the thinking of it, I can't be recallin' the sight of yous two together now for some time.
You wouldn't be leaving on account 'o' some falling out betwixt you two?
ESU
AVE

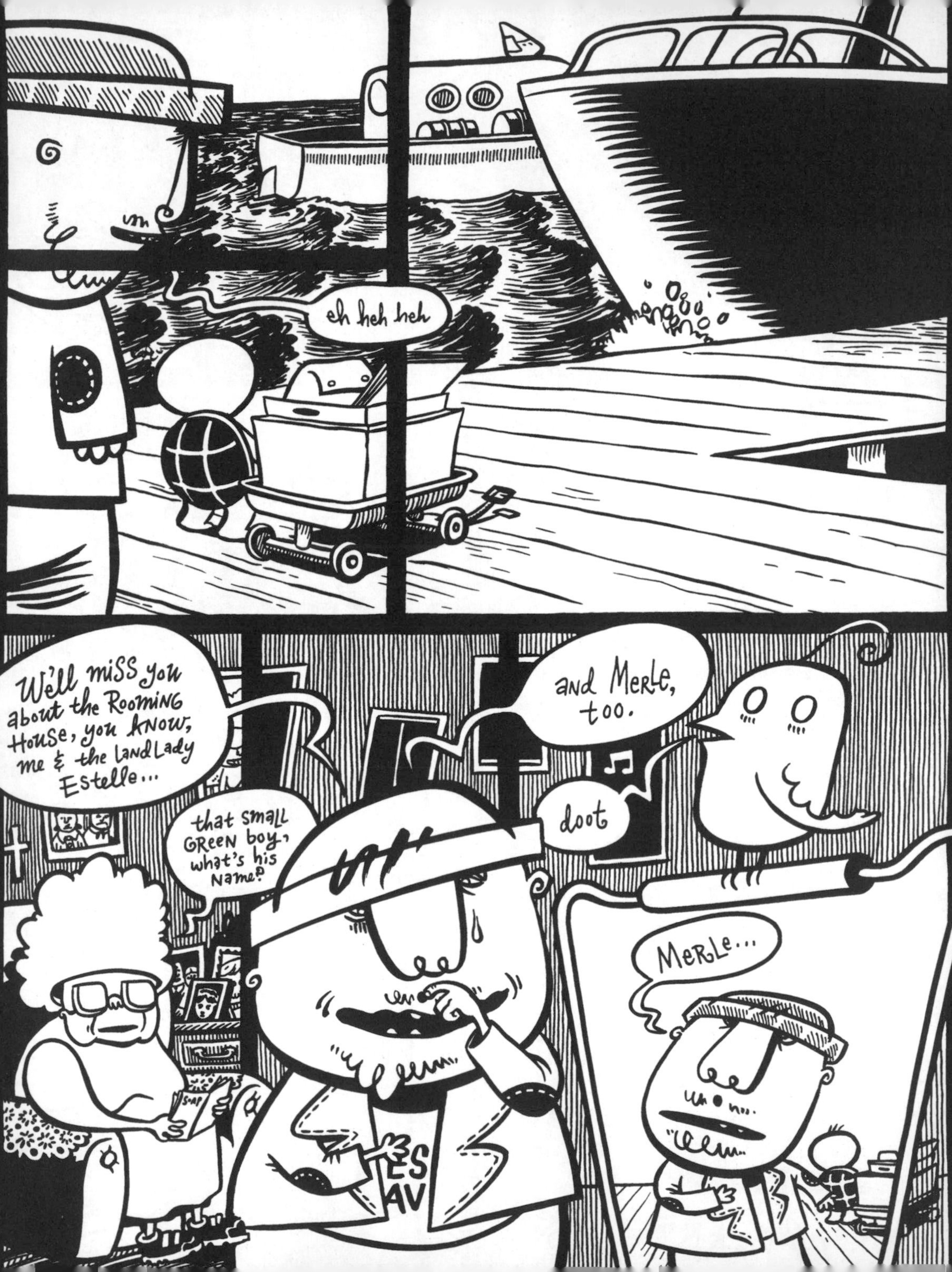
eh heh heh
We'll miss you about the Rooming House, you know, me & the landlady Estelle...
that small green boy, what's his name?
and Merle, too.
doot
Merle...
ES
AV

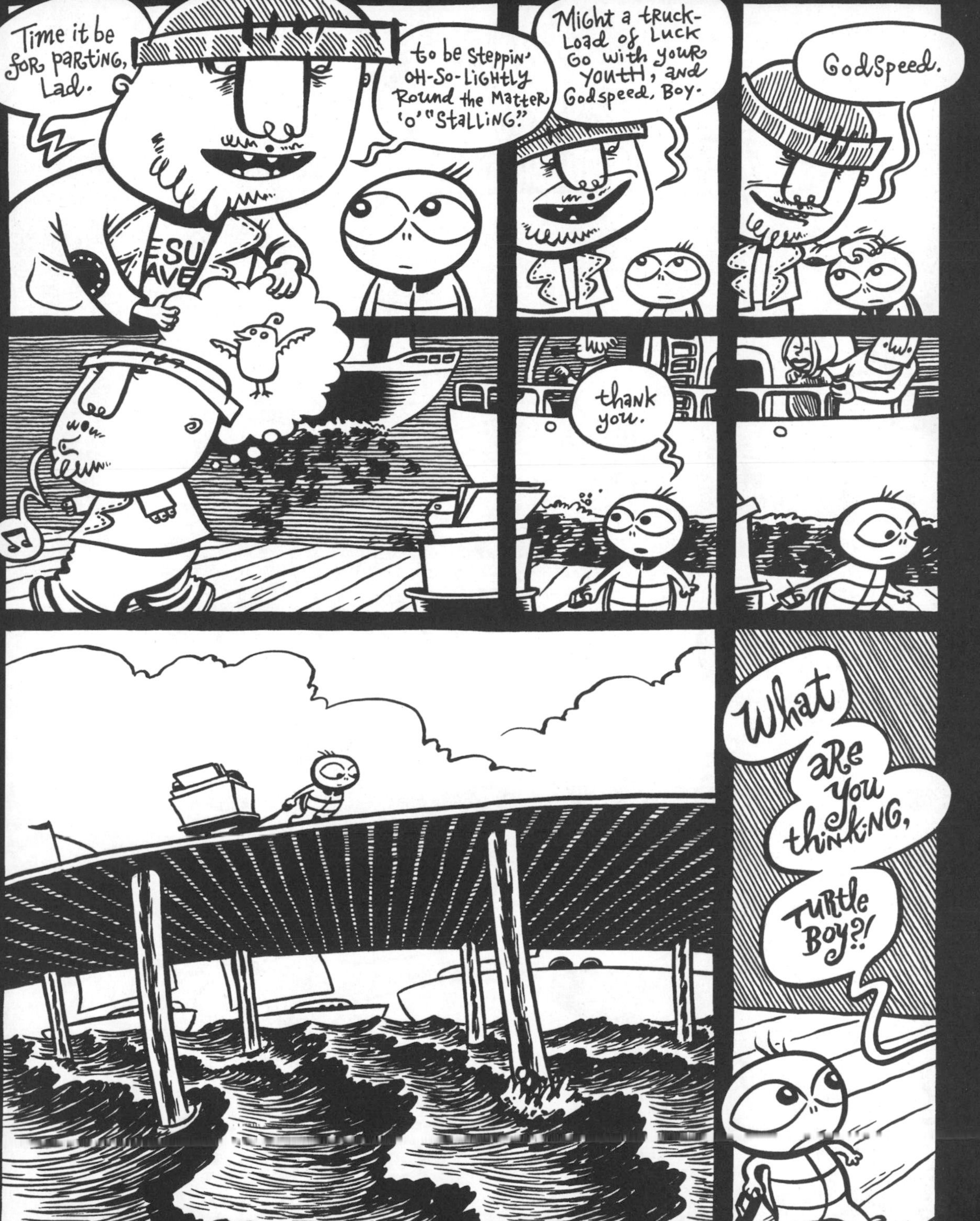

Time it be for parting, Lad.
to be steppin' oh-so-lightly Round the Matter 'o' "Stalling."
Might a truck-load of Luck go with your youth, and Godspeed, Boy.
Godspeed.
thank you.
What are you thinking, Turtle Boy?!

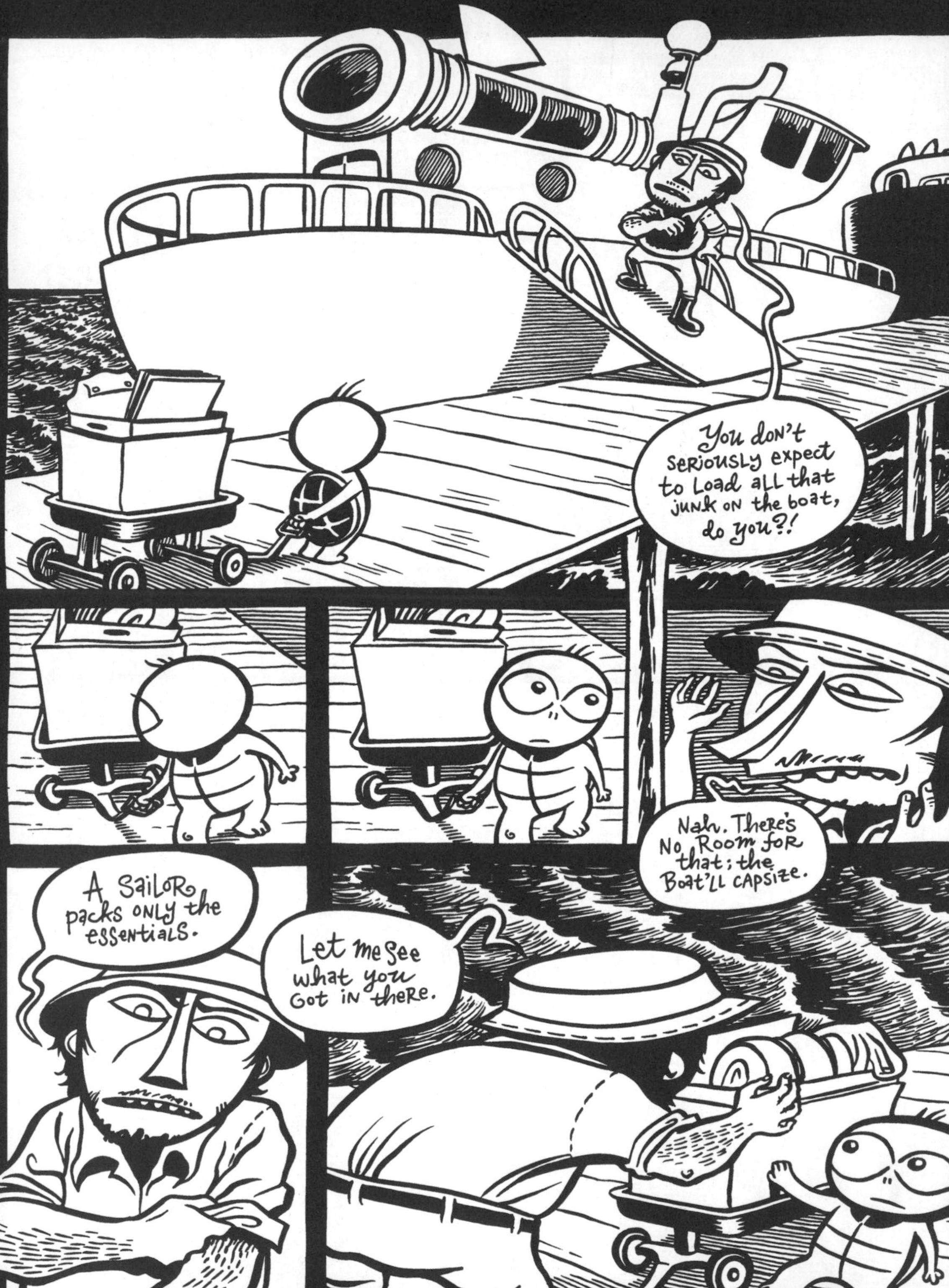
You don't seriously expect to load all that junk on the boat, do you?!
Nah. There's no room for that; the boat'll capsize.
A sailor packs only the essentials.
Let me see what you got in there.

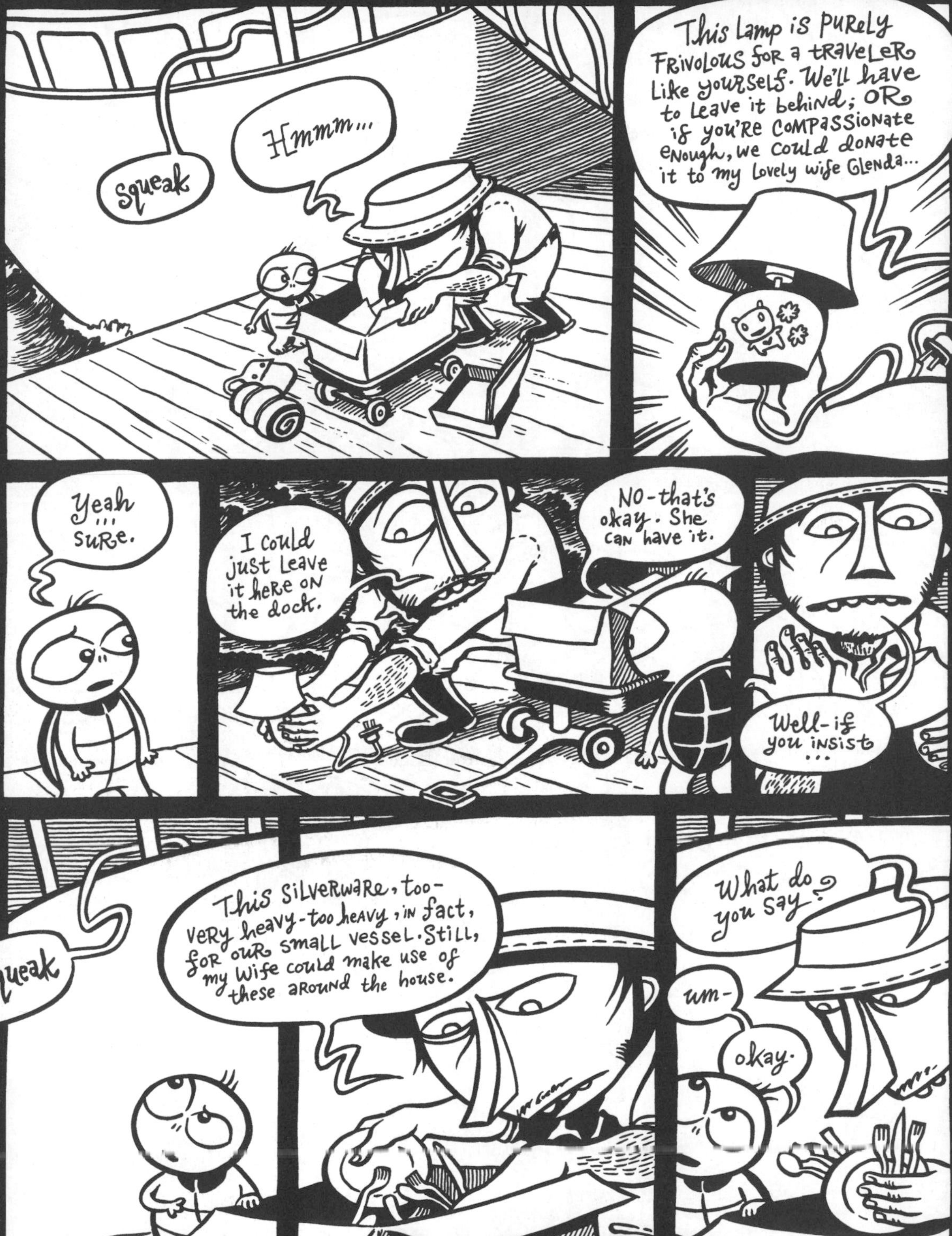
squeak
Hmmm...
This lamp is purely frivolous for a traveler like yourself. We'll have to leave it behind; or if you're compassionate enough, we could donate it to my lovely wife Glenda...
Yeah ... sure.
I could just leave it here on the dock.
No-that's okay. She can have it.
Well-if you insist ...
squeak
This silverware, too-very heavy-too heavy, in fact, for our small vessel. Still, my wife could make use of these around the house.
What do you say?
um-
okay.

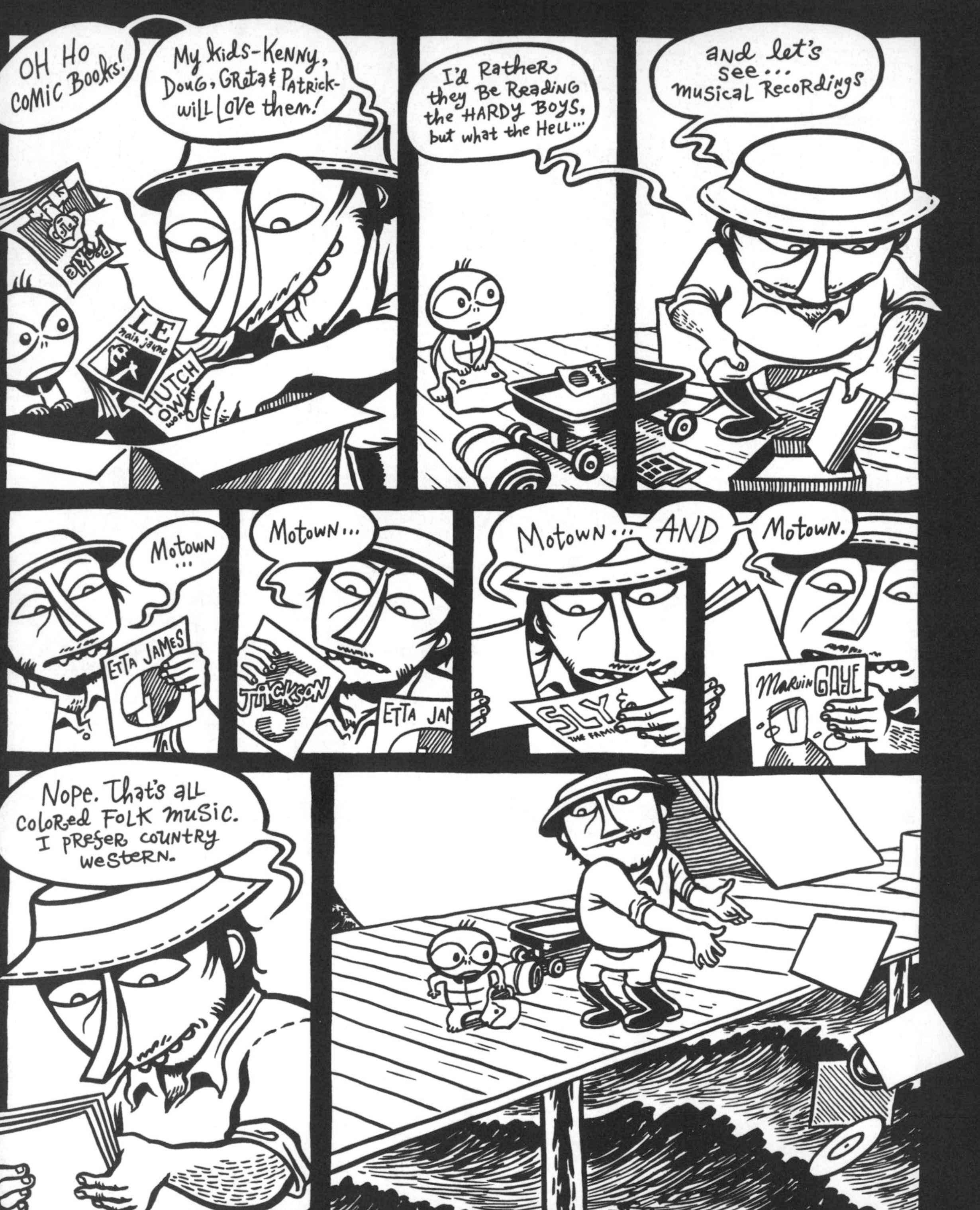
OH HO COMIC BOOKS!
My kids-Kenny, Doug, Greta & Patrick-will Love them!
I'd Rather they Be Reading the HARDY BOYS, but what the HELL...
and let's see... musical Recordings
Motown...
Motown...
Motown... AND Motown.
ETTA JAMES
JACKSON 5
ETTA JAM
SLY &
MARVIN GAYE
Nope. That's all colored folk music. I prefer country western.

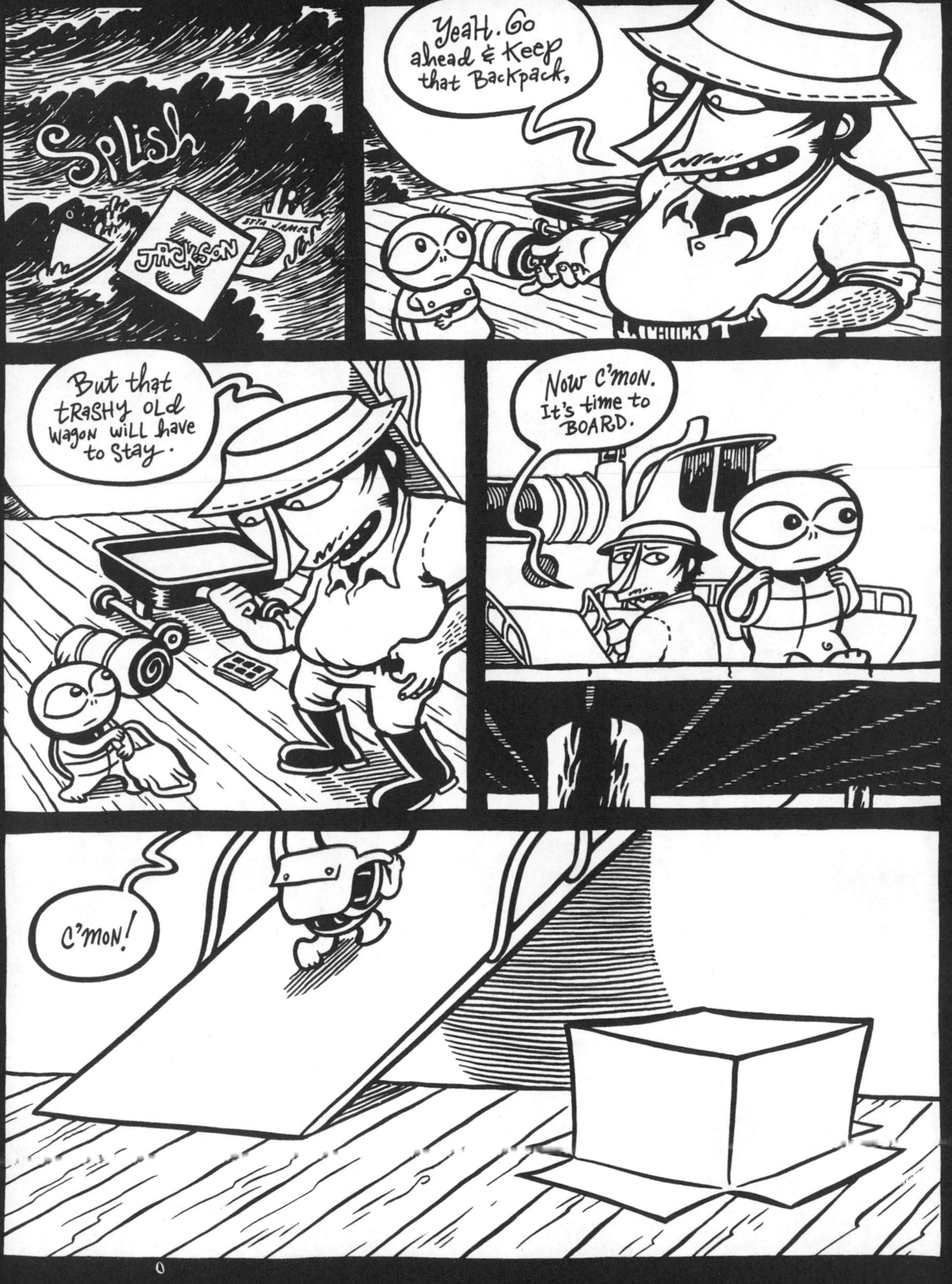
Splish
JACKSON 5
YeaH. Go ahead & Keep that Backpack,
CHUCK
But that trashy old wagon will have to stay.
Now C'mon. It's time to BOARD.
C'MON!

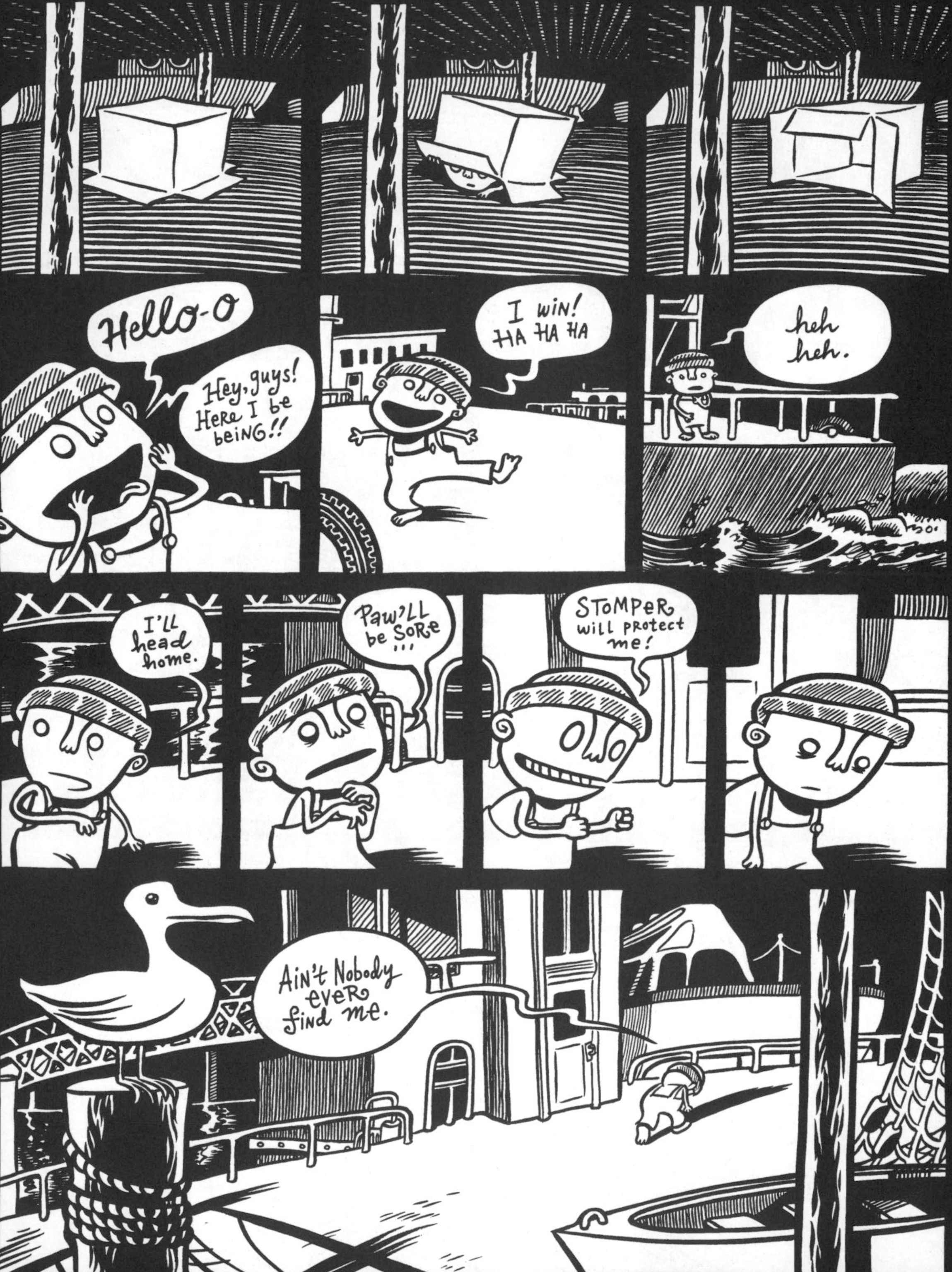
Hello-O
Hey, guys! Here I be being!!
I win! HA HA HA
heh heh.
I'LL head home.
Paw'LL be SORE ...
STOMPER will protect me!
Ain't Nobody ever find me.

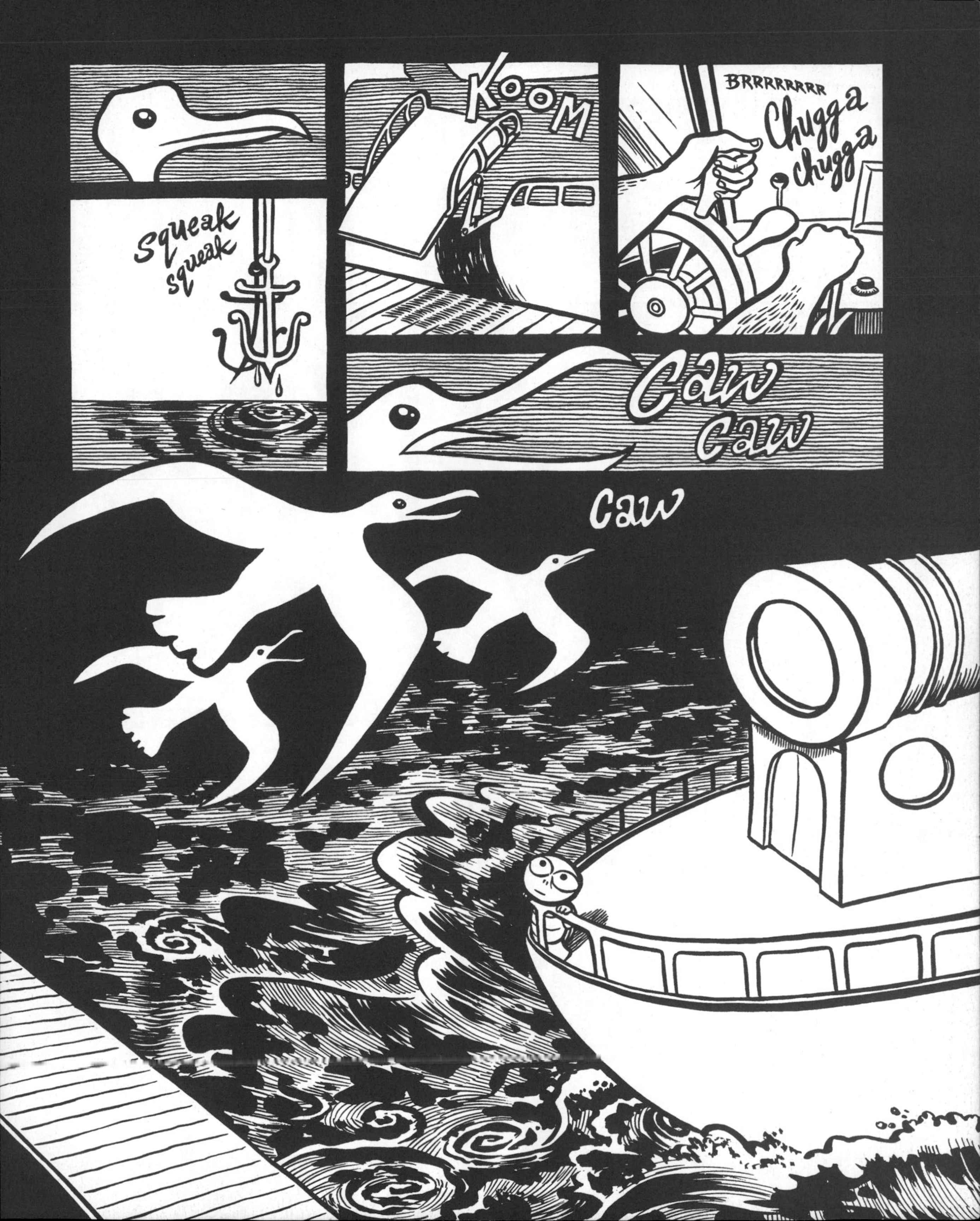
KOOM
BRRRRRRRR
Chugga chugga
squeak squeak
Caw caw
Caw

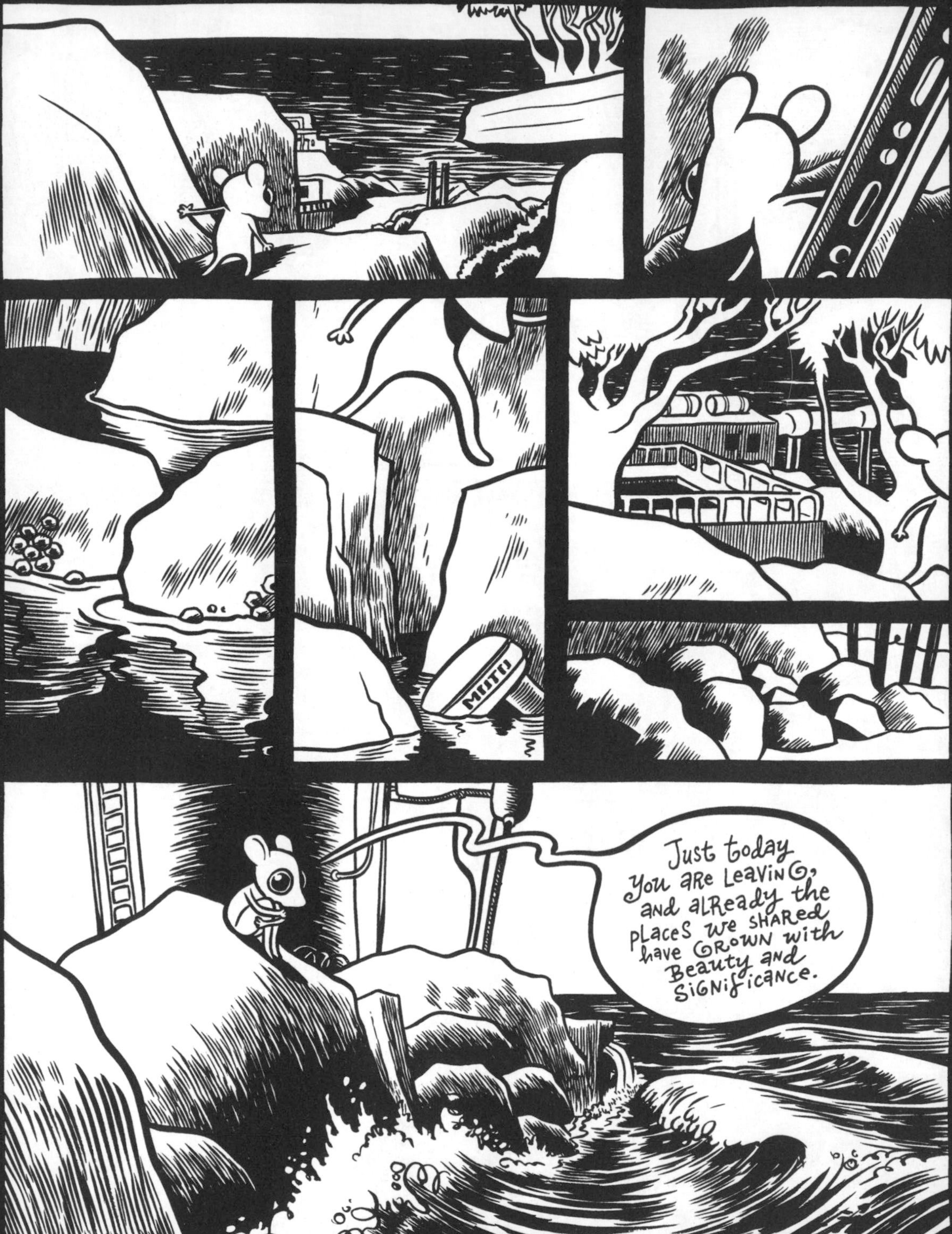
Just today you are leaving, and already the places we shared have grown with Beauty and significance.

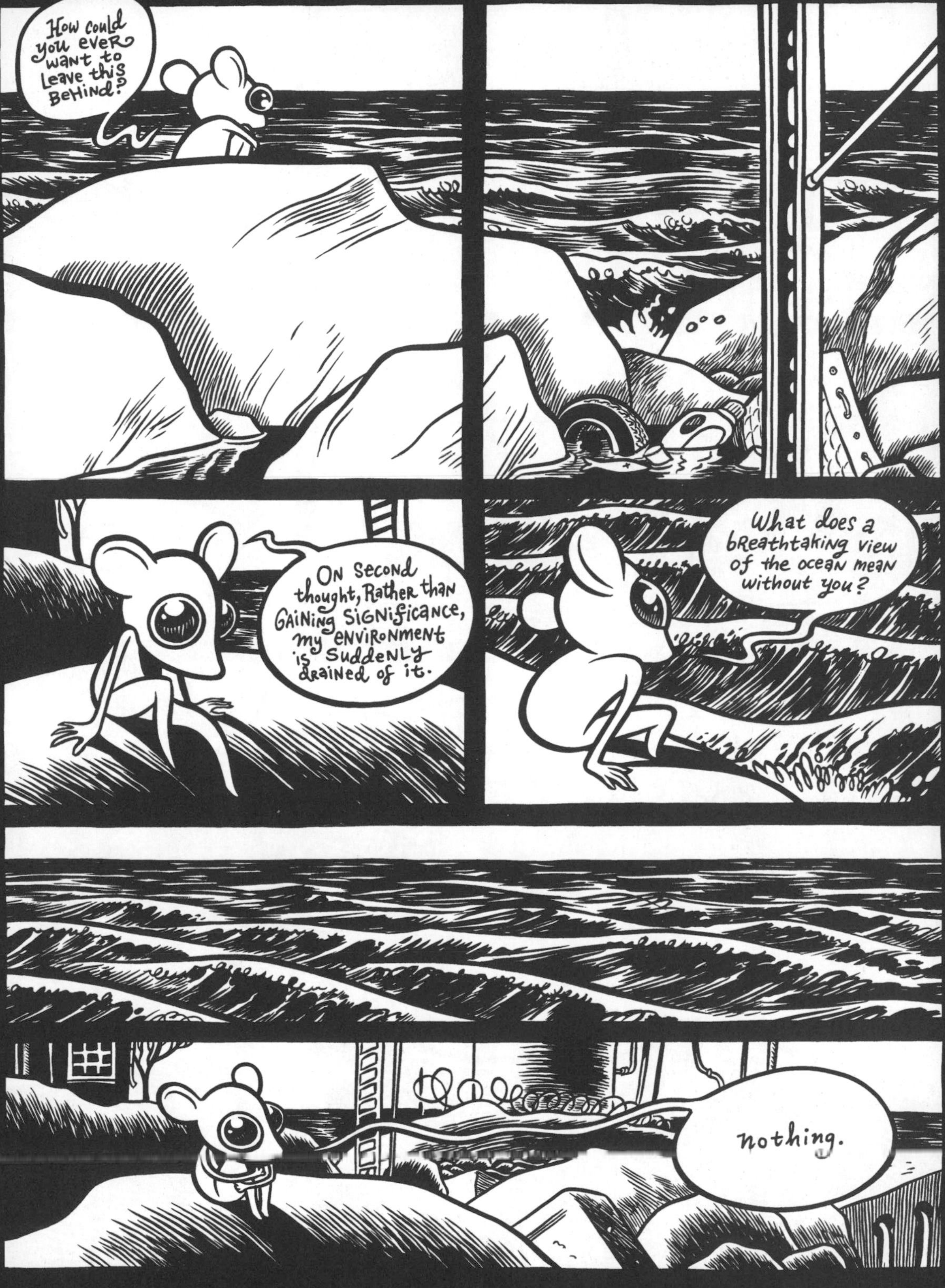
How could you ever want to leave this behind?
On second thought, rather than gaining significance, my environment is suddenly drained of it.
What does a breathtaking view of the ocean mean without you?
nothing.

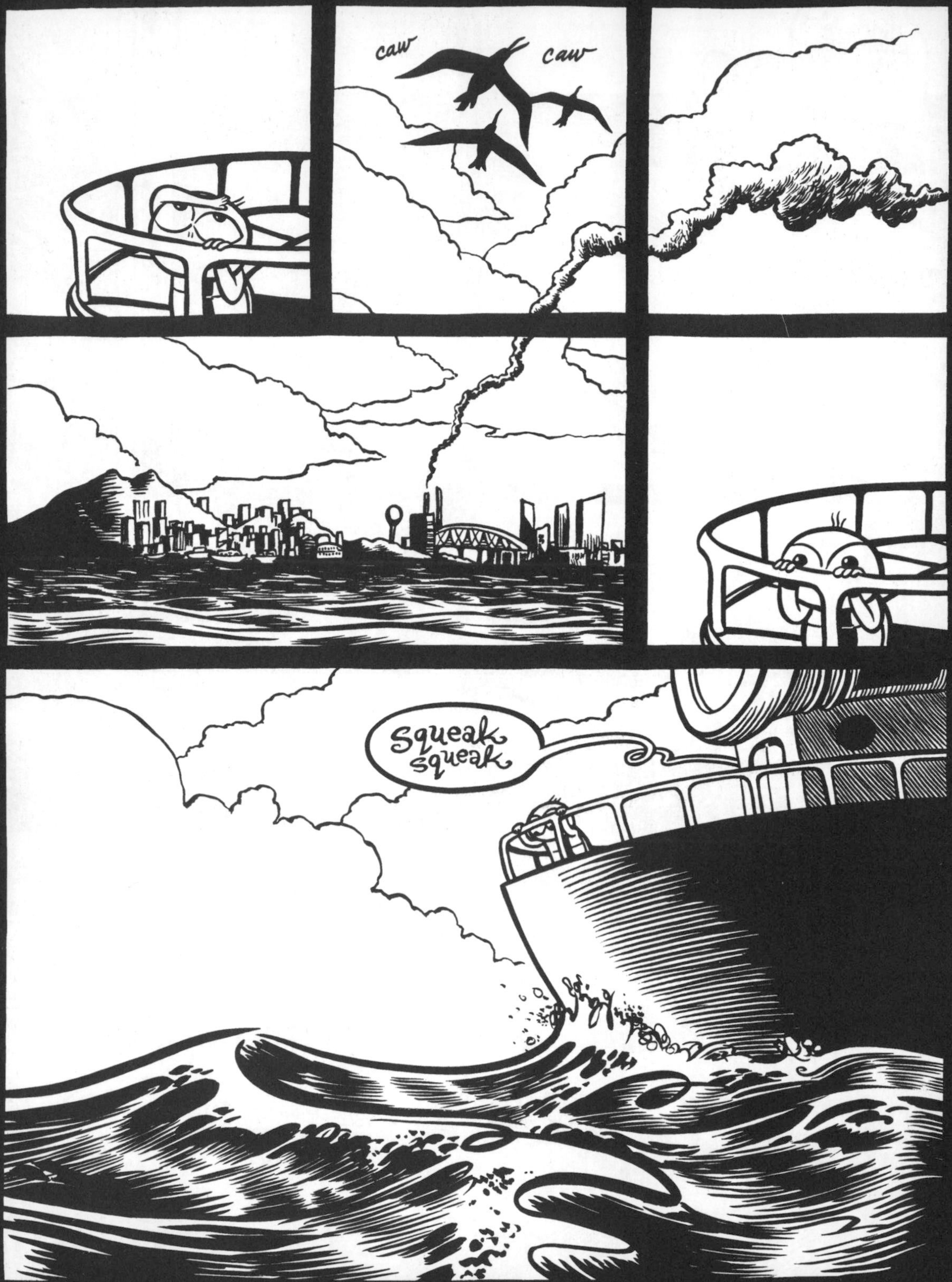
caw
caw
Squeak squeak

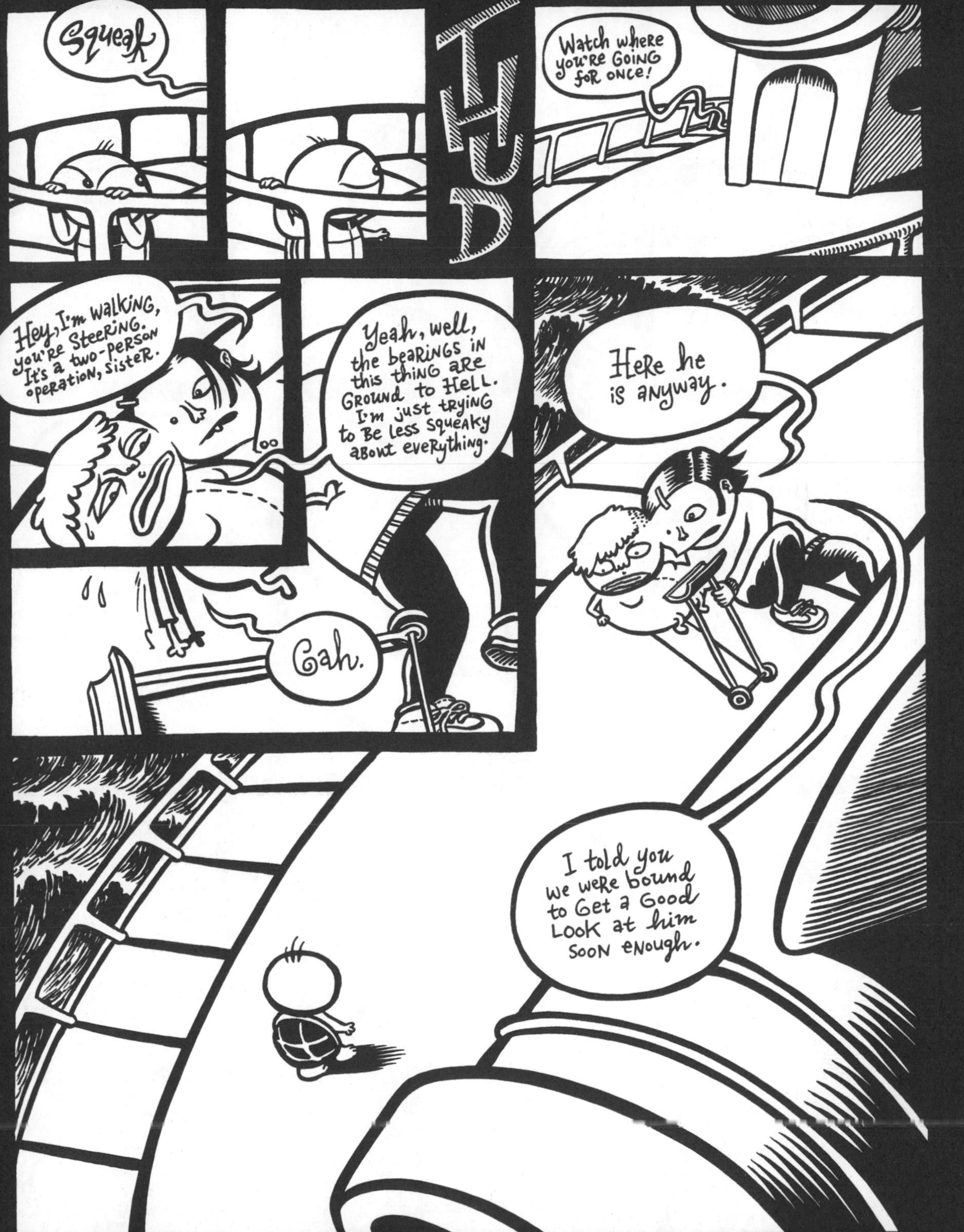
Squeak
THUD
Watch where you're GOING for once!
Hey, I'm WALKING, you're STEERING. It's a two-PERSON operation, SISTER.
Yeah, well, the bearings in this thing are GROUND to HELL. I'm just trying to be less squeaky about everything.
Gah.
Here he is anyway.
I told you we were bound to Get a Good Look at him soon enough.

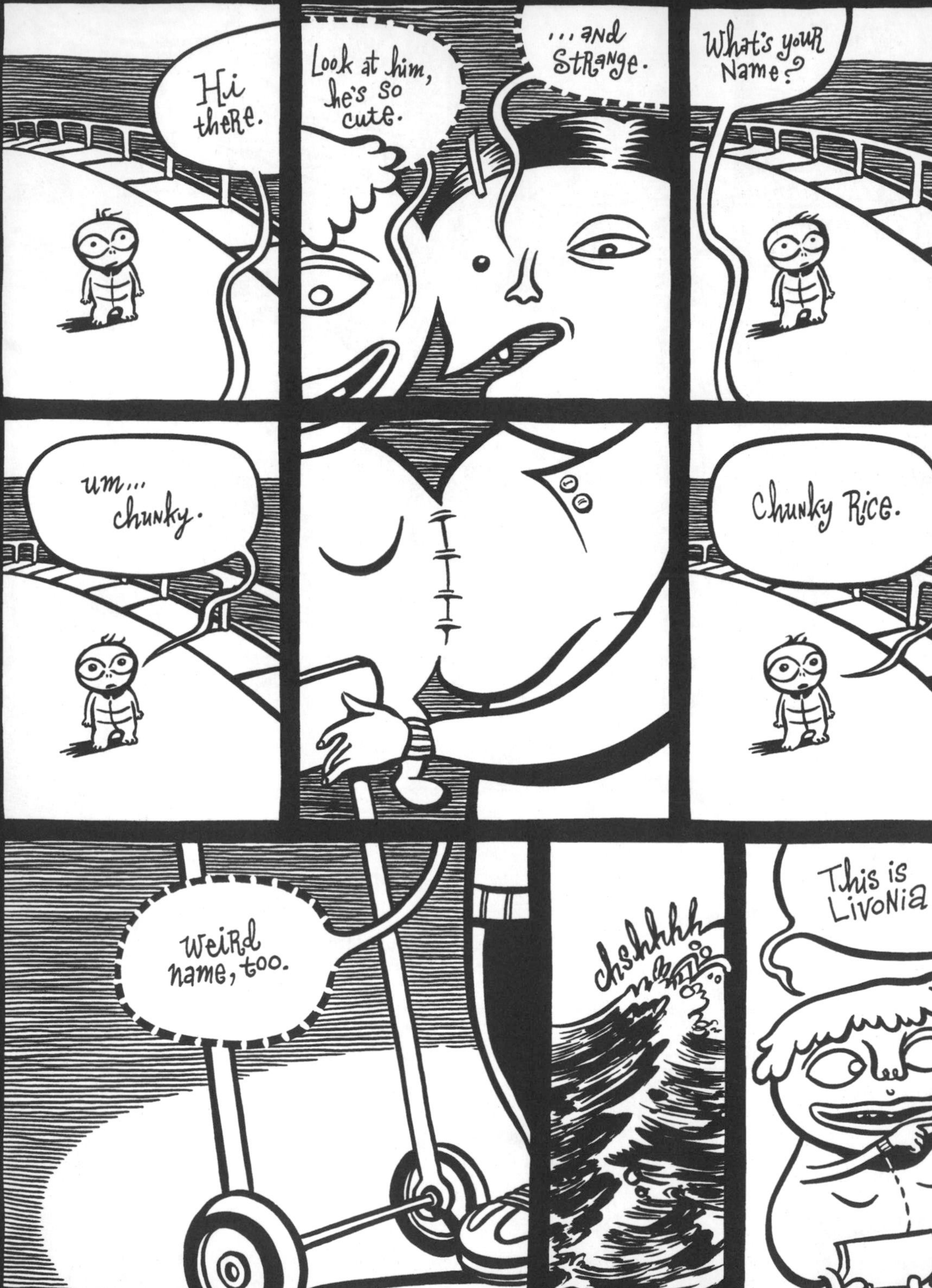

Hi there.
Look at him, he's so cute.
...and strange.
What's your Name?
um... chunky.
Chunky Rice.
Weird name, too.
chshhhh
This is Livonia,

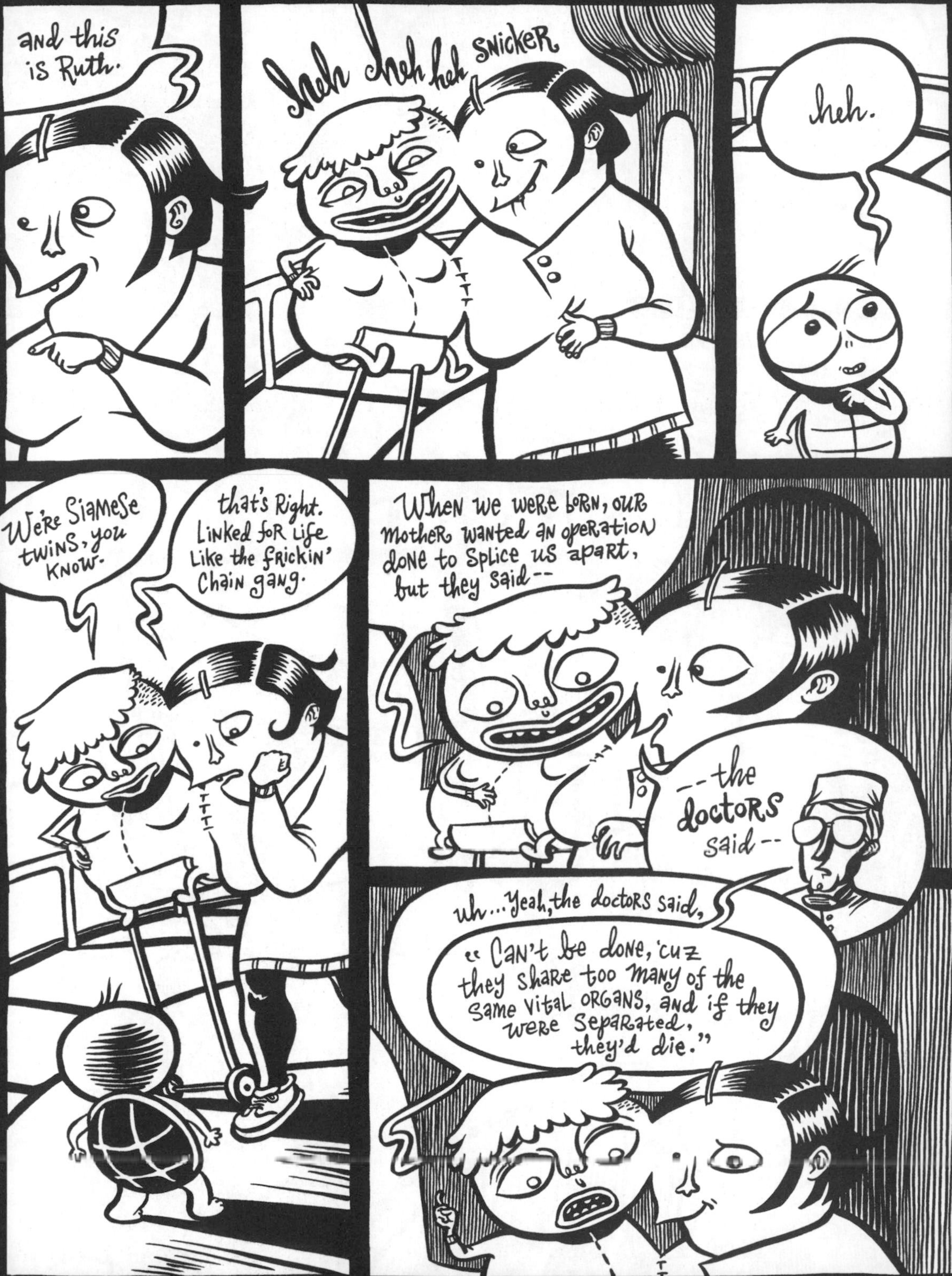
and this is Ruth.
heh heh heh SNICKER
heh.
We're Siamese twins, you know.
that's Right. Linked for life like the frickin' chain gang.
When we were born, our mother wanted an operation done to splice us apart, but they said--
--the doctors said--
uh... Yeah, the doctors said,
"Can't be done, 'cuz they share too many of the same vital organs, and if they were separated, they'd die."

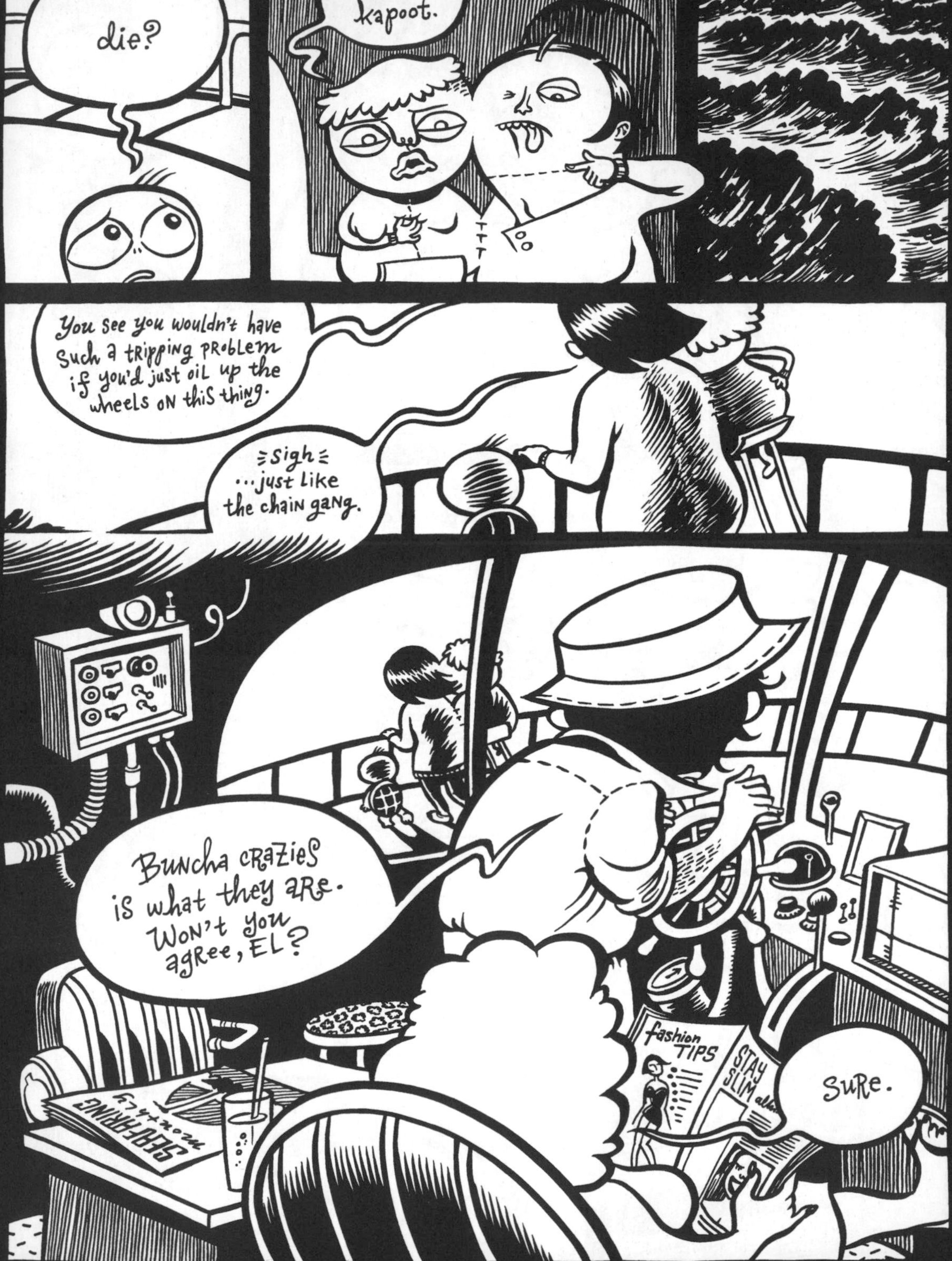
die?
kapoot.
You see you wouldn't have such a tripping problem if you'd just oil up the wheels on this thing.
sigh ...just like the chain gang.
Buncha crazies is what they are. Won't you agree, EL?
Sure.
fashion TIPS
STAY SLIM
SEAFARING monthly

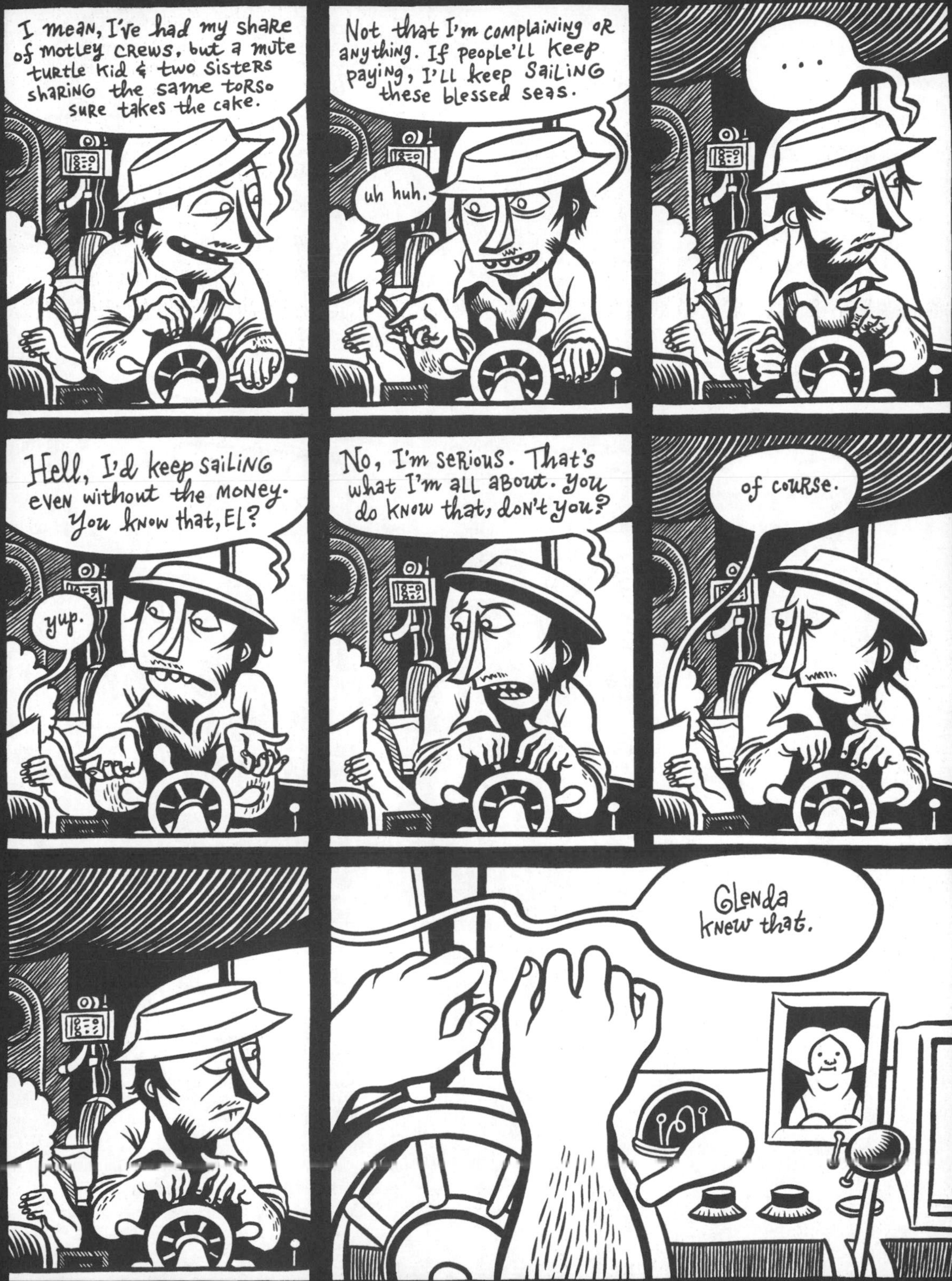
I mean, I've had my share of motley crews, but a mute turtle kid & two sisters sharing the same torso sure takes the cake.
Not that I'm complaining or anything. If people'll keep paying, I'll keep sailing these blessed seas.
uh huh.
...
Hell, I'd keep sailing even without the money. You know that, EL?
yup.
No, I'm serious. That's what I'm all about. You do know that, don't you?
of course.
Glenda knew that.

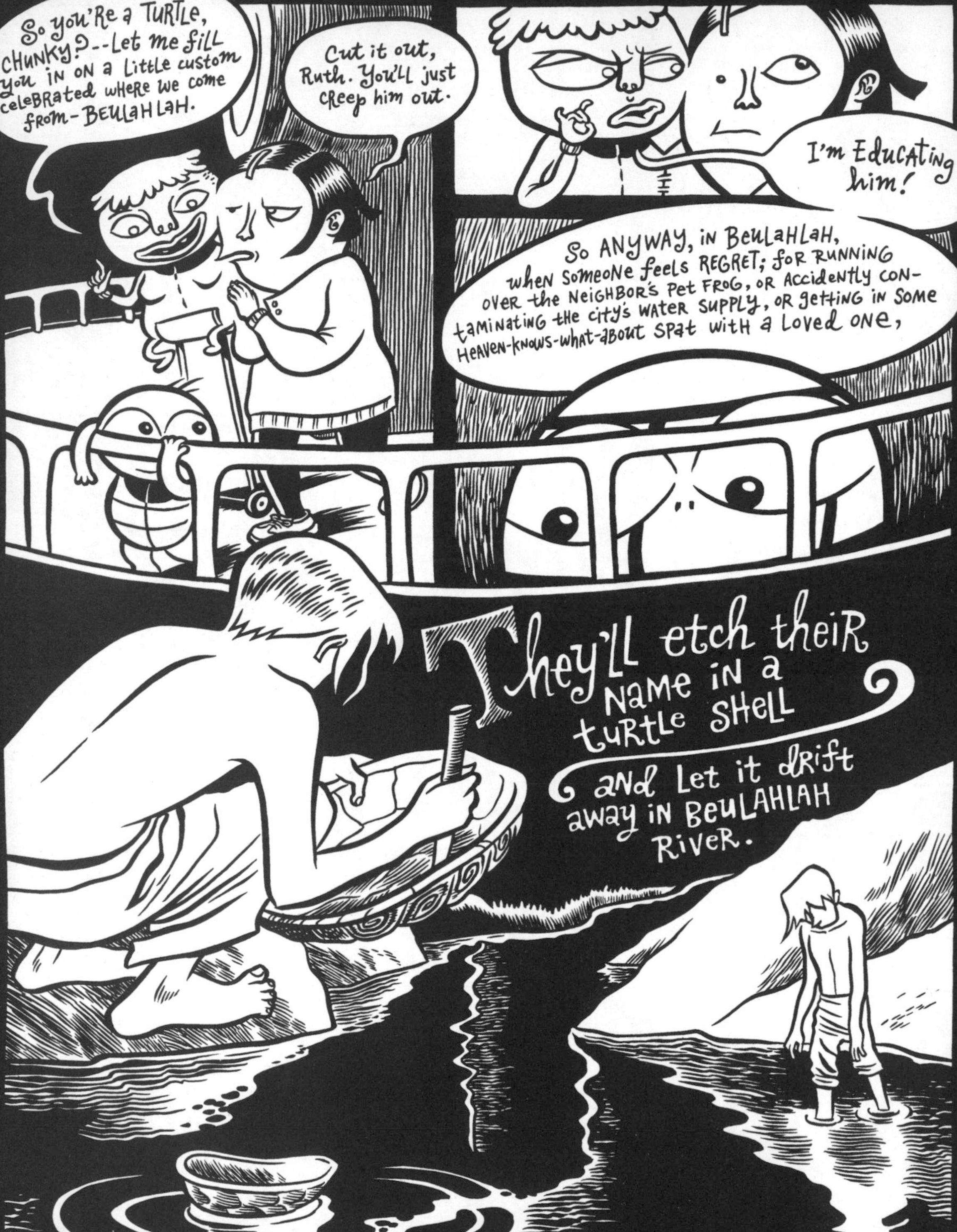
So you're a TURTLE, CHUNKY?--Let me fill you in on a little custom celebrated where we come from-BEULAHLAH.
Cut it out, Ruth. You'll just creep him out.
I'm Educating him!
So ANYWAY, in BEULAHLAH, when someone feels REGRET; for RUNNING over the NEIGHBOR'S Pet FROG, or Accidently contaminating the city's WATER SUPPLY, or getting in some Heaven-knows-what-about spat with a Loved one,
They'll etch their name in a turtle shell
and let it drift away in BEULAHLAH River.

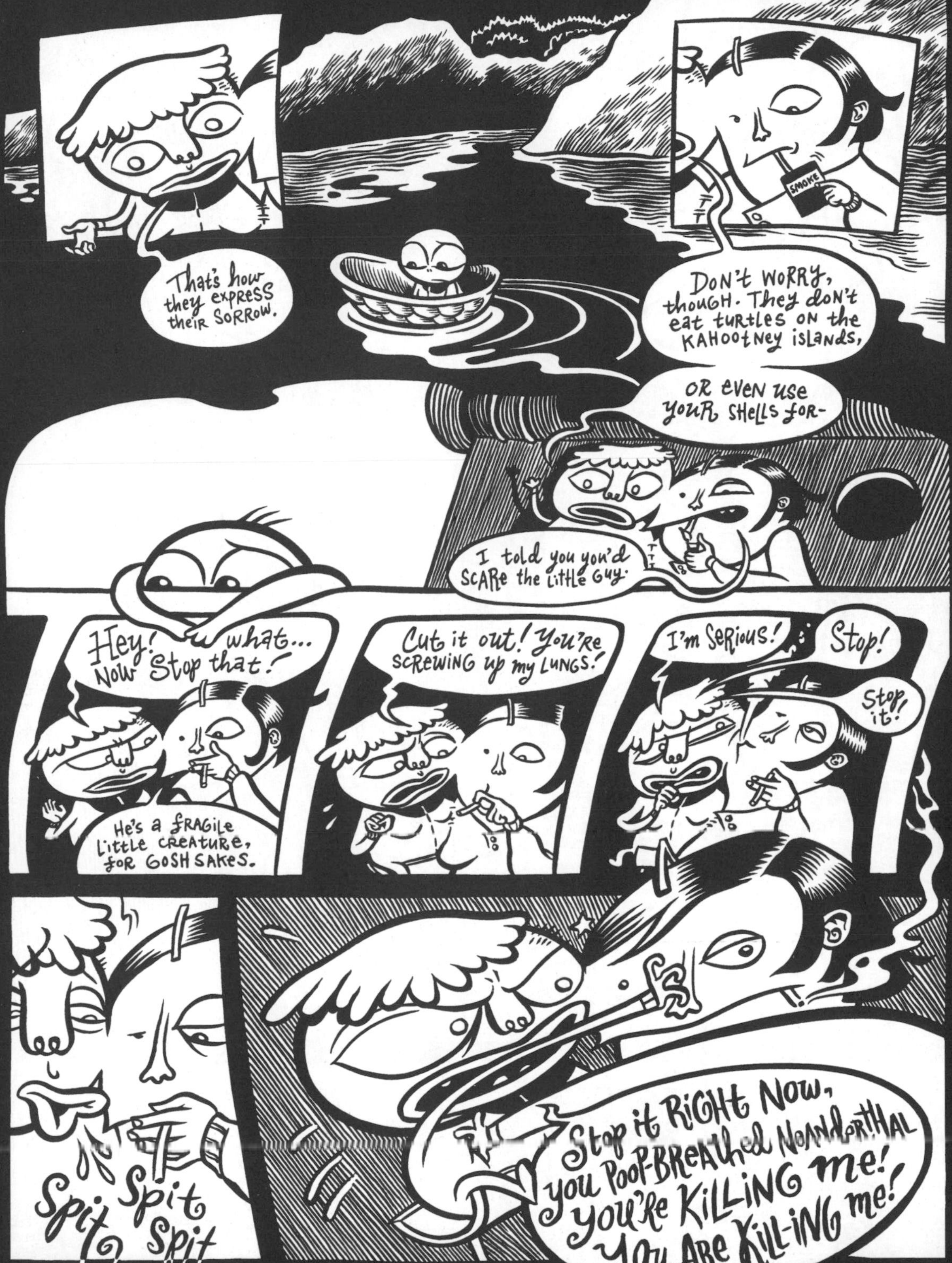

That's how they express their SORROW.
DON'T WORRY, though. They don't eat turtles on the KAHOOTNEY islands,
OR even use your shells for-
I told you you'd SCARE the Little Guy.
Hey! what... Now Stop that!
He's a fragile little creature, for GOSH SAKES.
Cut it out! You're SCREWING up my LUNGS!
I'm Serious!
Stop!
Stop it!
Spit Spit Spit Spit
Stop it RIGHT NOW, you POOP-BREATHED NEANDERTHAL you're KILLING me! You ARE KILL-ING me!

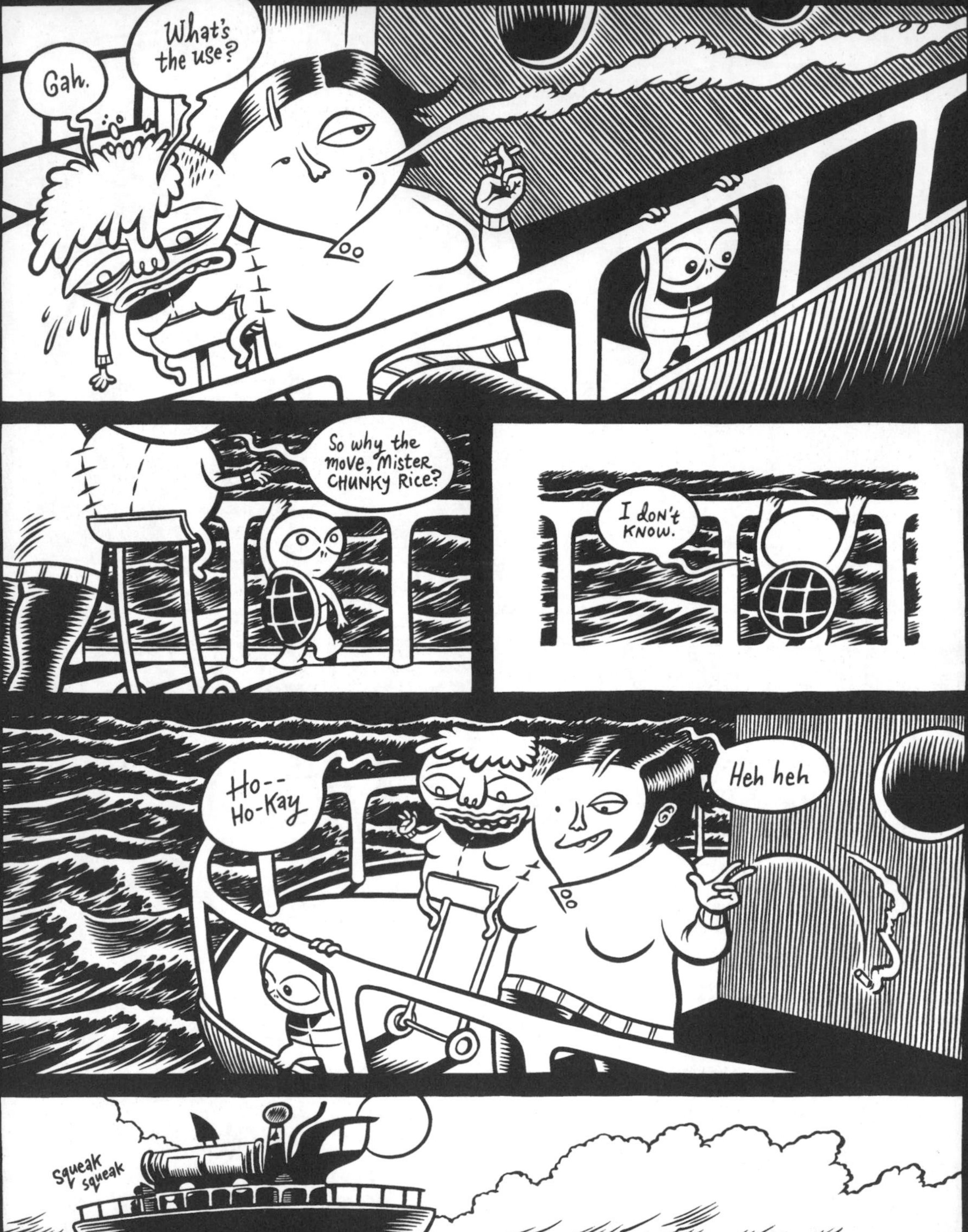
Gah.
What's the use?
So why the move, Mister CHUNKY Rice?
I don't know.
Ho-- Ho-Kay
Heh heh
squeak squeak

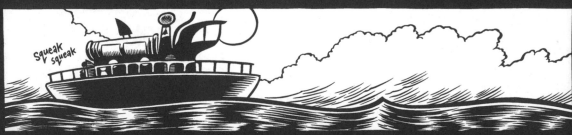

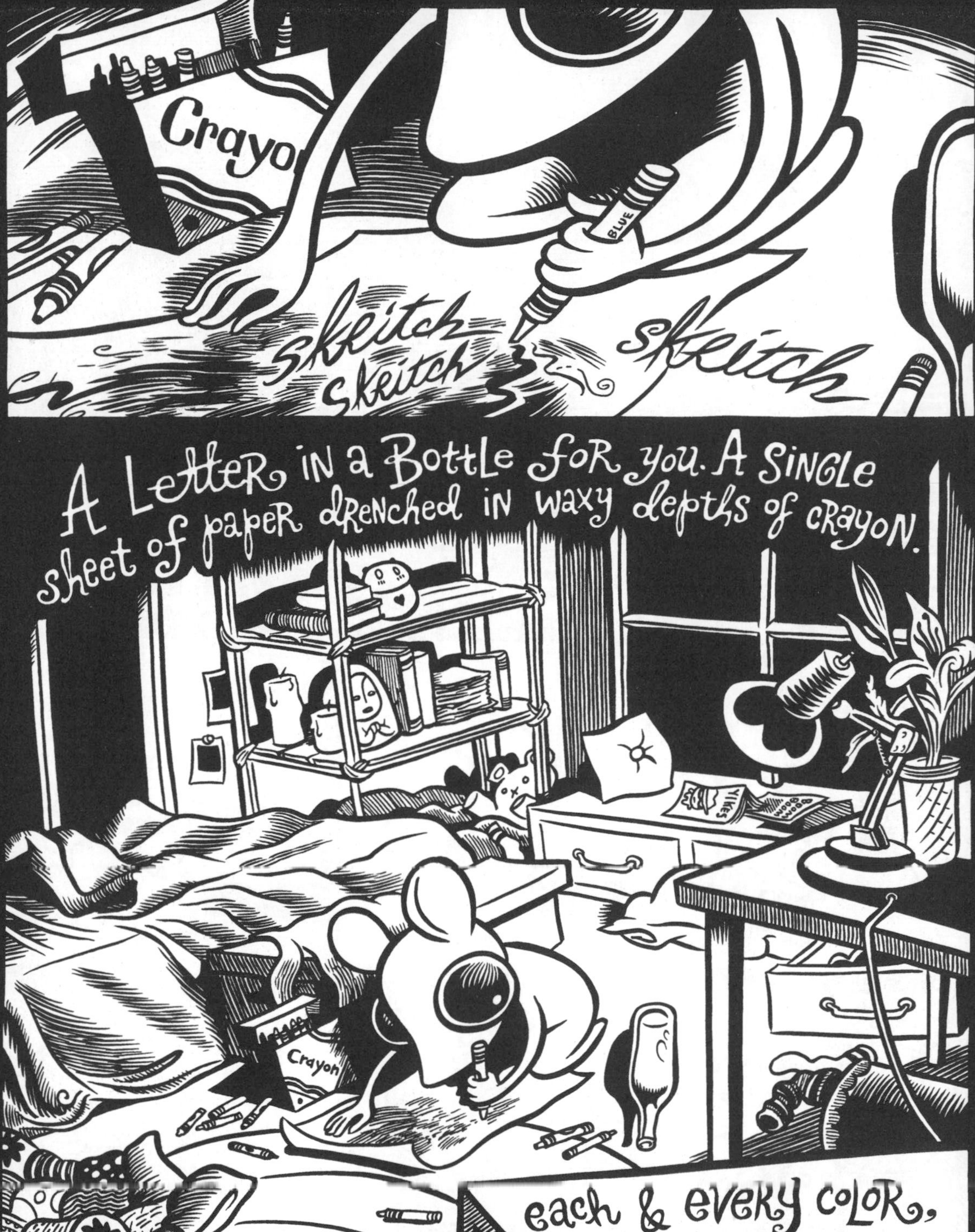
Crayo
BLUE
skritch
skritch
skritch
skritch
A Letter in a Bottle for you. A single sheet of paper drenched in waxy depths of crayon.
YIKES
Crayon
each & every color, but no words.

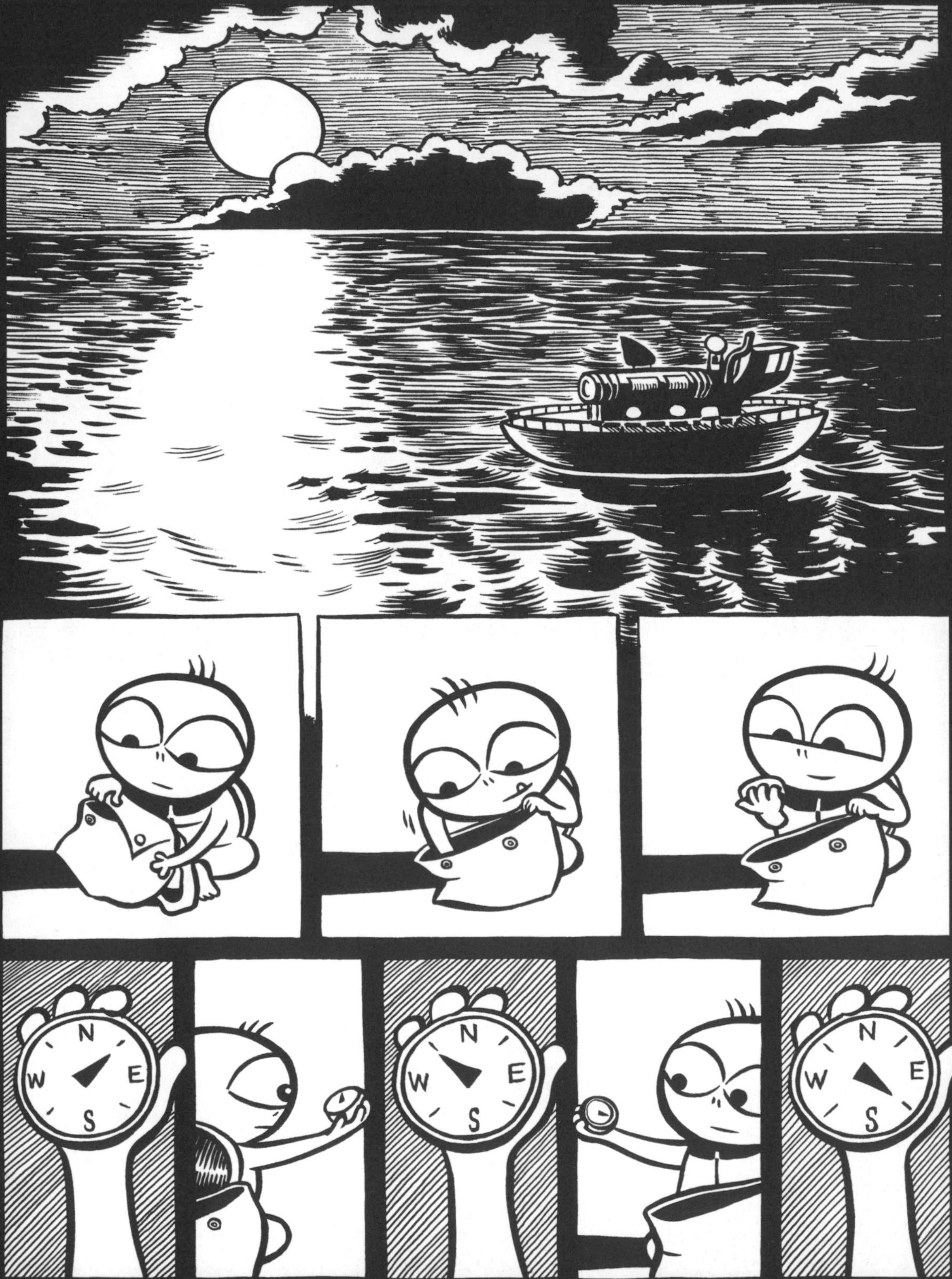
N
W
E
S
N
W
E
S
N
W
E
S

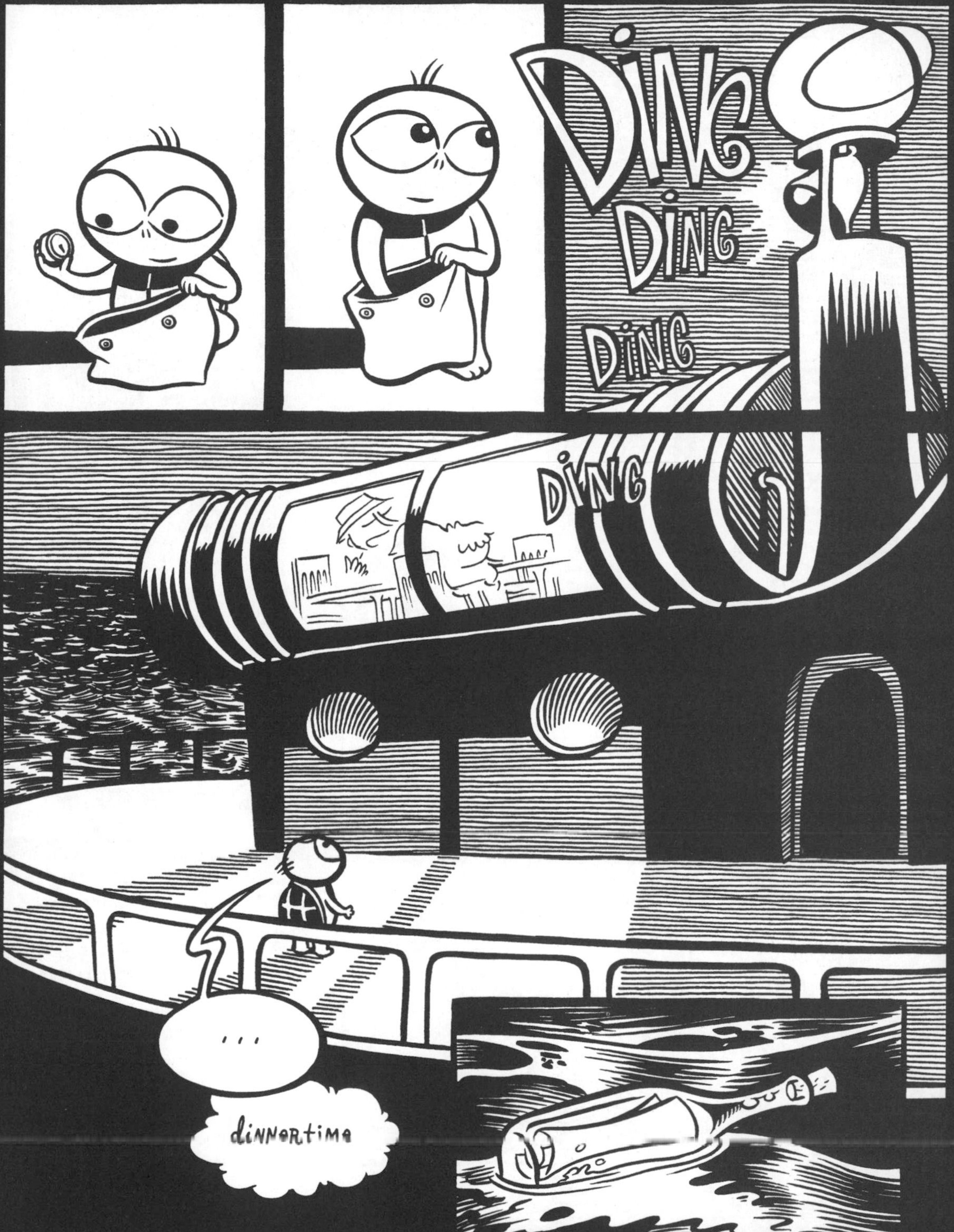
DING
DING
DING
DING
...
dinnertime

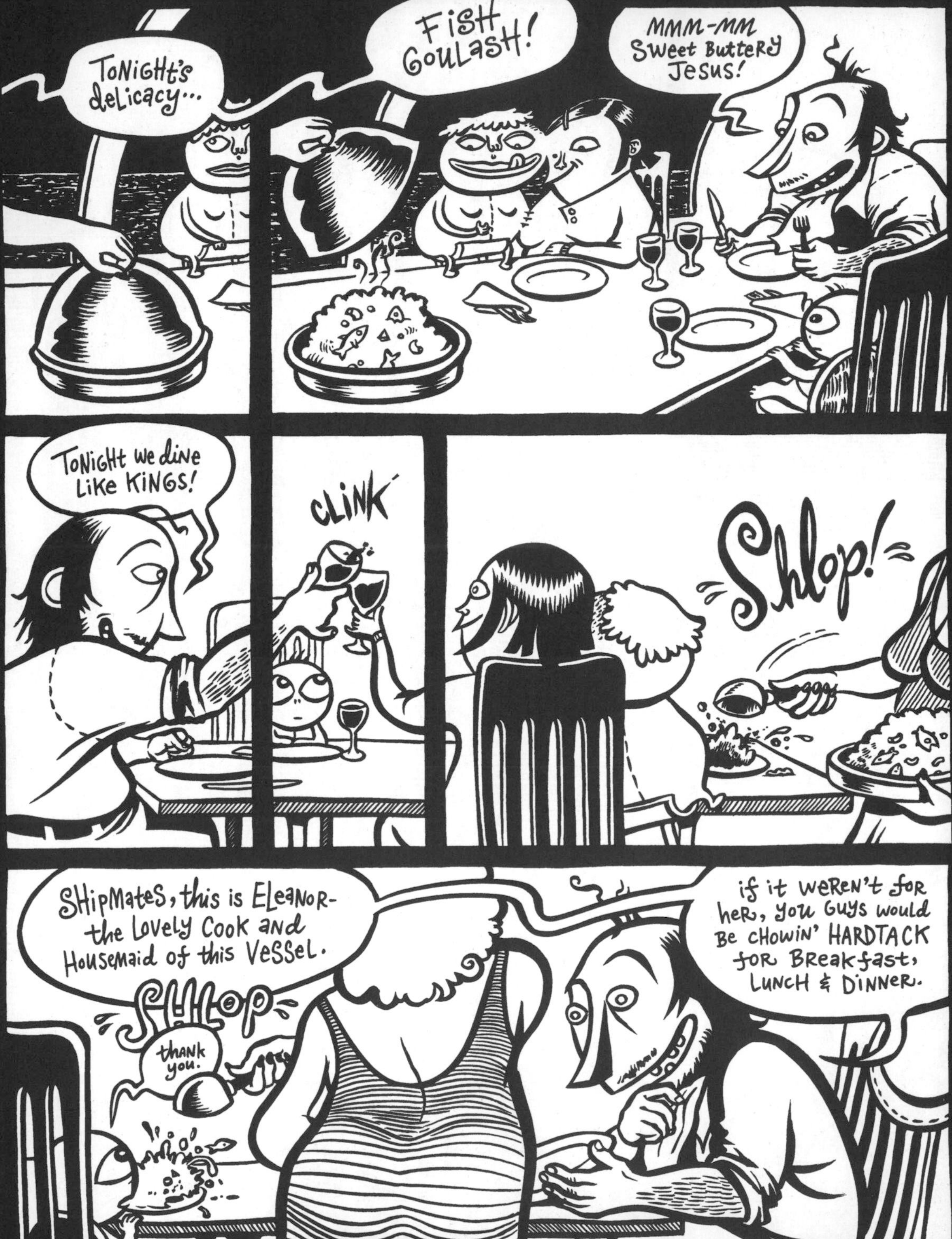

TONIGHT'S delicacy...
FISH GOULASH!
MMM-MM Sweet Buttery Jesus!
TONIGHT we dine like KINGS!
CLINK
SHLOP!
SHIPMATES, this is ELEANOR- the Lovely Cook and Housemaid of this VESSEL.
SHLOP
thank you.
if it WEREN'T for her, you GUYS would BE CHOWIN' HARDTACK for Breakfast, LUNCH & DINNER.

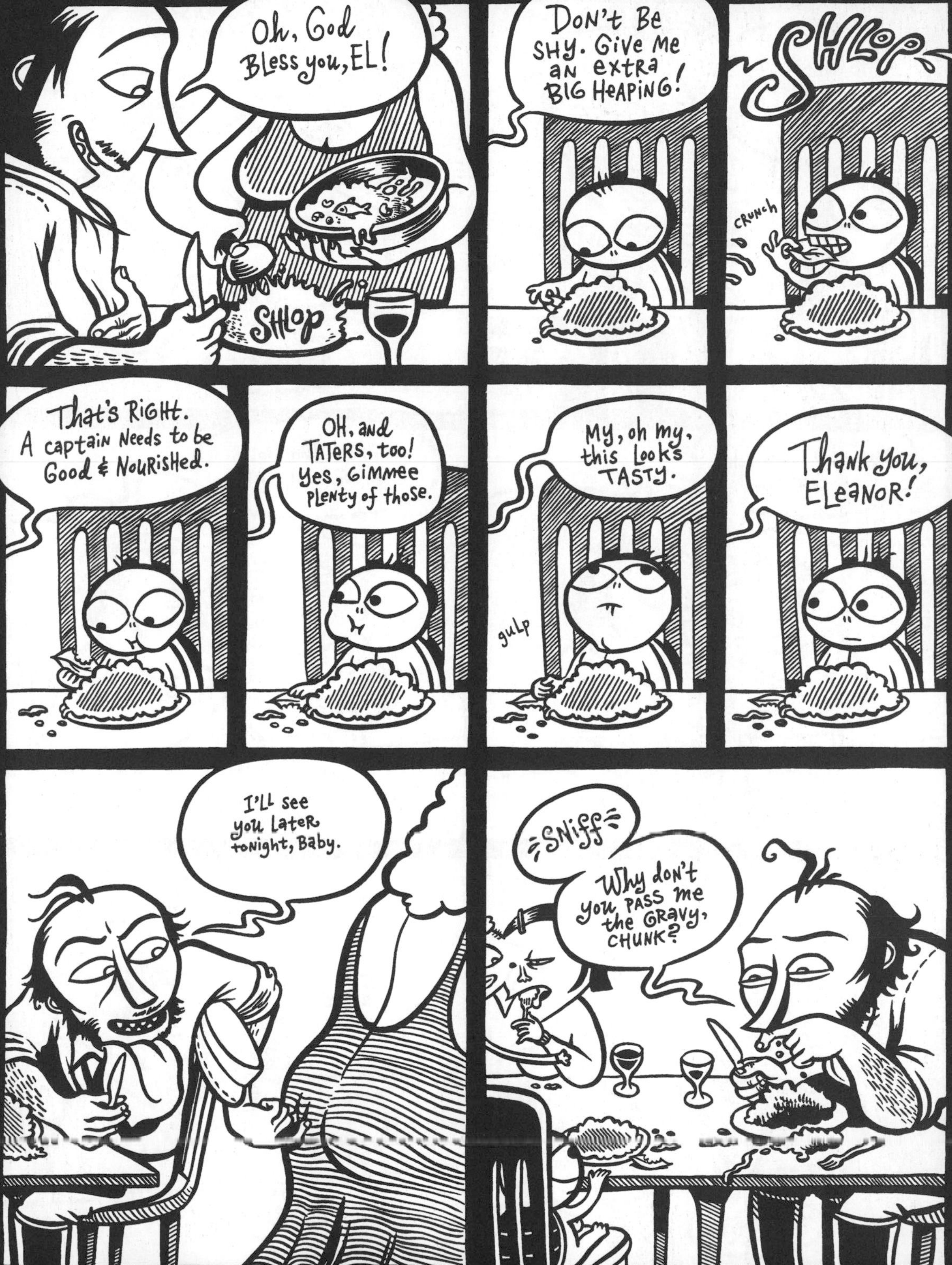
Oh, God Bless you, EL!
SHLOP
Don't Be SHY. Give Me an extra BIG HeaPING!
SHLOP
CRUNCH
That's RIGHT. A captain Needs to be Good & NouRisHed.
OH, and TATERS, too! Yes, GIMMee PLenty of those.
My, oh my, this Looks TASTY.
gulp
Thank you, ELeanor!
I'LL see you Later tonight, Baby.
SNiff
Why don't you PASS me the GRAVY, CHUNK?

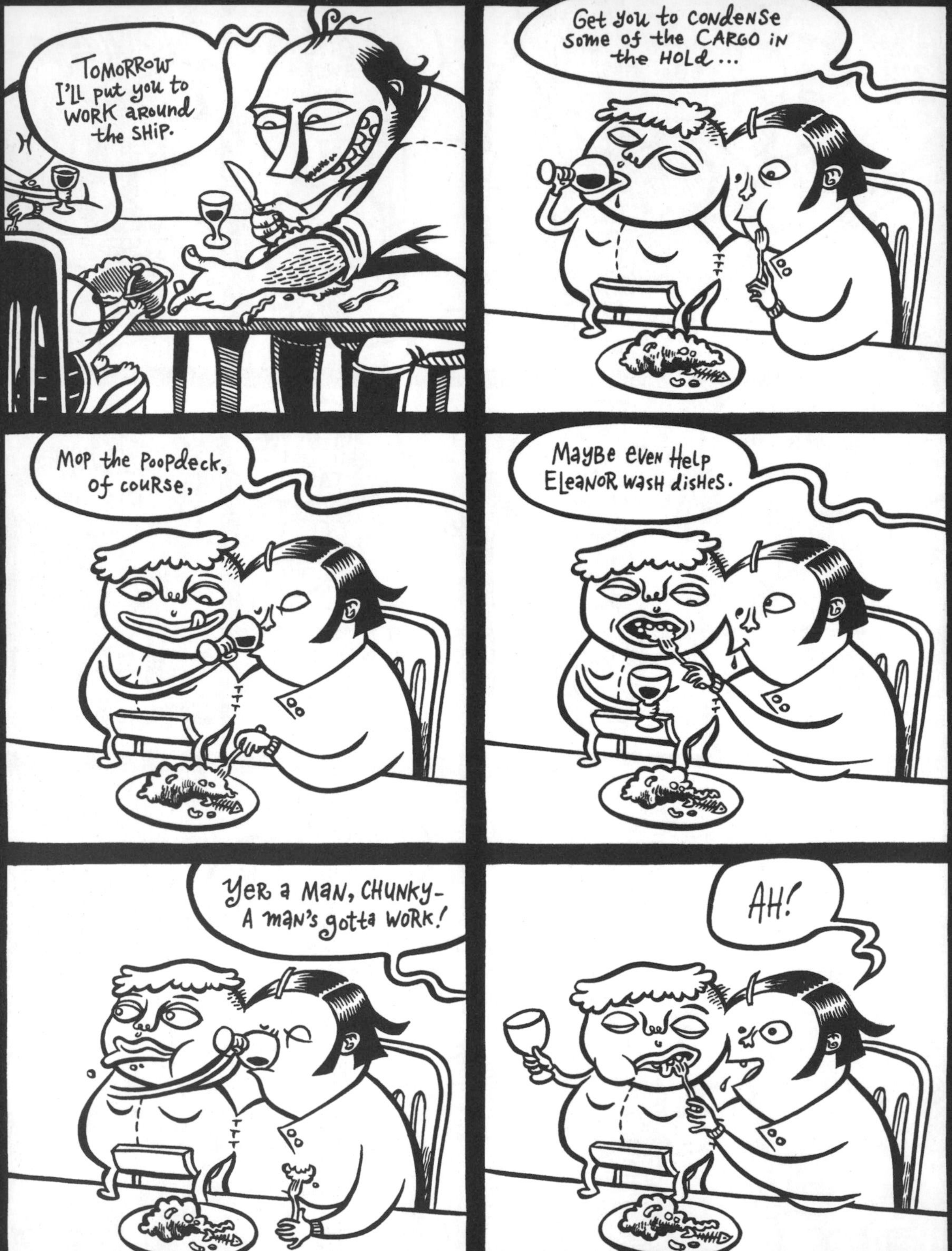
TOMORROW I'LL put you to WORK around the SHIP.
Get you to CONDENSE some of the CARGO IN the HOLD...
Mop the Poopdeck, of course,
MayBE EVEN Help ELEANOR WASH dishes.
Yer a MAN, CHUNKY- A man's gotta WORK!
AH!

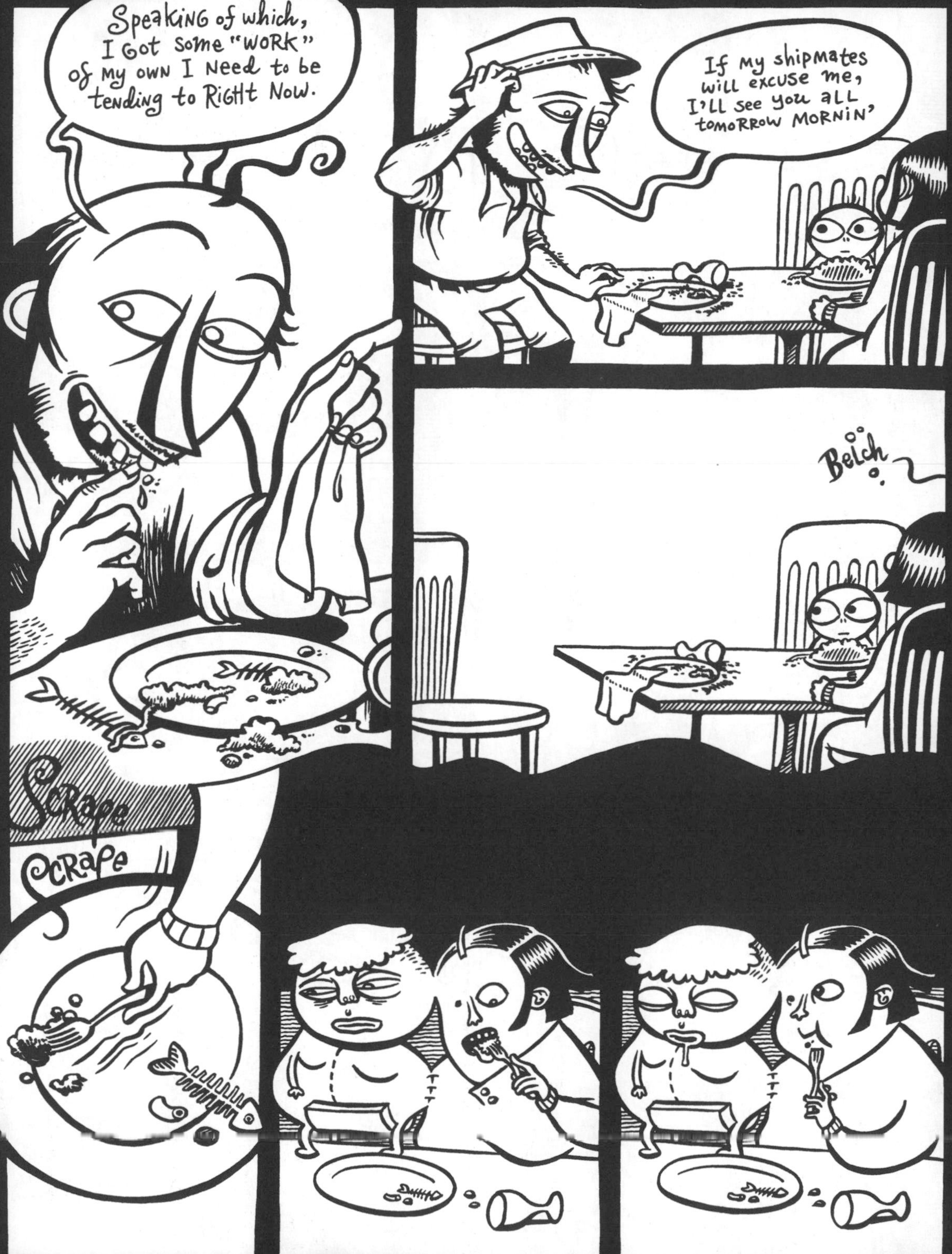

Speaking of which, I Got some "WORK" of my own I Need to be tending to RIGHt Now.
If my shipmates will excuse me, I'll see you all tomorrow MORNIN'
Belch
Scrape
Scrape

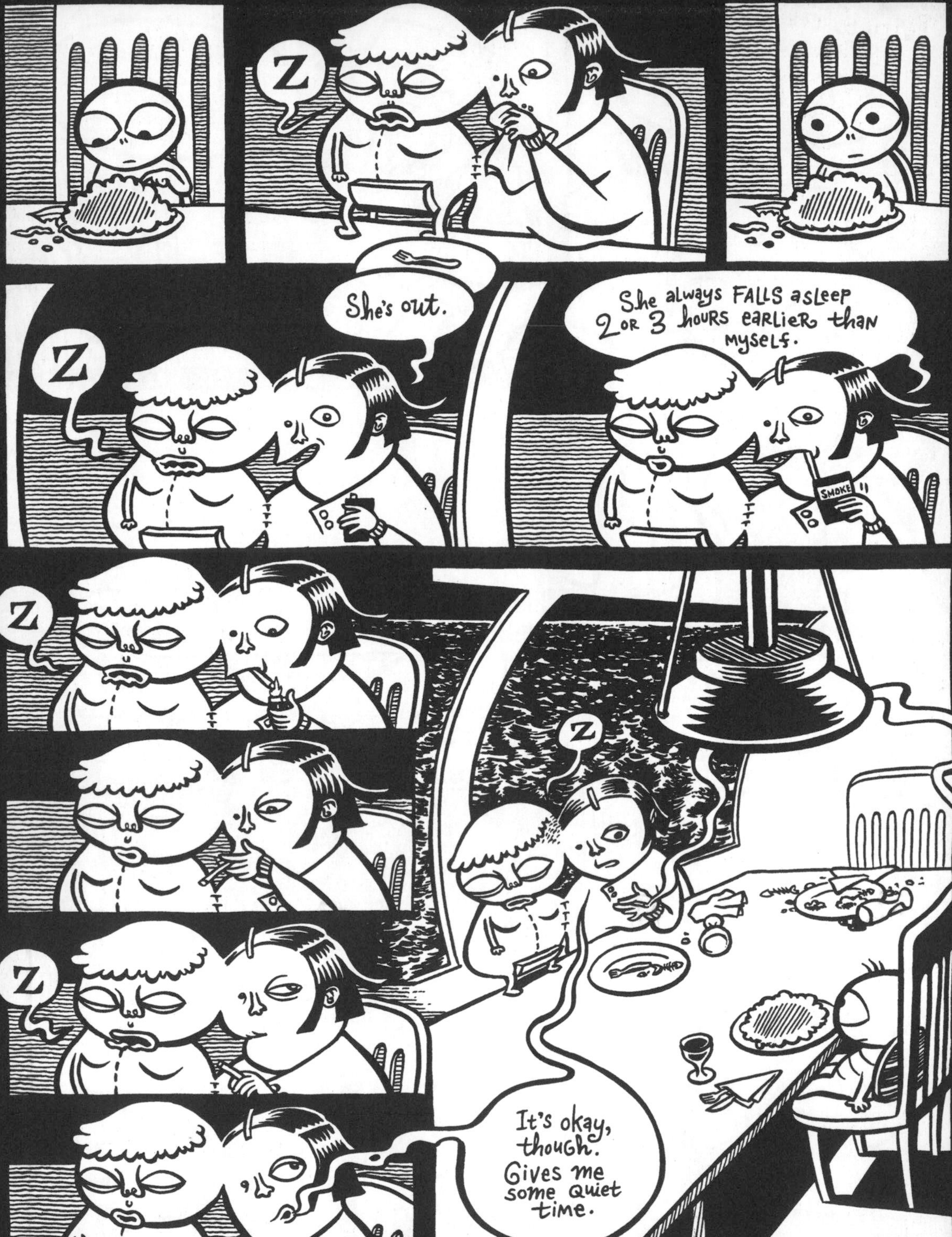

Z
Z
She's out.
She always FALLS asleep 2 or 3 hours earlier than myself.
SMOKE
Z
Z
Z
It's okay, though. Gives me some quiet time.

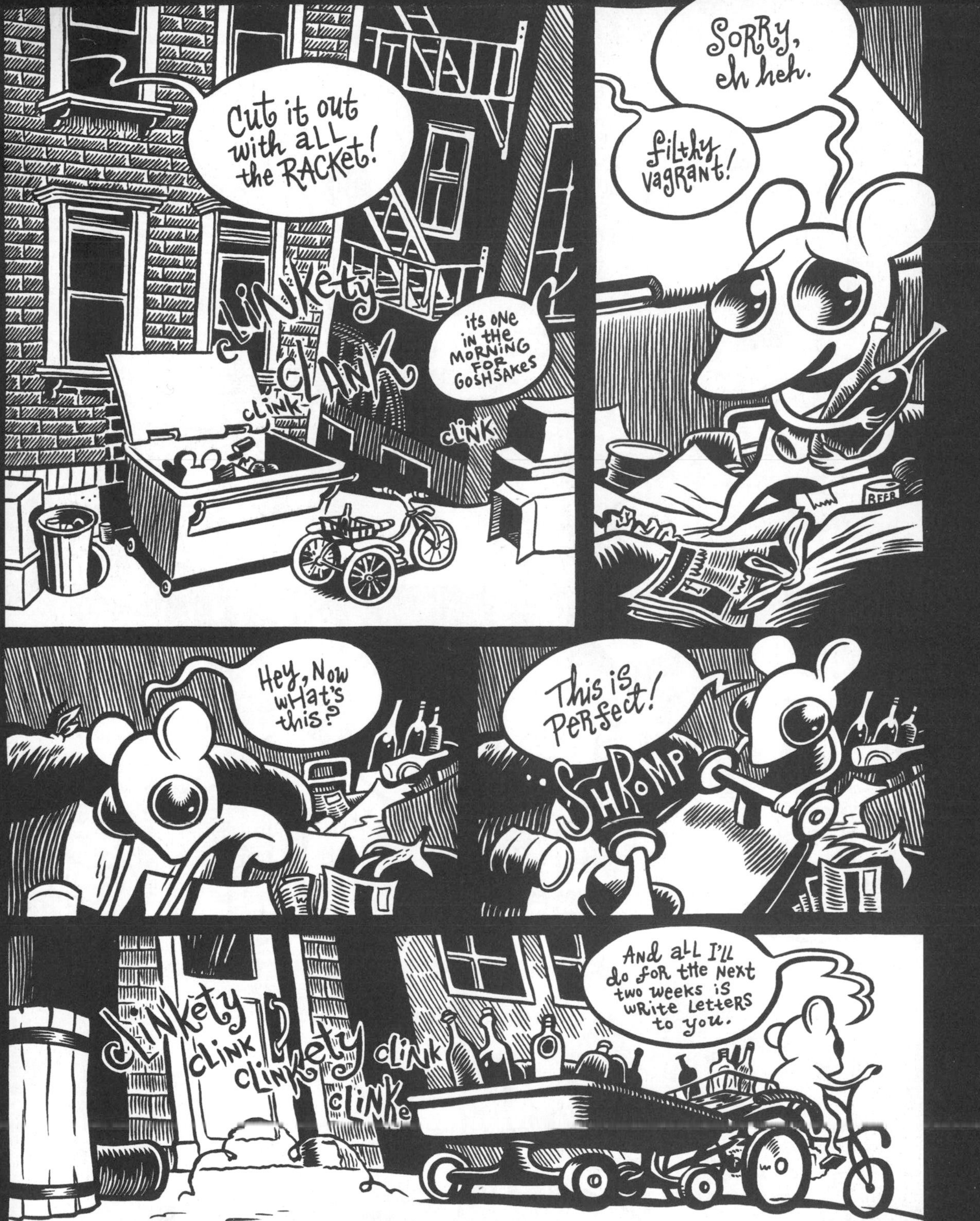
Cut it out with all the RACKET!
clinkety
clink
CLANK
clink
its ONE in the MORNING FOR GOSHSAKES
clink
SORRY, eh heh.
filthy vagrant!
BEER
Hey, Now what's this?
This is Perfect!
SHROMP
clinkety
clink
clinkety
clink
clink
clink
And all I'll do for the next two weeks is write letters to you.

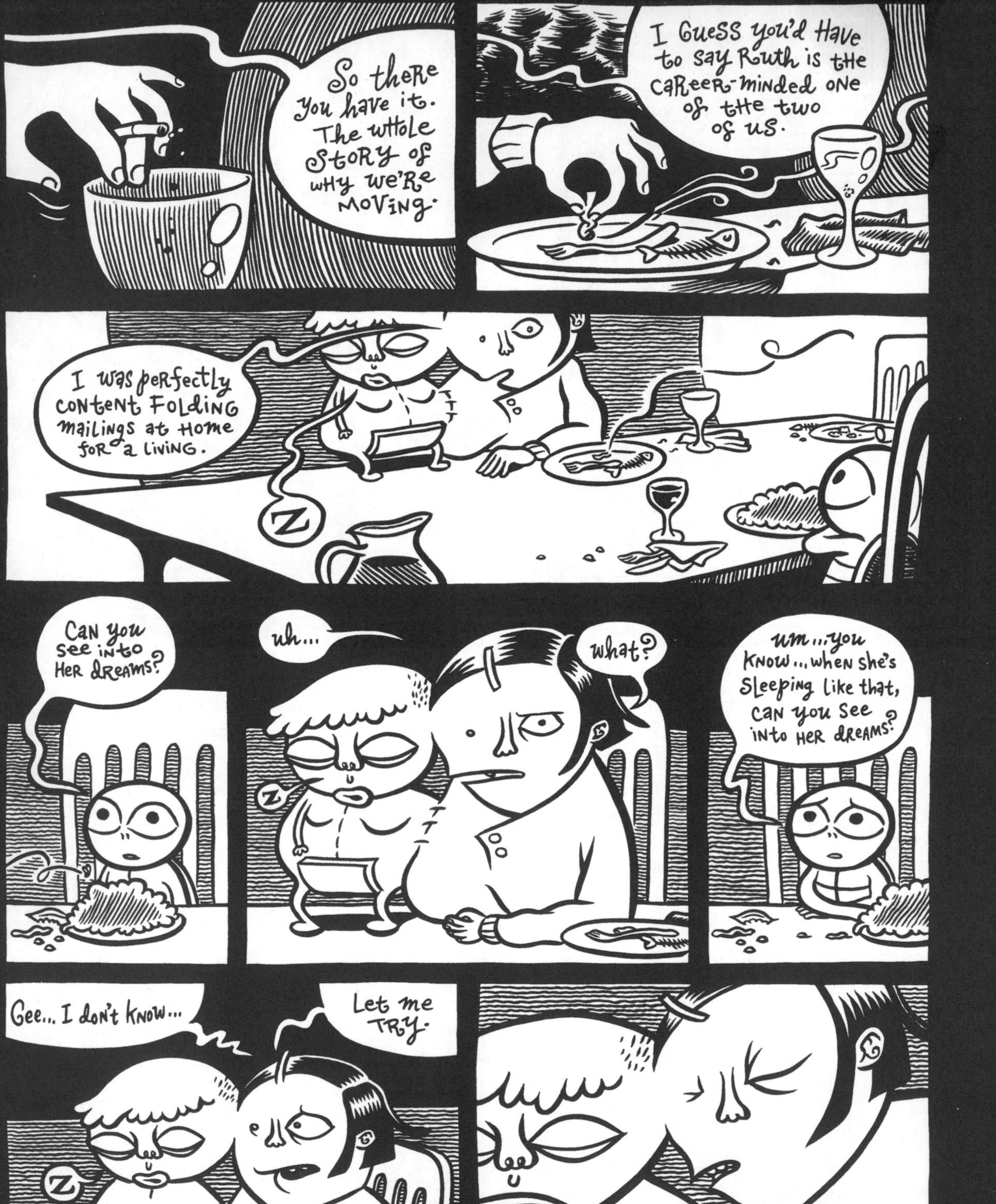
So there you have it. The whole story of why we're moving.
I guess you'd have to say Ruth is the career-minded one of the two of us.
I was perfectly content folding mailings at home for a living.
Can you see into her dreams?
uh...
what?
um...you know...when she's sleeping like that, can you see into her dreams?
Gee... I don't know...
Let me TRY.

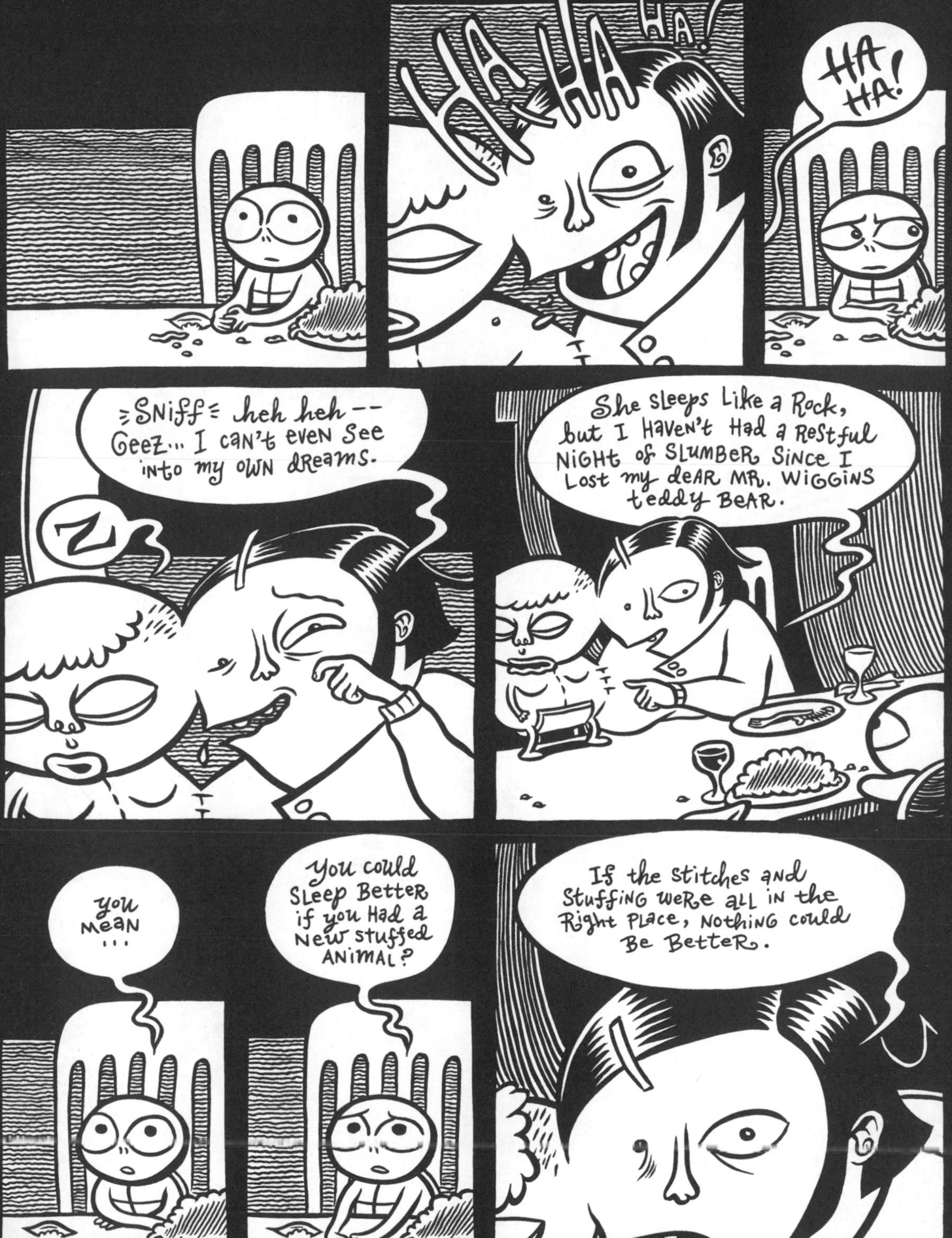
HA HA HA HA!
HA HA!
SNIFF heh heh -- Geez... I can't even see into my own dreams.
Z
She sleeps like a rock, but I haven't had a restful night of slumber since I lost my dear Mr. Wiggins teddy bear.
You mean...
You could sleep better if you had a new stuffed animal?
If the stitches and stuffing were all in the right place, nothing could be better.

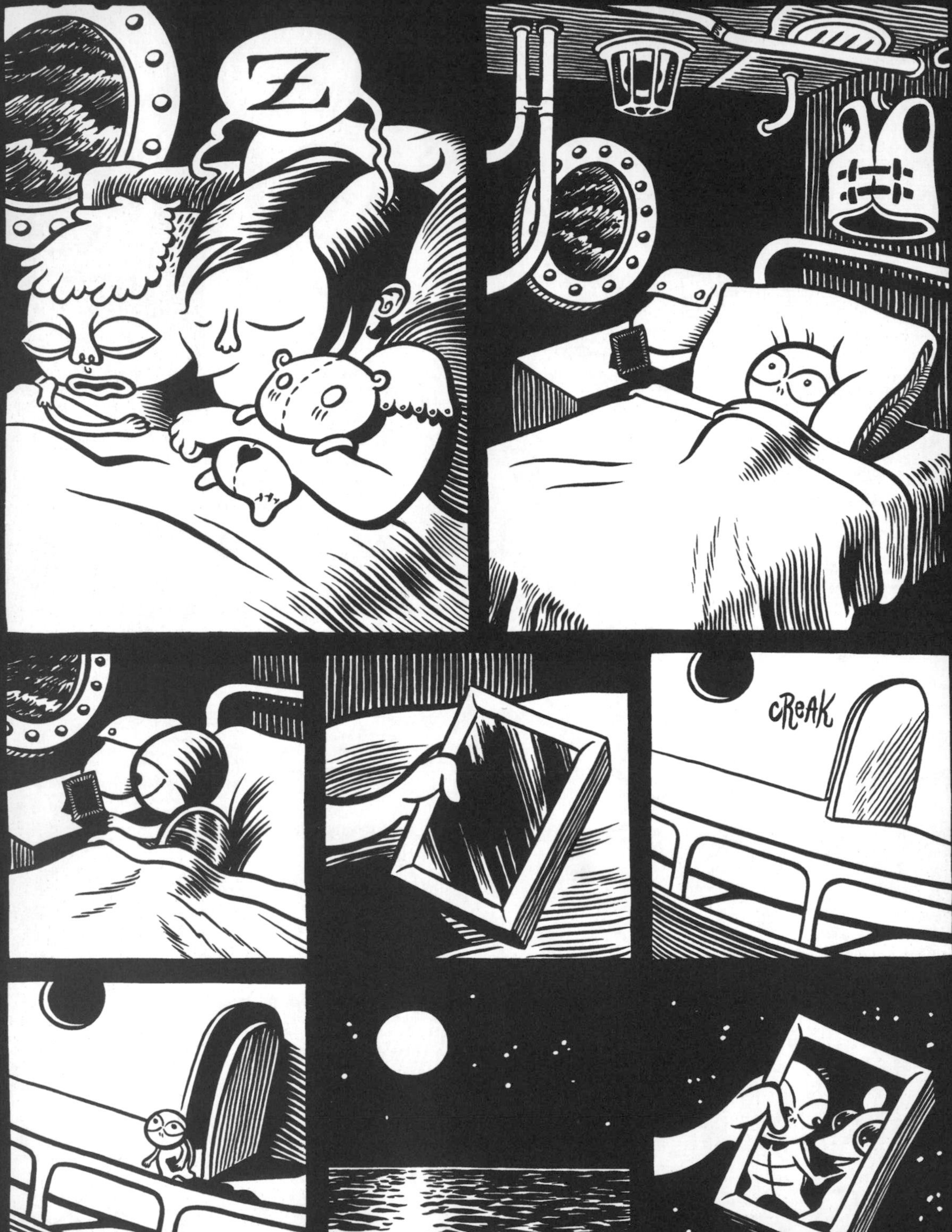
Z
CReAK

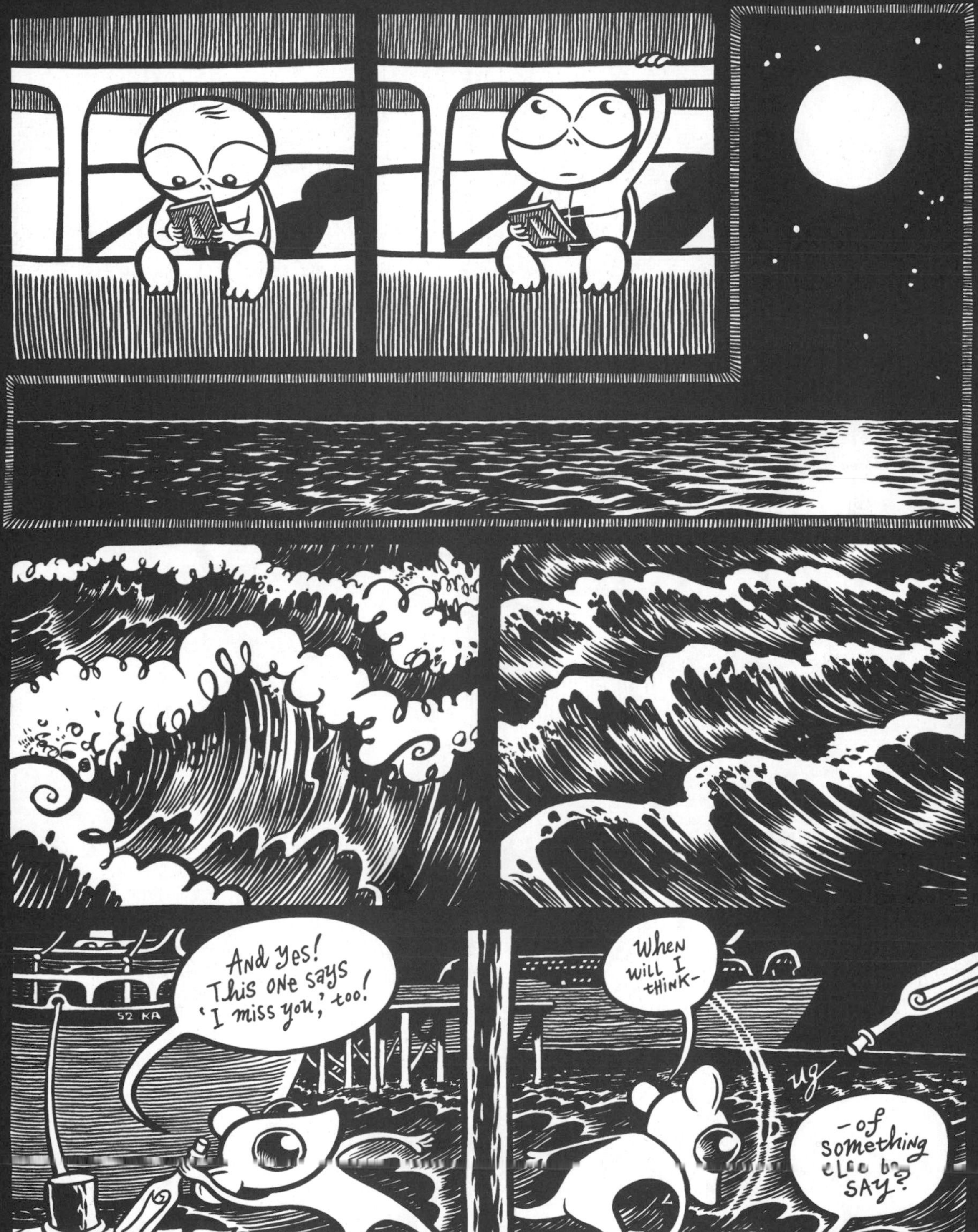

And yes! This one says 'I miss you,' too!
52 KA
When will I think-
-of something
SAY?

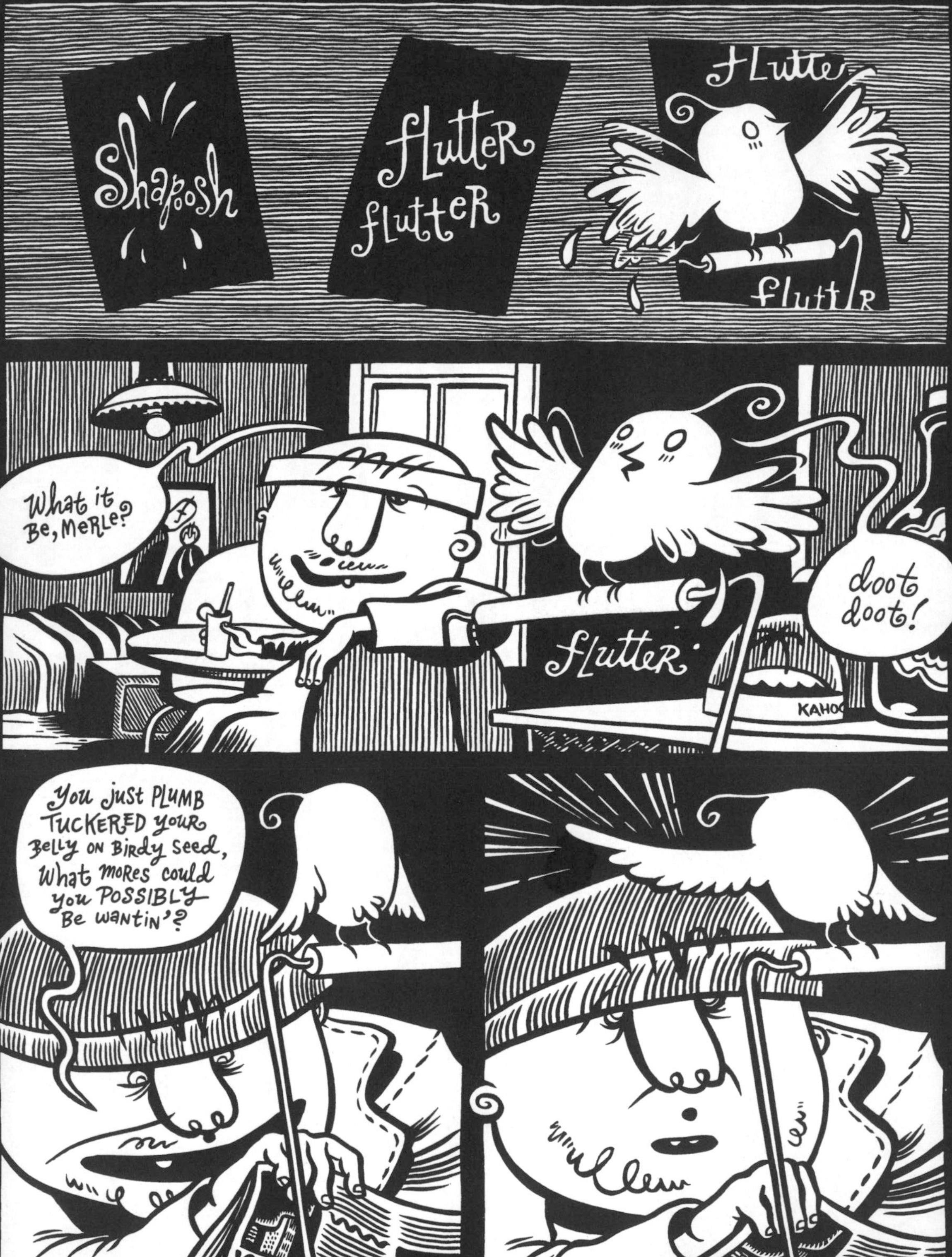
Shaposh
flutter flutter
flutte
flutt R
What it Be, Merle?
doot doot!
flutter
KAHO
You just PLUMB TUCKERED your Belly on Birdy seed, What mores could you POSSIBLY Be wantin'?

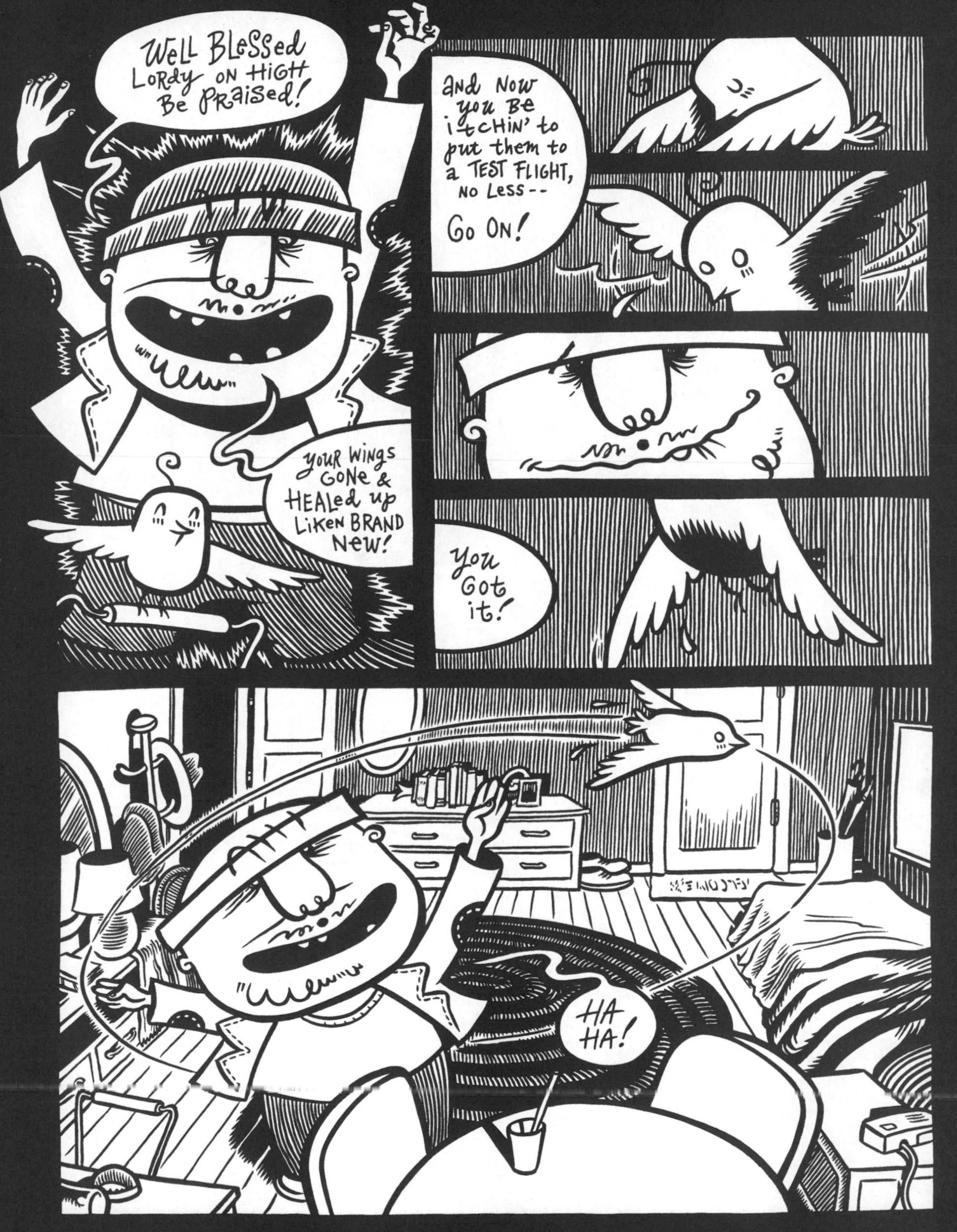

WeLL BLeSSed LORdy ON HIGH Be PRaiSed!
youR WiNgS GONe & HEALed up LiKeN BRAND New!
and NOW you Be itCHIN' to put them to a TEST FLIGHT, NO LESS --
Go ON!
you Got it!
HA HA!

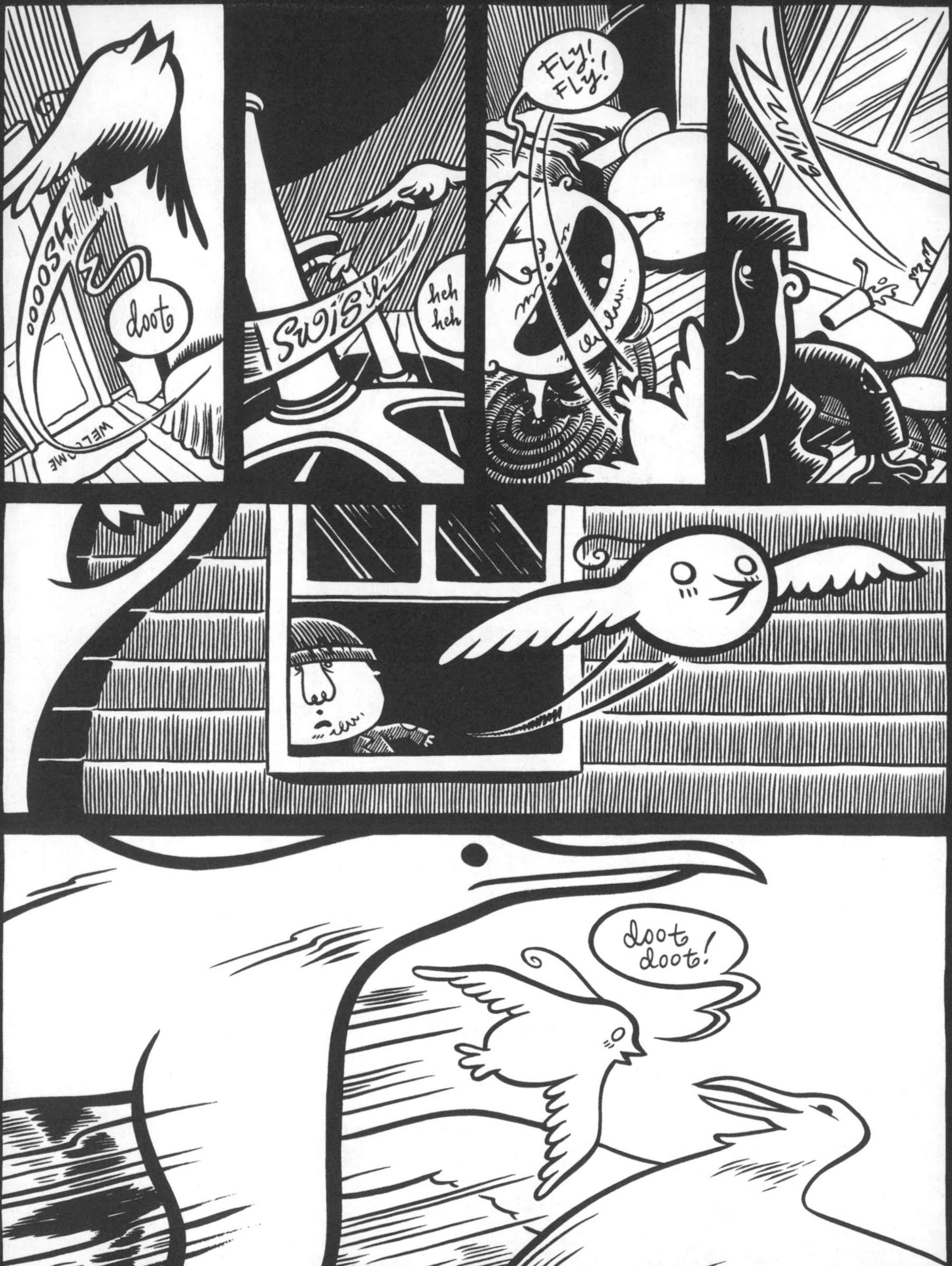
oooooSH
doot
SWISH
heh heh
FLY! FLY!
ZWING
doot doot!

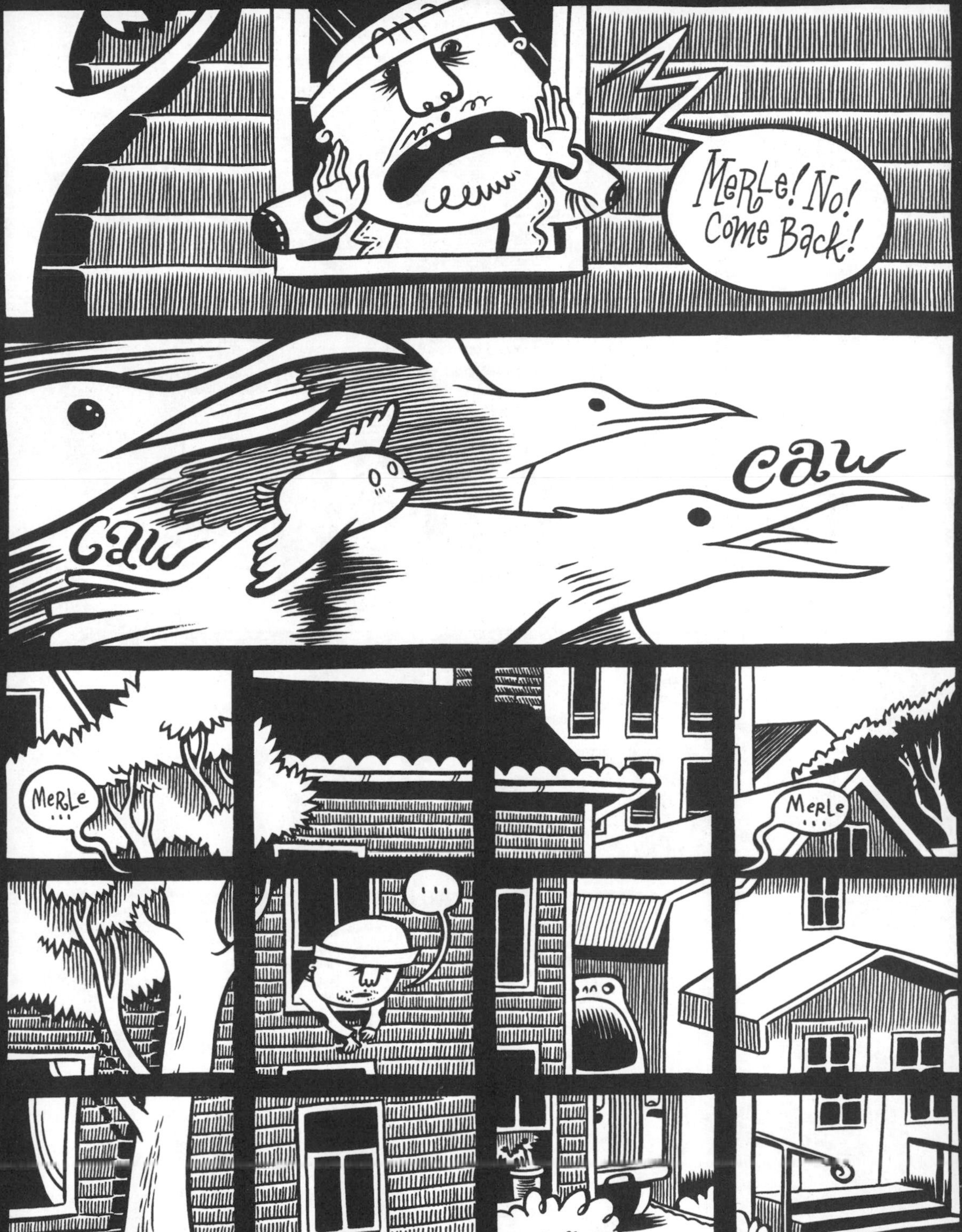
Merle! No! Come Back!
caw
caw
Merle ...
Merle ...
...

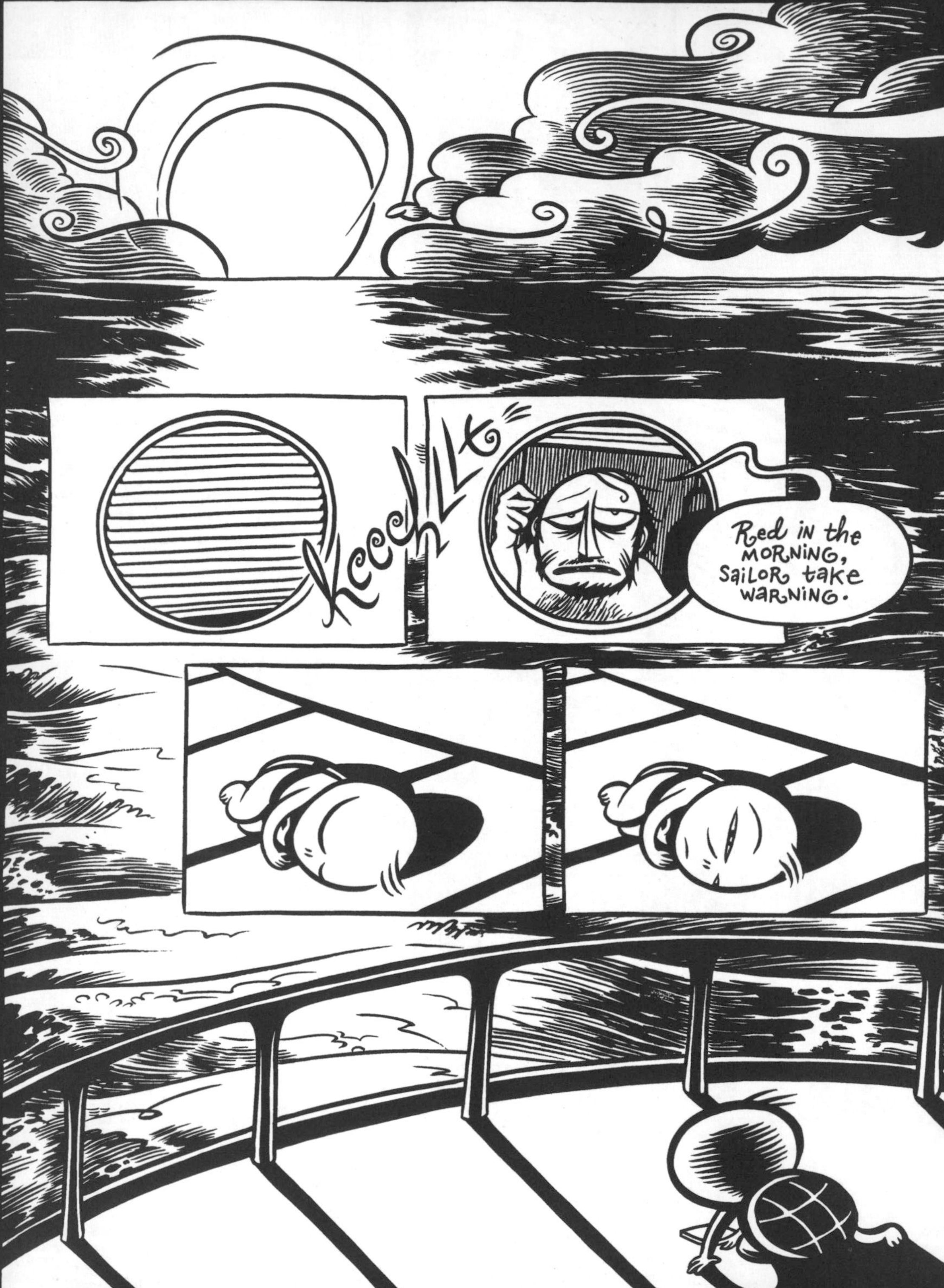
KCCCHLLt
Red in the MORNING, Sailor take WARNING.

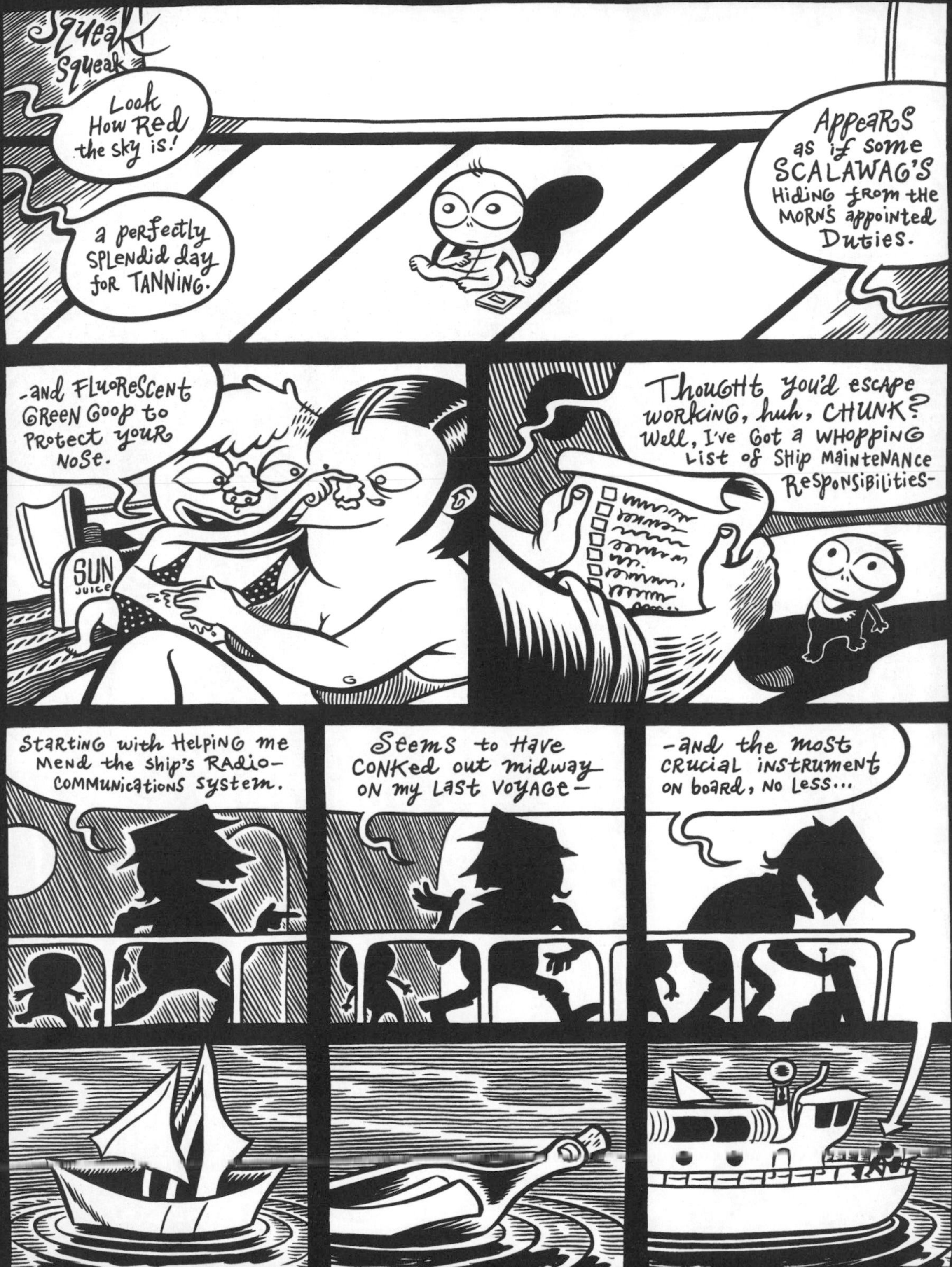
Squeak
Squeak
Look How Red the sky is!
a perfectly splendid day for TANNING.
Appears as if some SCALAWAG'S Hiding from the MORN'S appointed Duties.
-and FLUORESCENT GREEN GOOP to PROTECT YOUR NOSE.
SUN JUICE
Thought you'd escape working, huh, CHUNK? Well, I've Got a WHOPPING List of Ship Maintenance Responsibilities-
STARTING with Helping me Mend the ship's RADIO-COMMUNICATIONS system.
Seems to Have CONKED out midway ON my LAST VOYAGE-
-and the most crucial instrument on board, No Less...

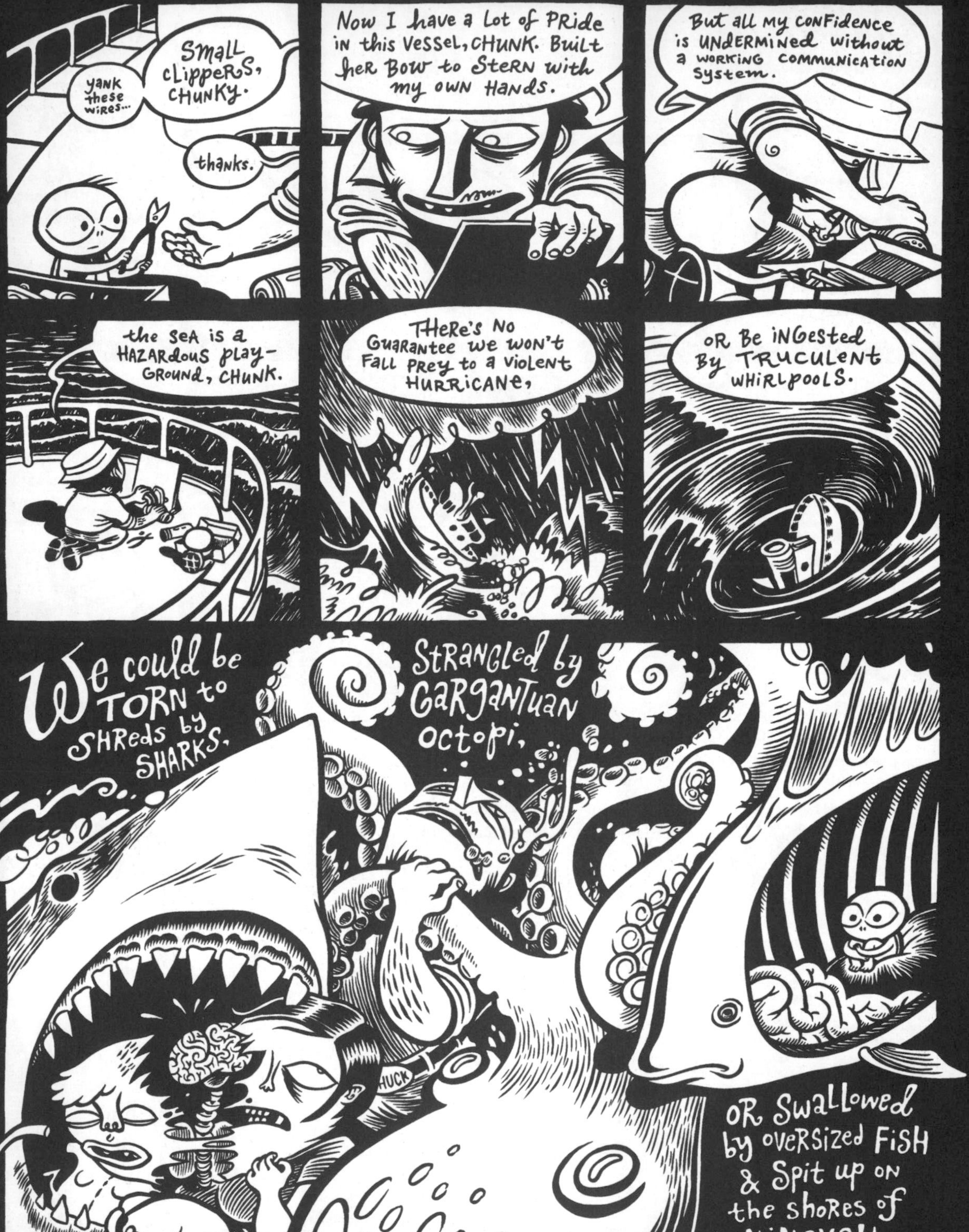

yank these wires...
SMALL CLIPPERS, CHUNKY.
thanks.
Now I have a Lot of PRide in this VESSEL, CHUNK. Built her Bow to STERN with my OWN HANDS.
But all my CONFIDENCE is UNDERMINED without a WORKING COMMUNICATION SYSTEM.
the SEA is a HAZARDOUS PLAY-GROUND, CHUNK.
THERE'S NO GUARANTEE WE WON'T FALL PREY to a VIOLENT HURRICANE,
OR BE INGESTED By TRUCULENT WHIRLPOOLS.
We could be TORN to SHReds by SHARKS,
STRANGLED by GARGANTUAN octopi,
HUCK
OR SwalLowed by oversized FISH & Spit up ON the shores of NINEVAH.

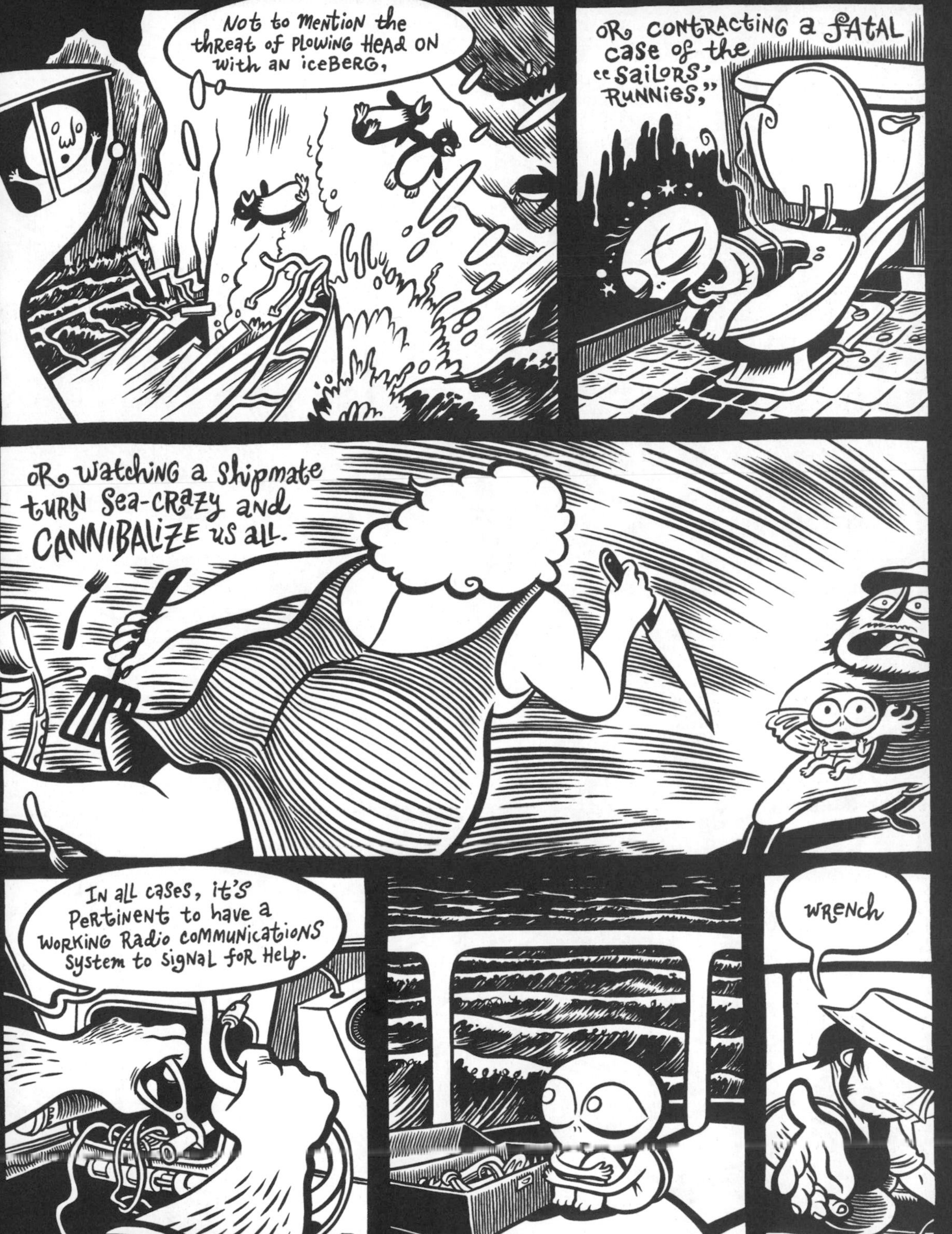
Not to mention the threat of plowing head on with an iceberg,
or contracting a fatal case of the "Sailors' Runnies,"
or watching a shipmate turn sea-crazy and cannibalize us all.
In all cases, it's pertinent to have a working radio communications system to signal for help.
WRENCH

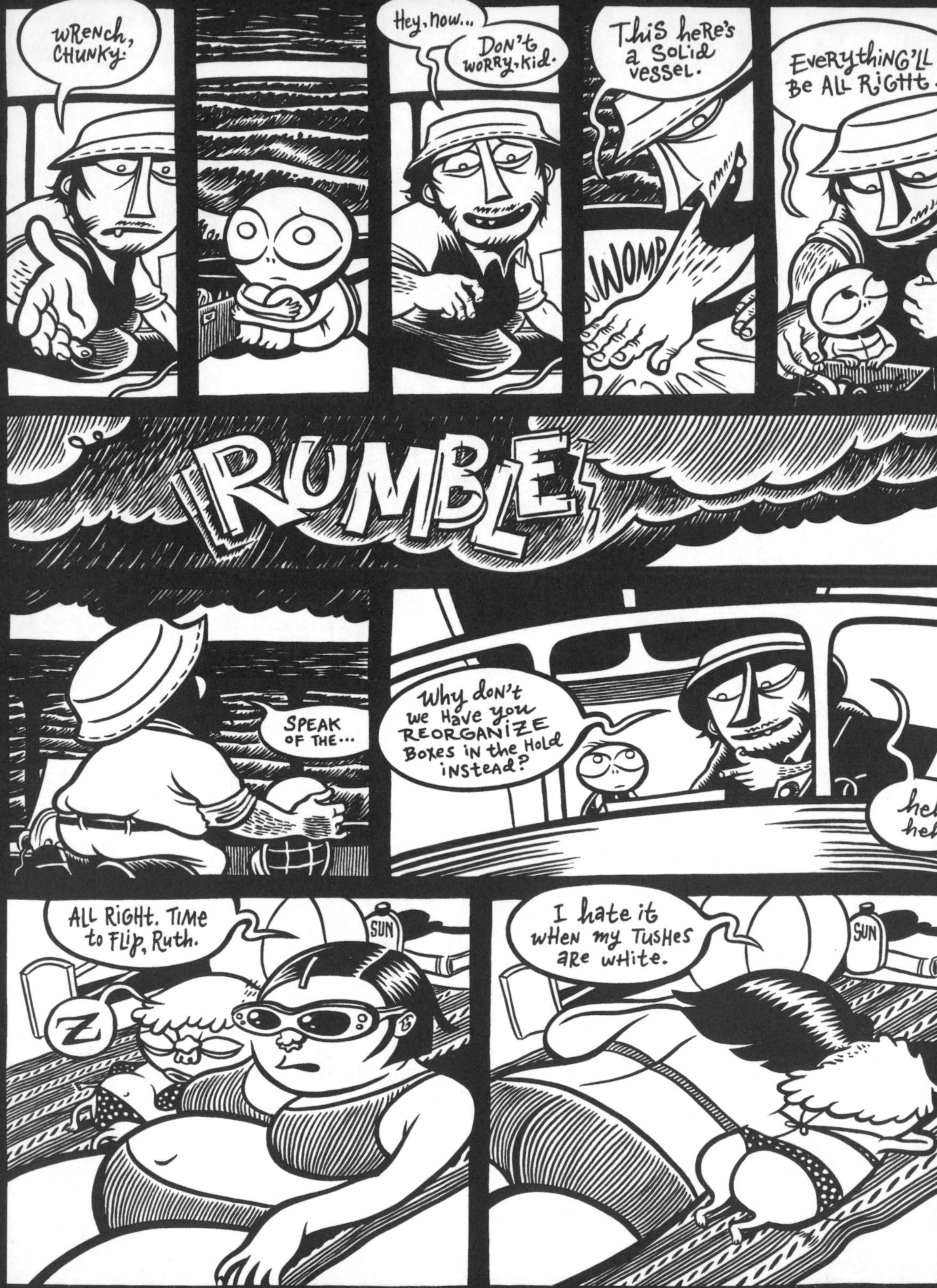
Wrench, Chunky.
Hey, now...
Don't worry, kid.
This here's a solid vessel.
WOMP
Everything'll be all right.
RUMBLE
Speak of the...
Why don't we have you reorganize boxes in the hold instead?
heh heh
All right. Time to flip, Ruth.
Z
SUN
I hate it when my tushes are white.
SUN

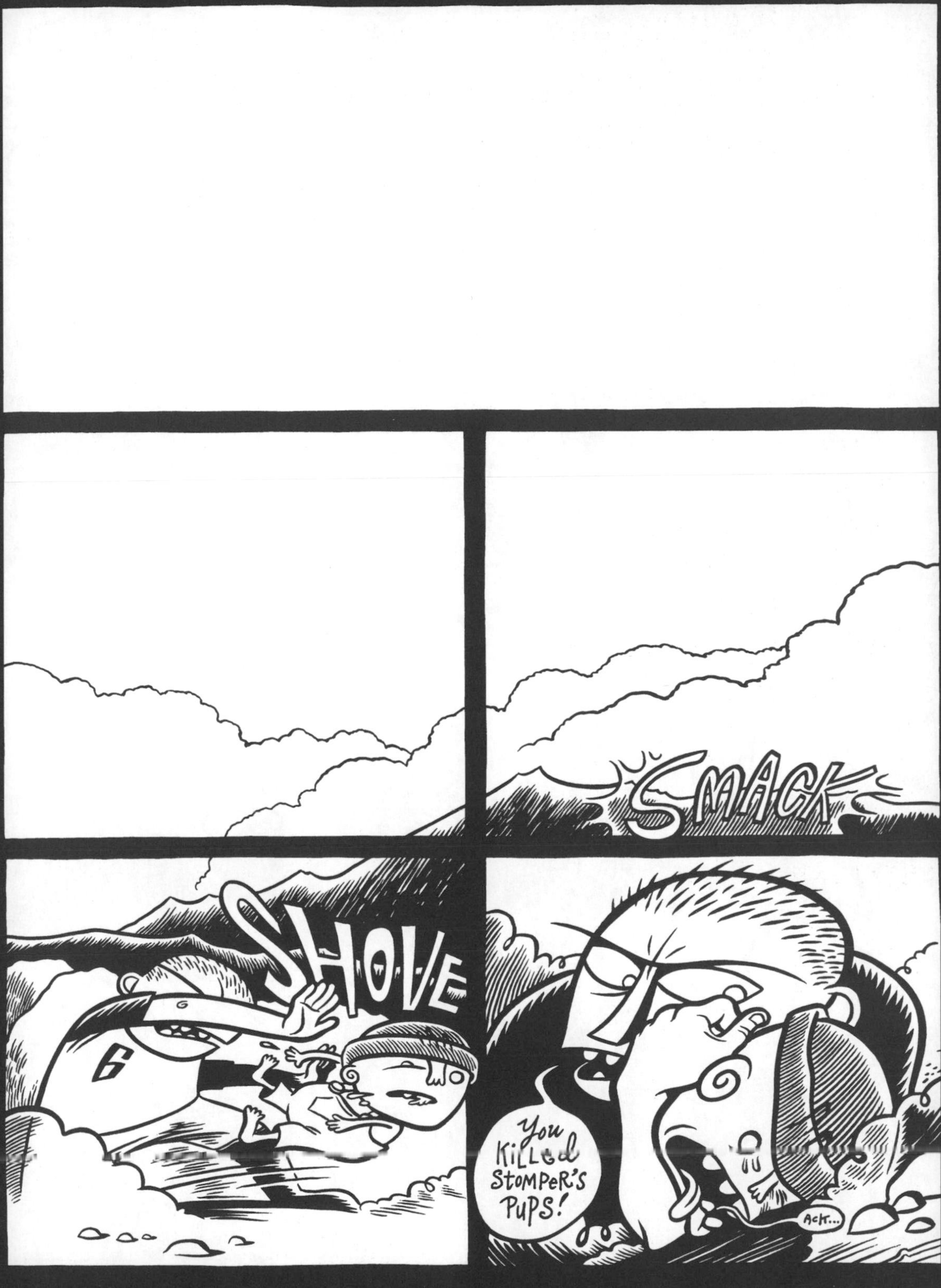
SMACK
SHOVE
You KILLed STOMPER'S PUPS!
ACK...

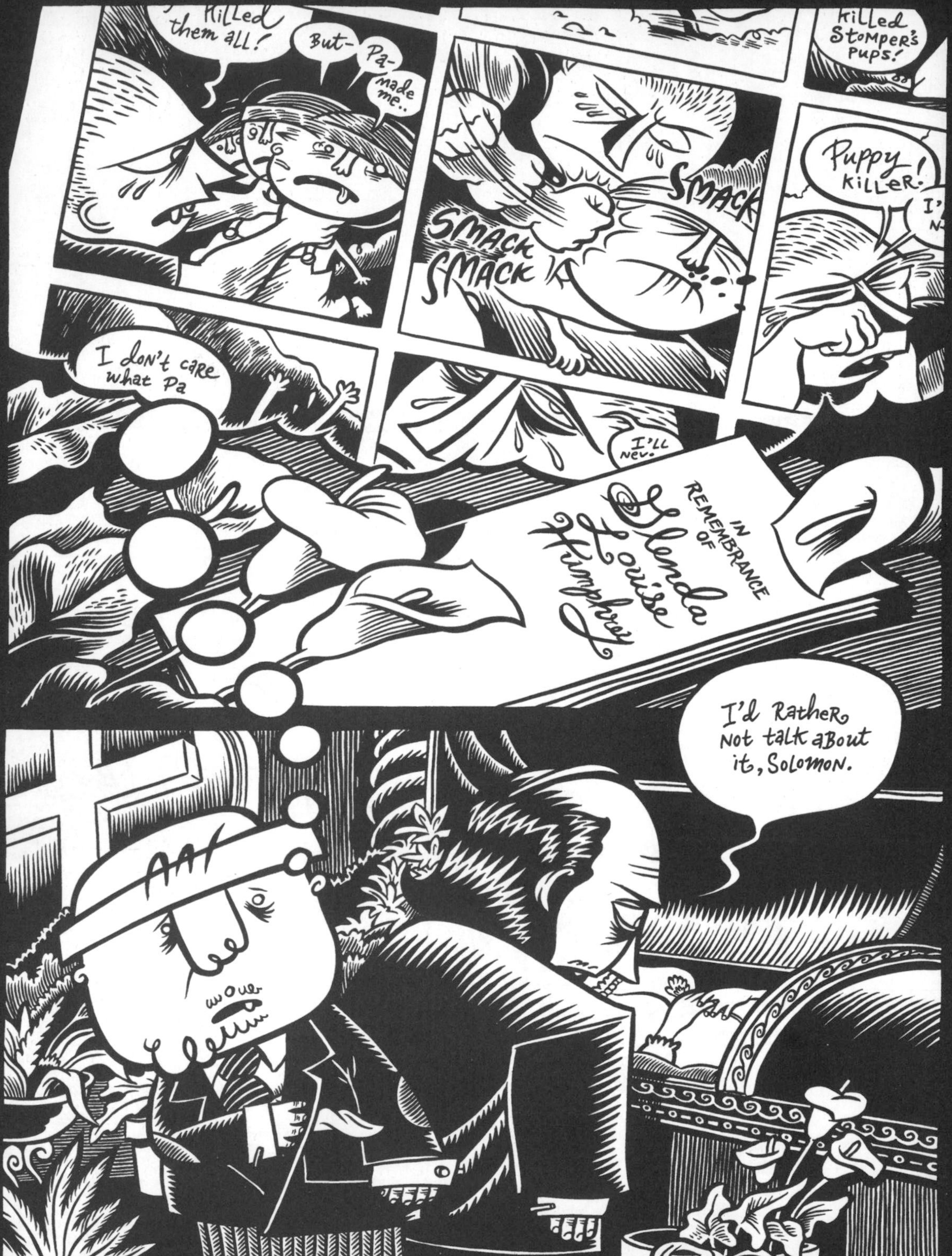

Killed them all!
But-
Pa- made me..
killed Stomper's pups!
SMACK
SMACK SMACK
Puppy! Killer!
I don't care what Pa
I'll nev.
IN REMEMBRANCE OF Glenda Louise Humphrey
I'd Rather Not talk about it, Solomon.

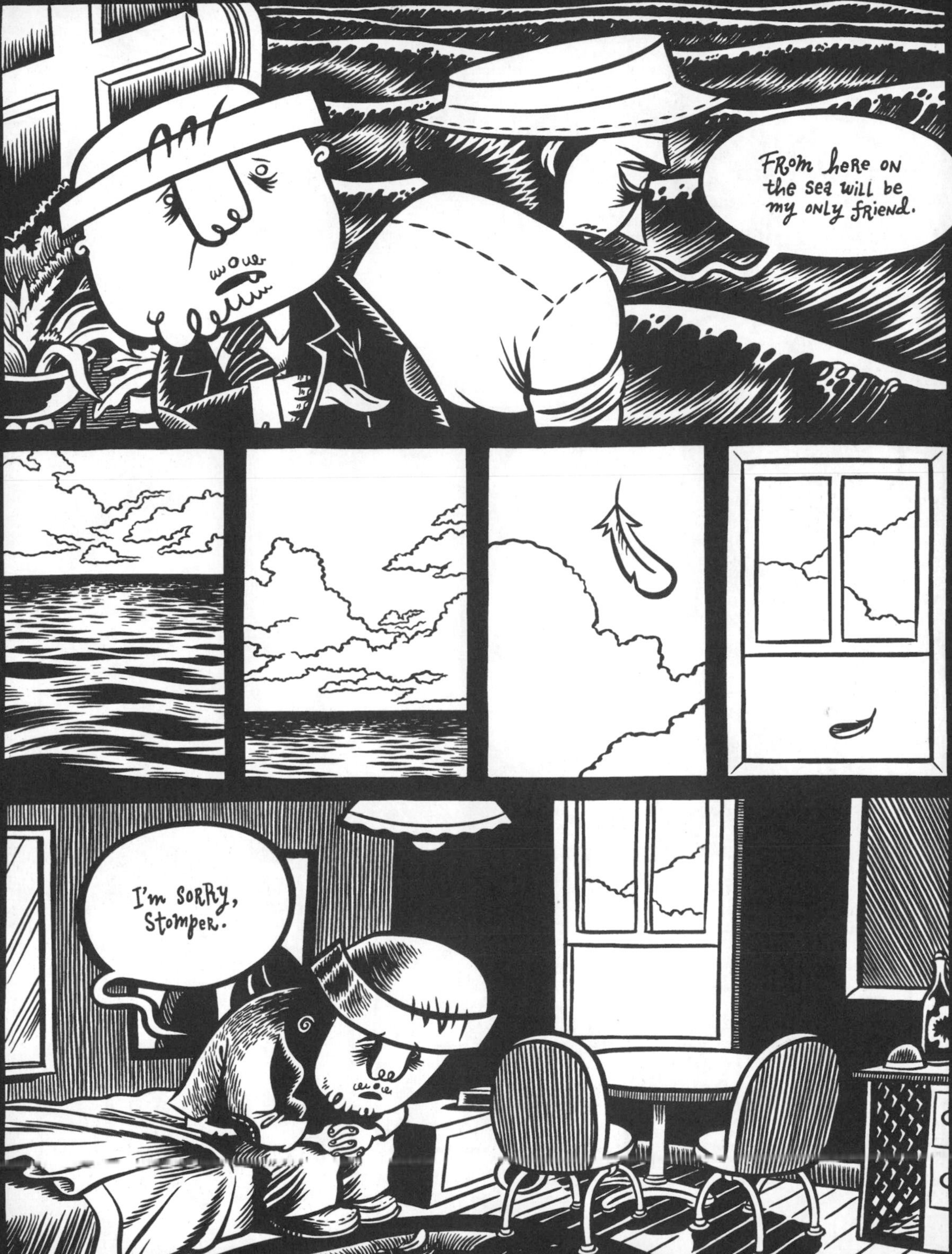
FROM here ON the sea will be my ONLY friend.
I'm SORRY, Stomper.

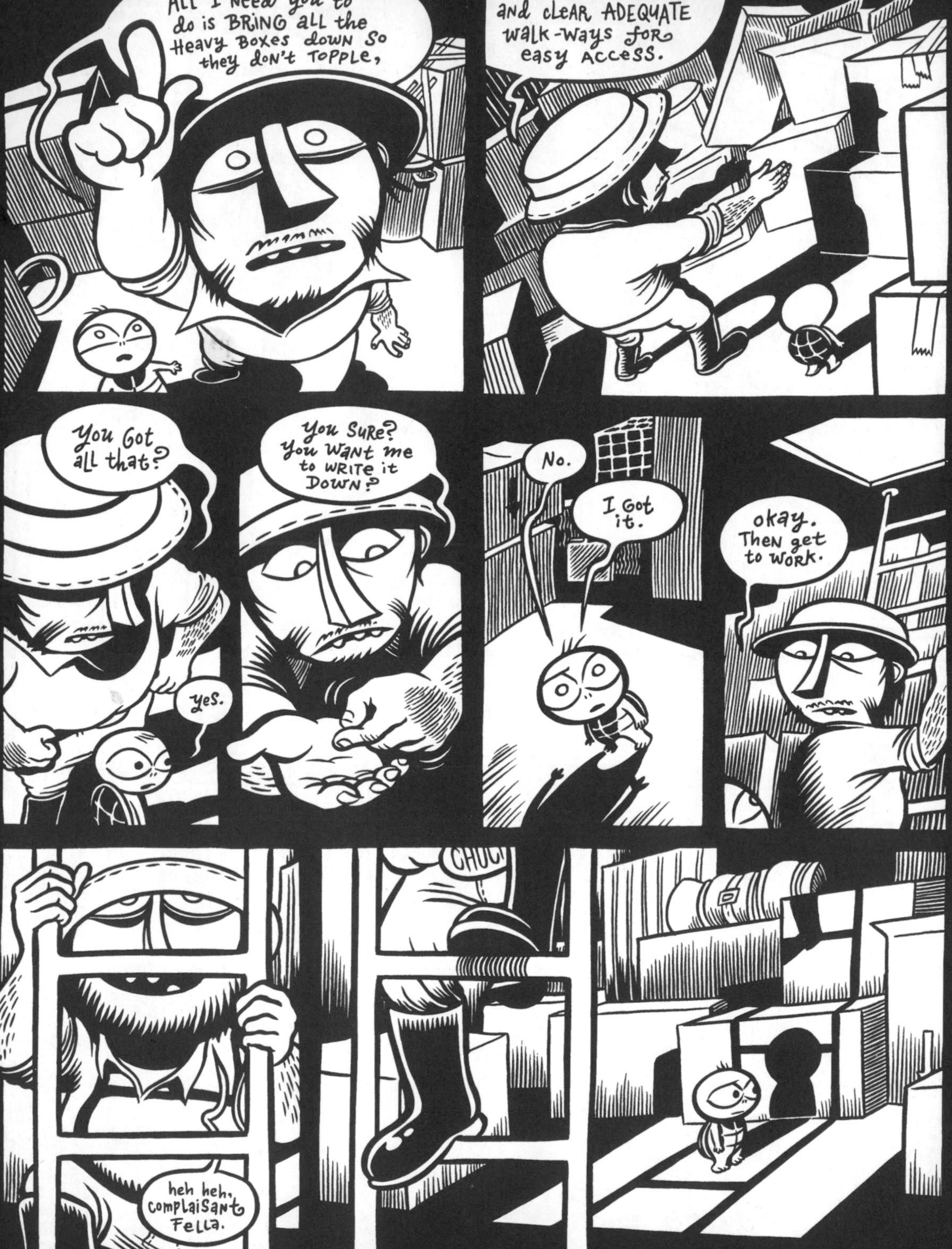
ALL I Need you to do is BRING all the Heavy Boxes down so they don't TOPPLE,
and clear ADEQUATE walk-ways for easy ACCESS.
You Got all that?
yes.
You SURE? You WANT me to WRITE it DOWN?
No.
I Got it.
okay. Then get to work.
heh heh. complaisant fella.

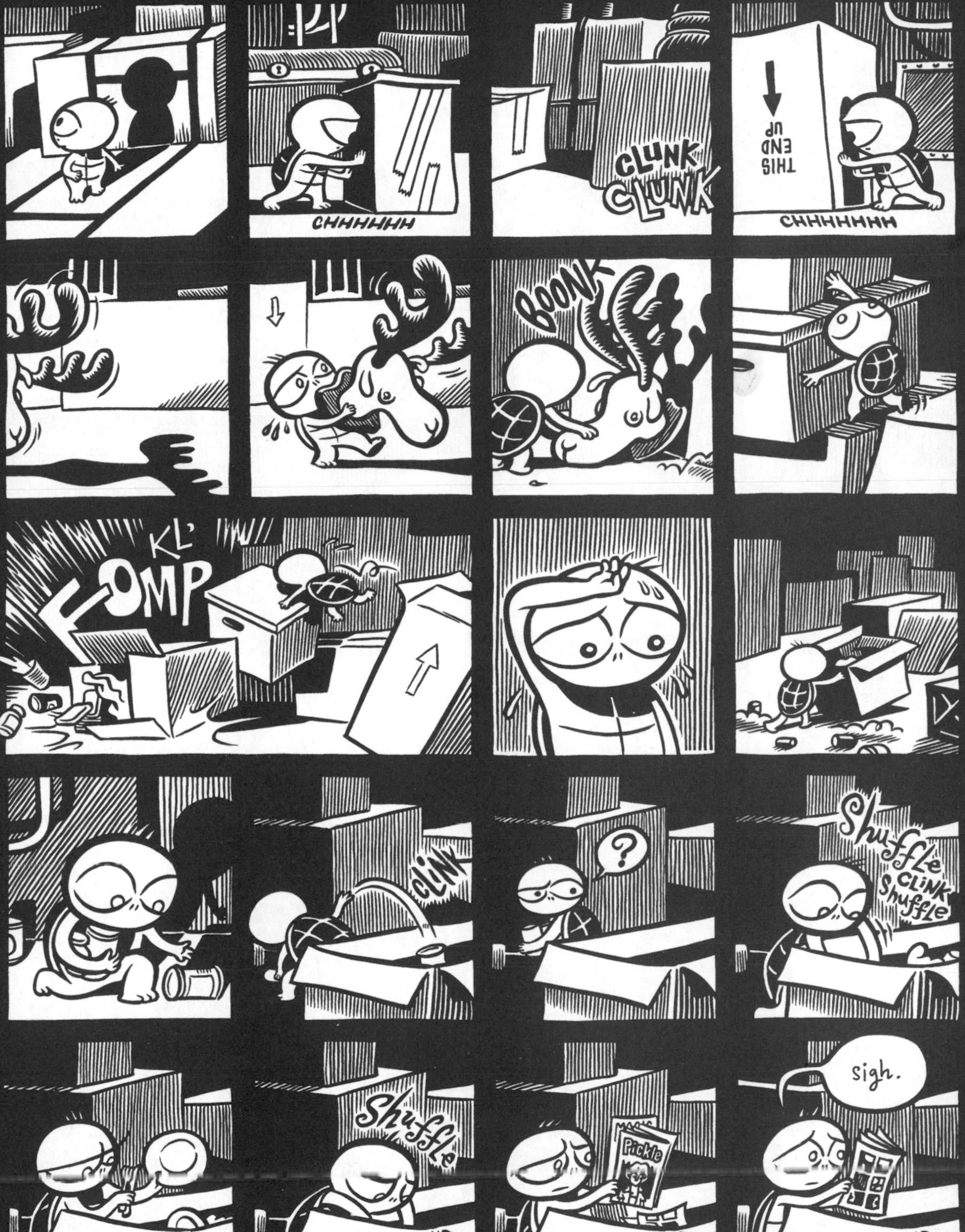
CHHHHHH
CLUNK
CLUNK
THIS END UP
CHHHHHHH
BOONK
KL'
FOMP
CLINK
?
Shuffle
CLINK
Shuffle
Shuffle
Pickle
sigh.

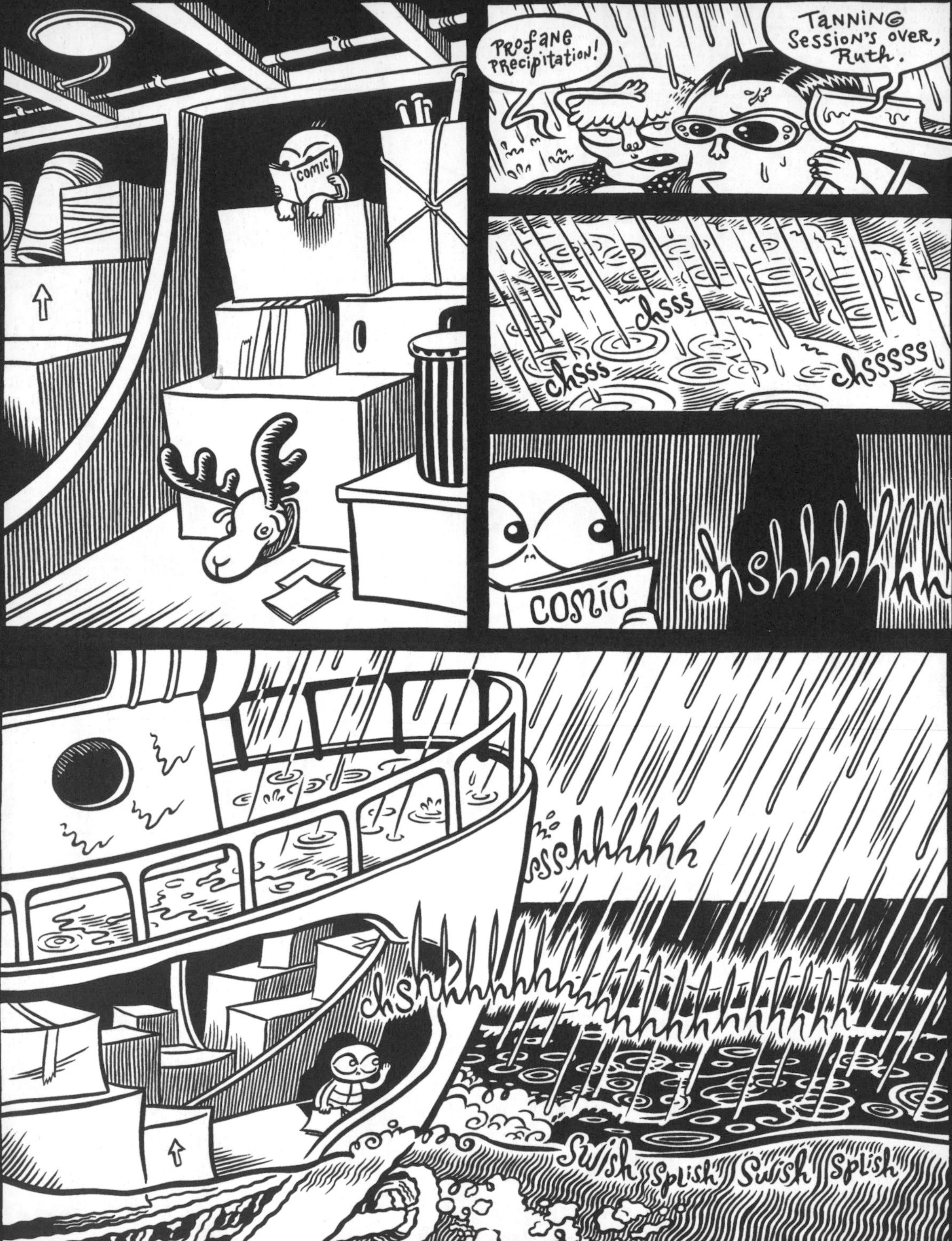
COMIC
Profane Precipitation!
Tanning Session's over, Ruth.
chsss
chsss
chsssss
COMIC
chshhhhhhh
sshhhhhhh
chshhhhhhhhhhhhhhhhhhhhhhhhh
Swish Splish Swish Splish

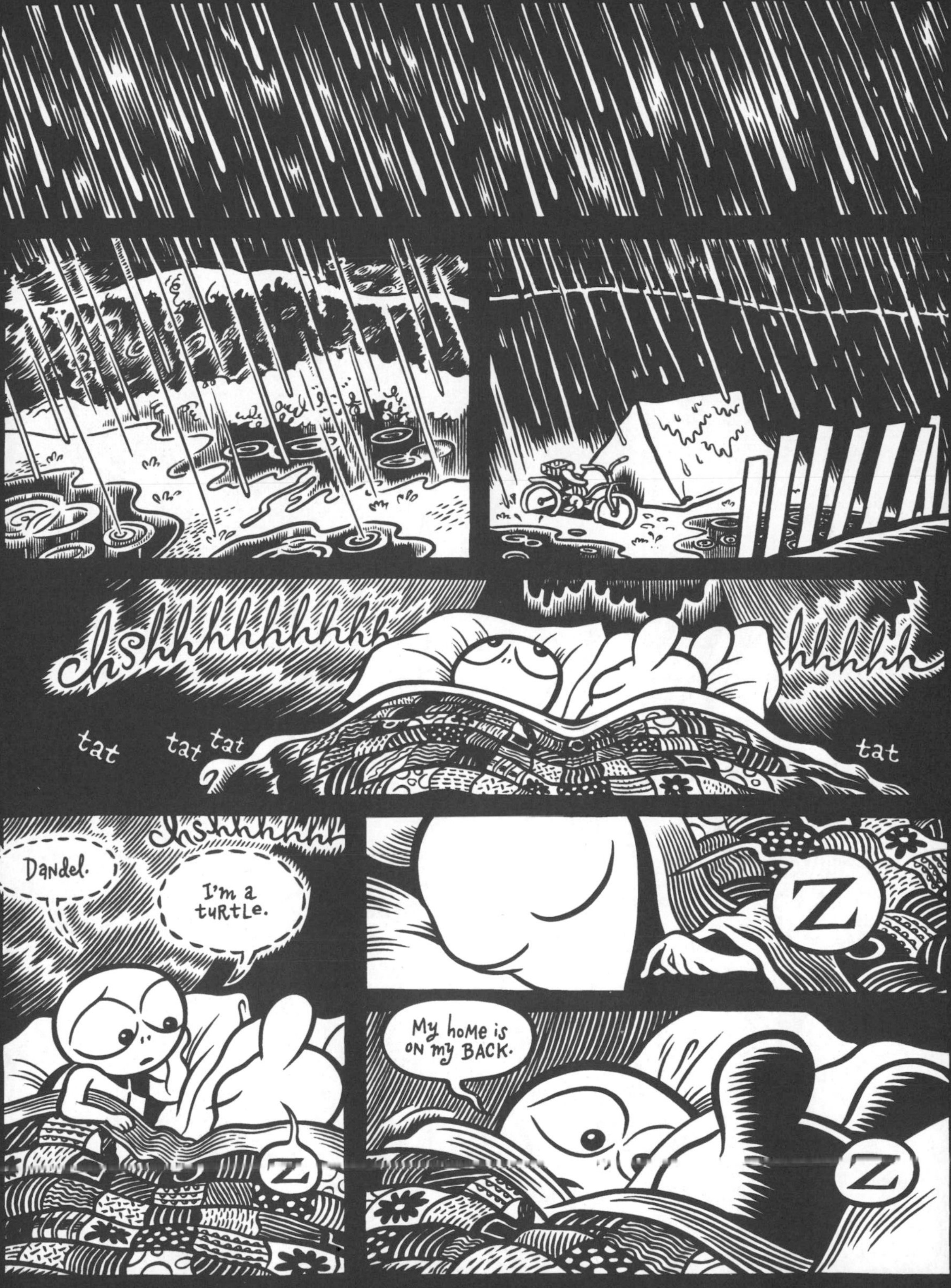
chshhhhhhhhhh
hhhhh
tat
tat tat
tat
chshhhhhh
Dandel.
I'm a turtle.
Z
Z
My home is on my BACK.
Z

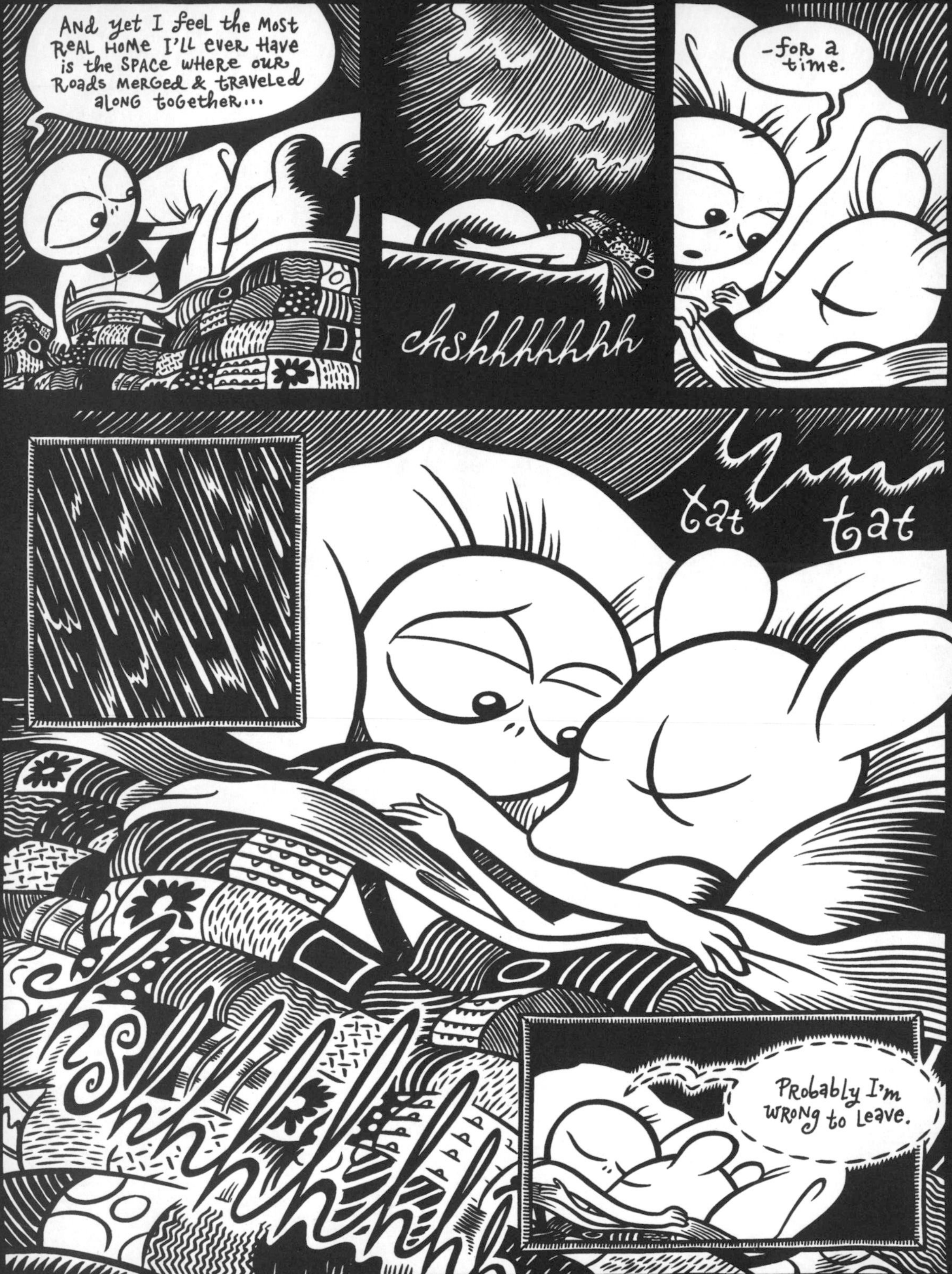
And yet I feel the most real home I'll ever have is the space where our roads merged & traveled along together...
chshhhhhhhh
-for a time.
tat tat
hshhhhhhhhh
Probably I'm wrong to leave.

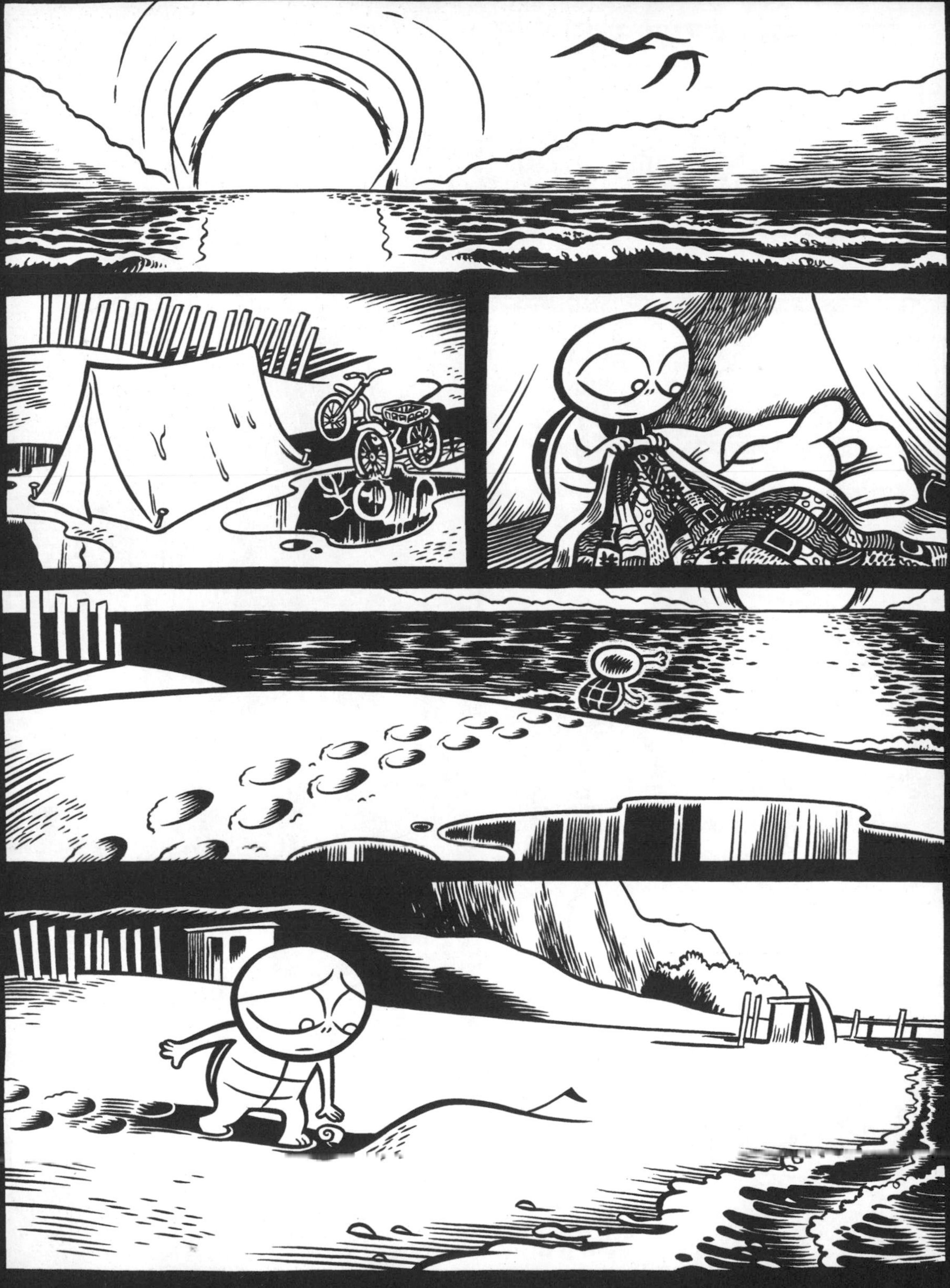

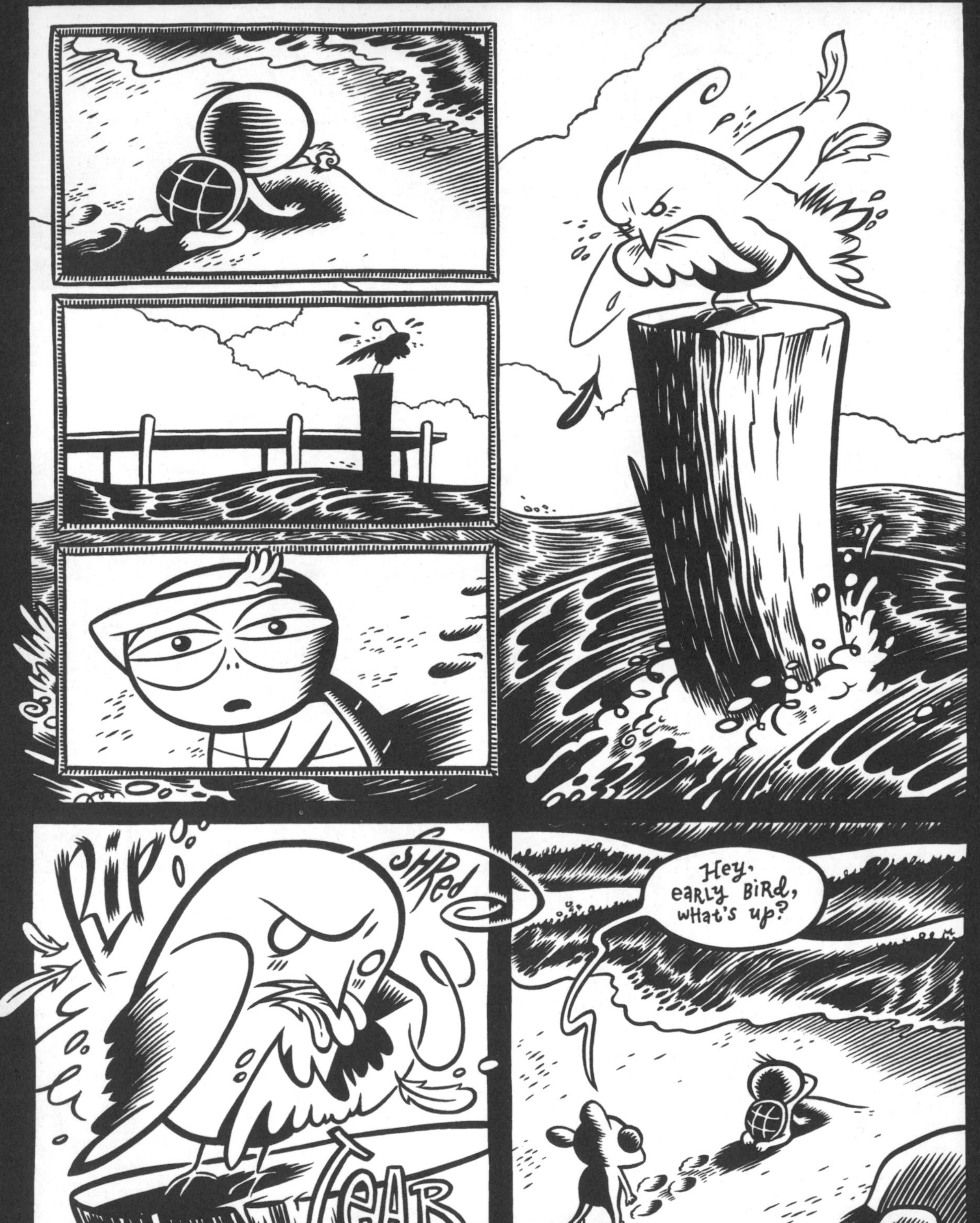
Rip
SHRed
Tear
Hey, early bird, what's up?

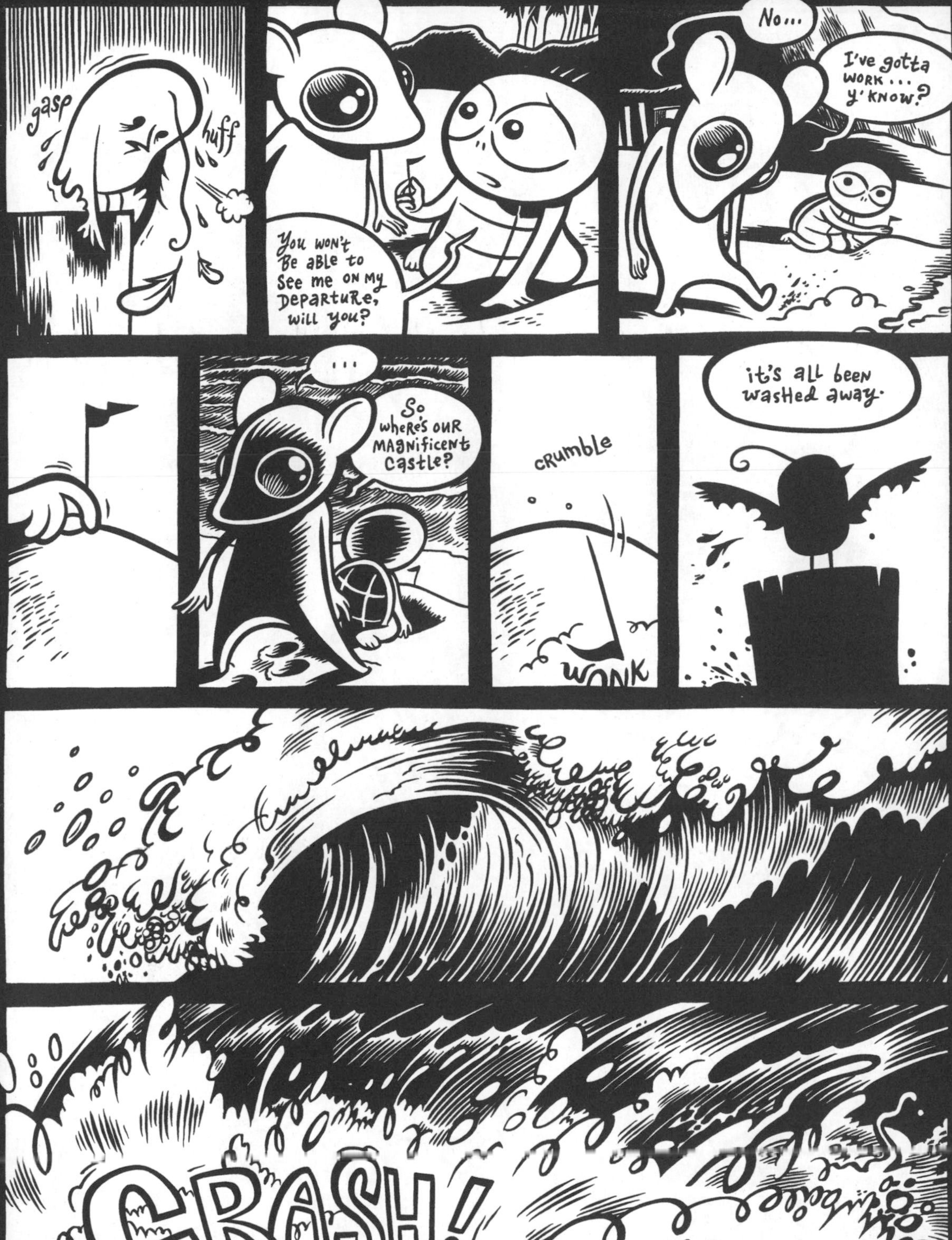

gasp
huff
You won't Be able to See me on my Departure, will you?
No...
I've gotta work... y' know?
...
So where's our magnificent castle?
crumble
WONK
it's all been washed away.
CRASH!

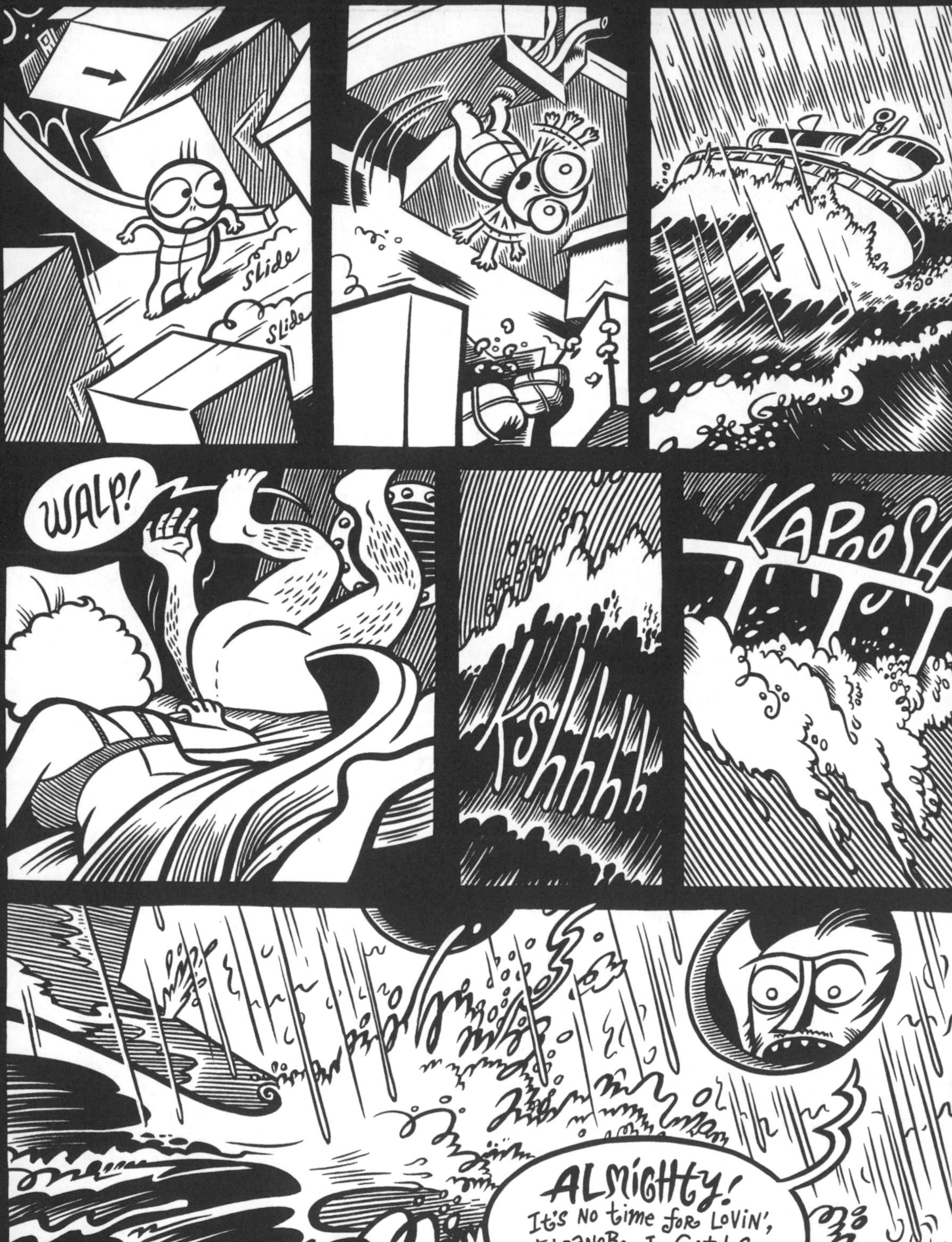
SLIDE
SLIDE
WALP!
K-SHHHHH
KAPOOSH
ALMIGHTY!
IT'S NO TIME FOR LOVIN', ELEANOR. I GOTTA GET TO THE HELM!

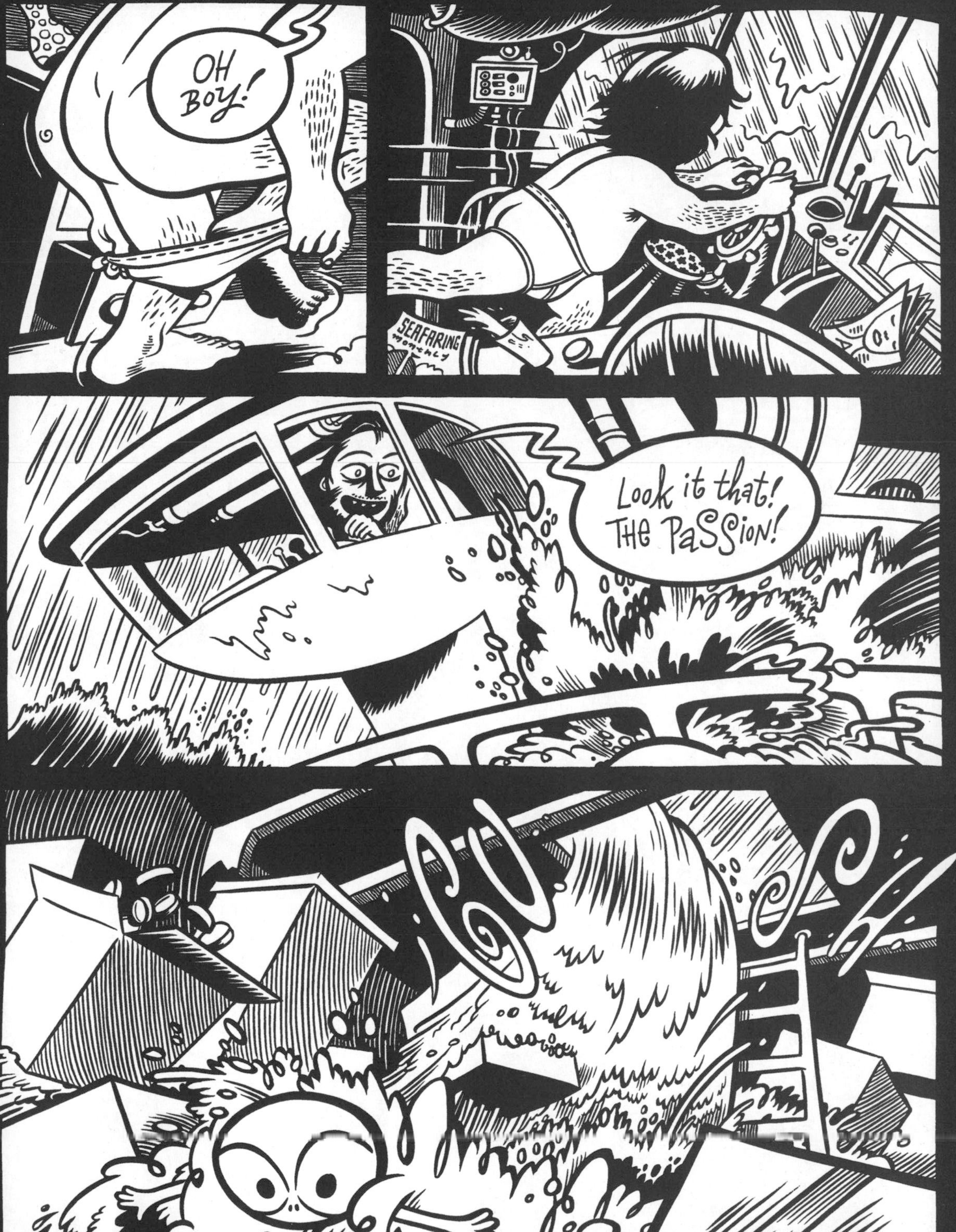
OH BOY!
SEAFARING MONTHLY
Look it that! THE PaSSion!

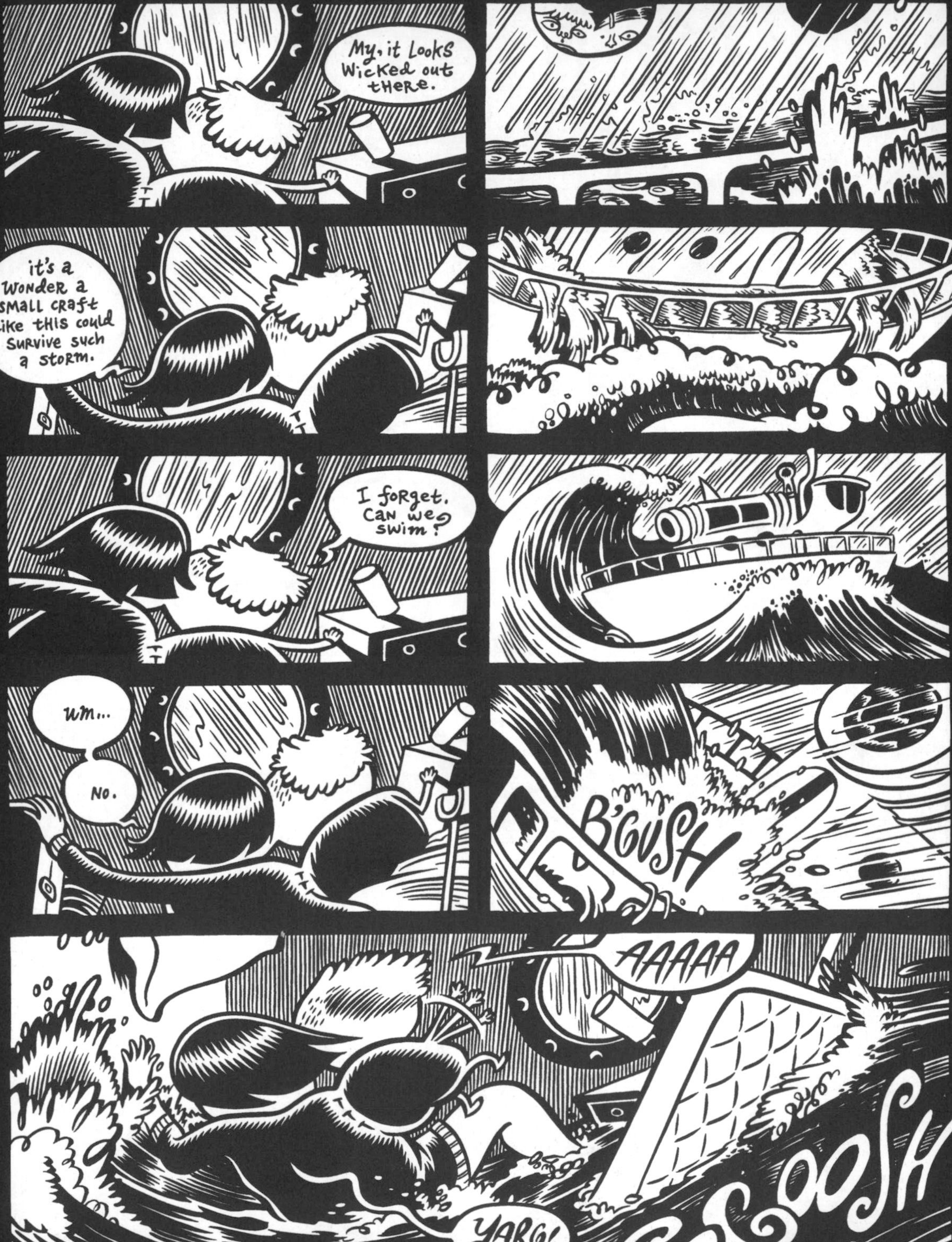
My, it Looks Wicked out there.
it's a wonder a small craft like this could survive such a storm.
I forget. Can we swim?
um...
No.
B'GUSH!
AAAAA
YARG!
SCOOSH

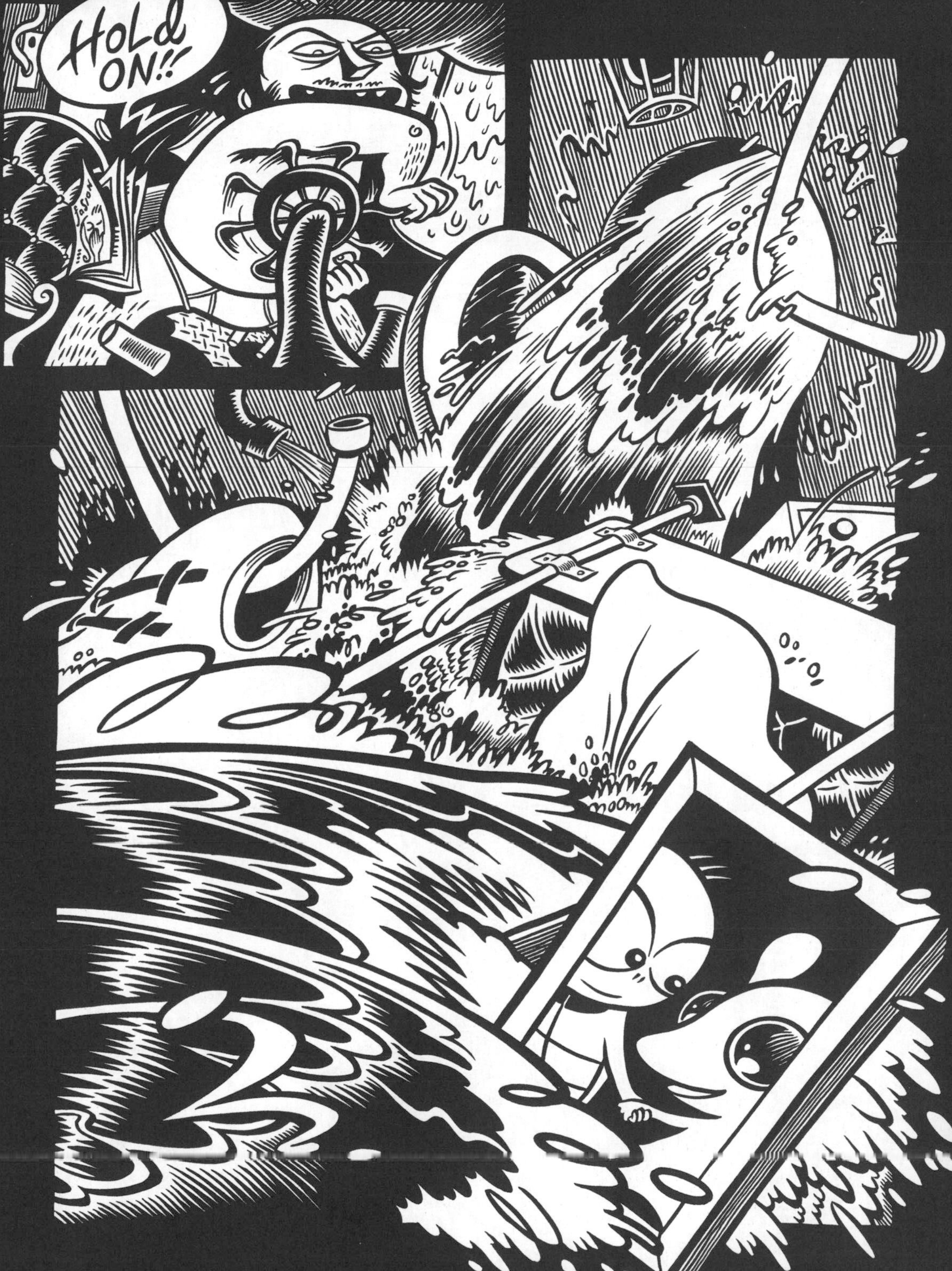
HOLD ON!!

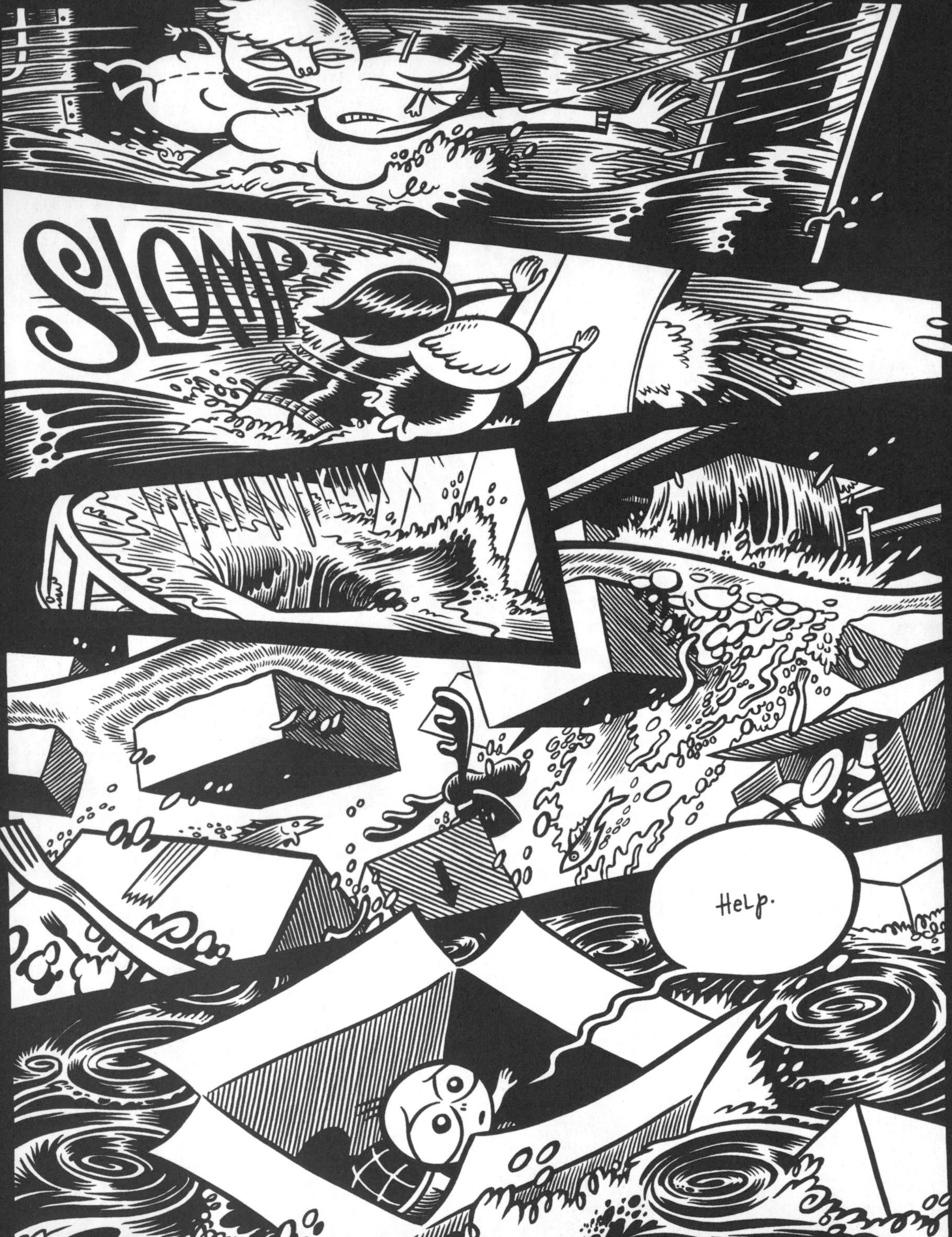
SLOMP
Help.

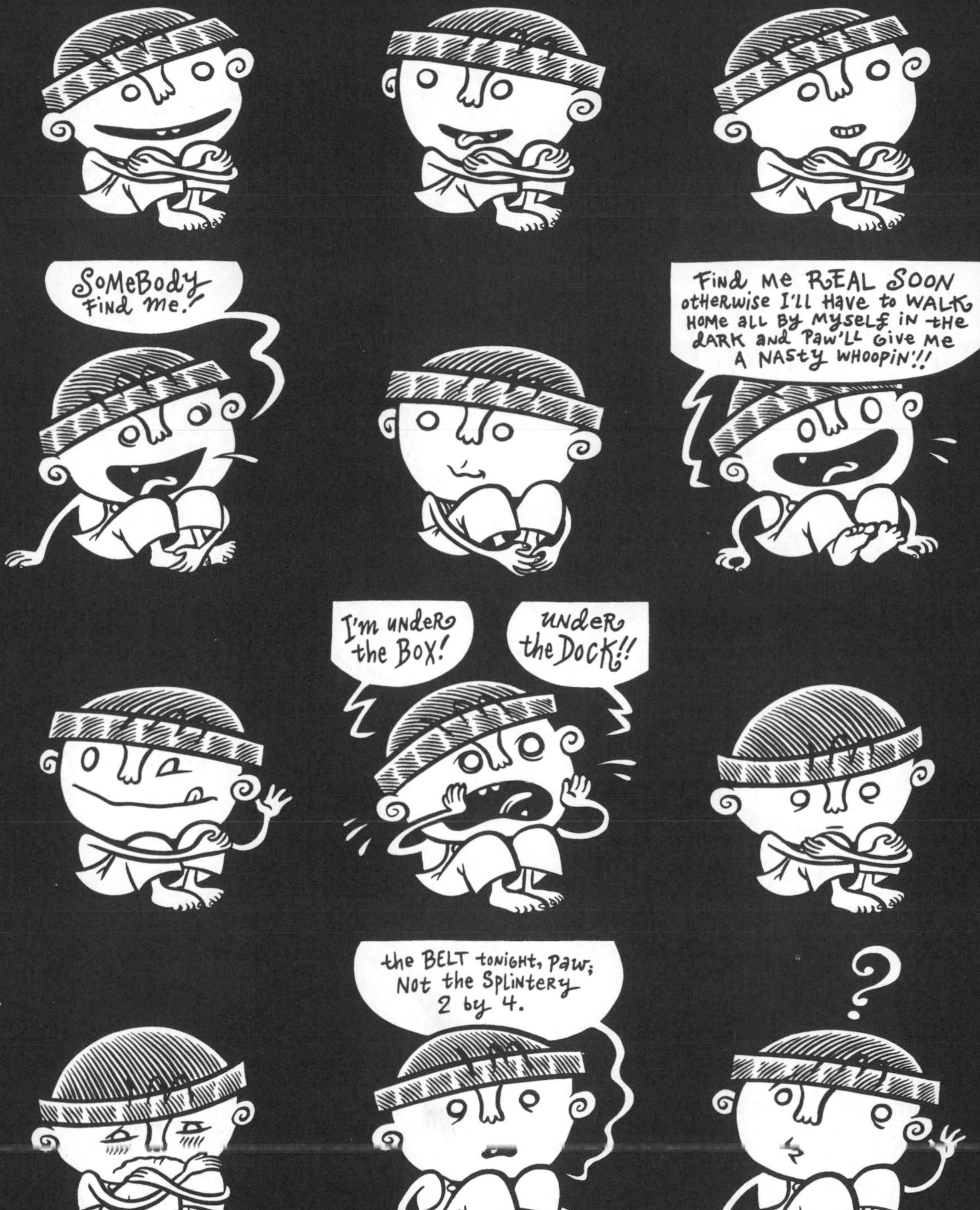
SoMeBody Find me.!
Find Me REAL SOON otherwise I'LL Have to WALK Home all by MySELF in the DARK and PAW'LL Give Me A NASty WHOOPIN'!!
I'm under the Box!
under the Dock!!
the BELT tonight, Paw; Not the Splintery 2 by 4.
?

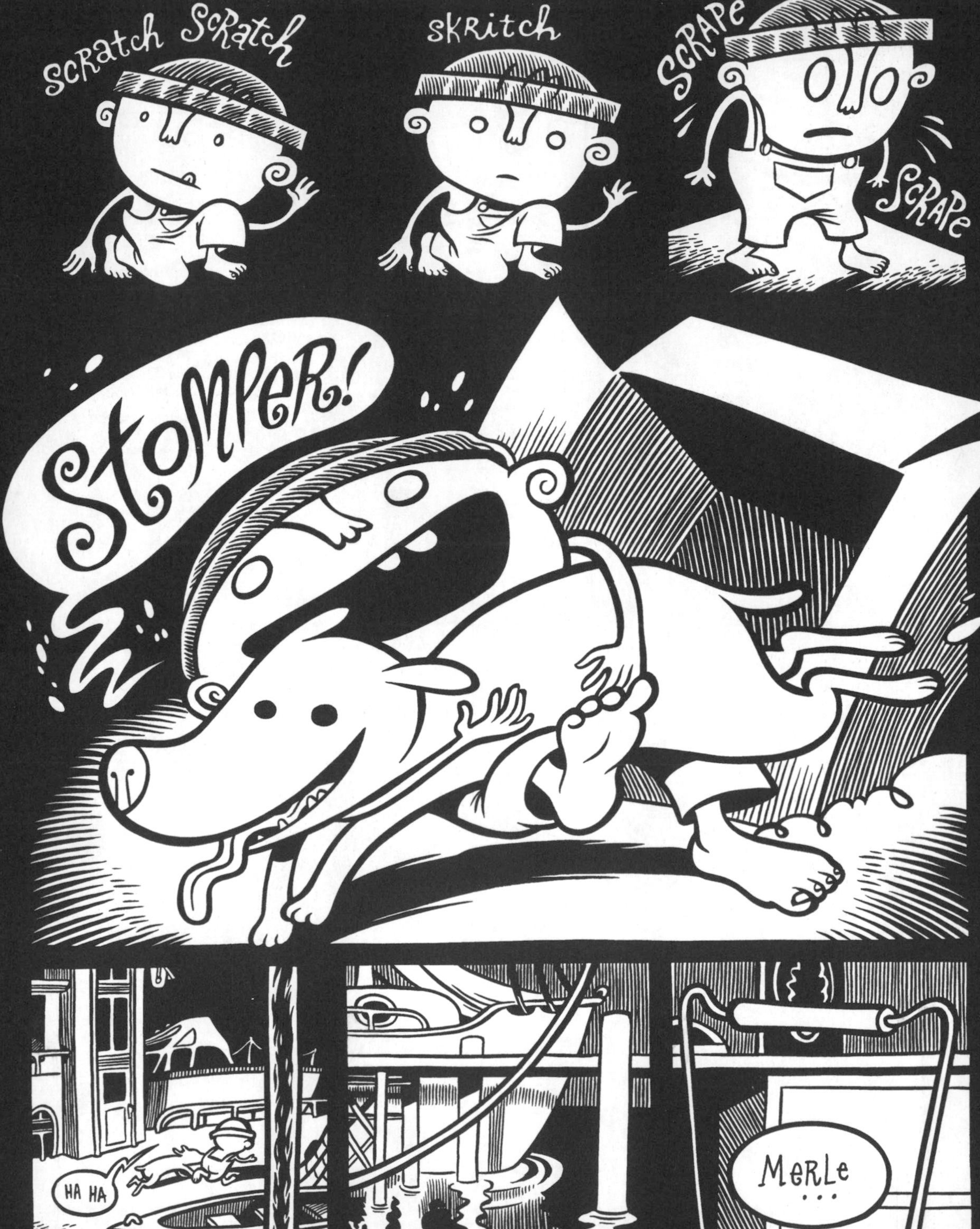
SCRATCH SCRATCH
SKRITCH
SCRAPE
SCRAPE
STOMPER!
HA HA
MERLE
...

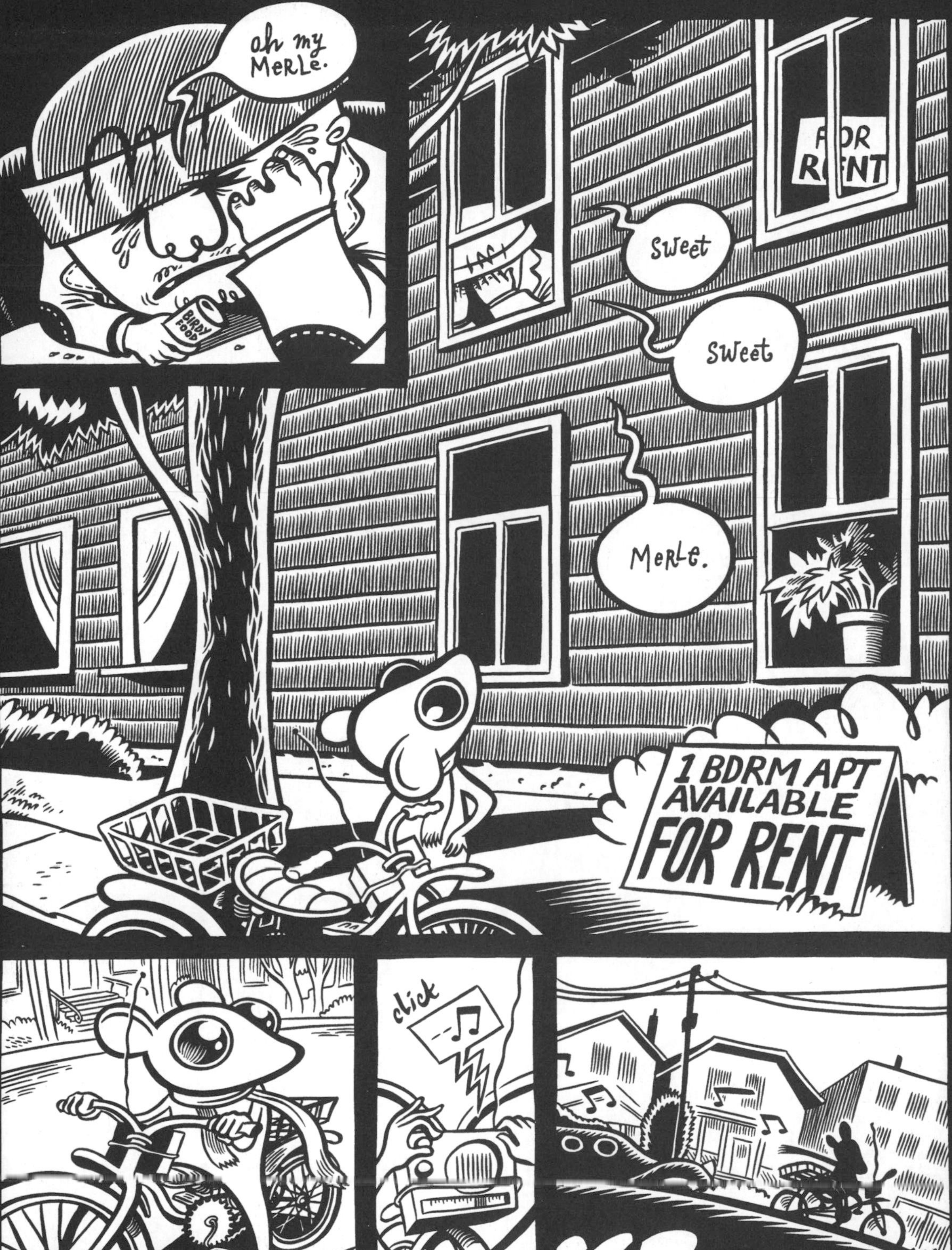
oh my Merle.
BIRDY FOOD
FOR RENT
sweet
sweet
Merle.
1 BDRM APT AVAILABLE FOR RENT
click

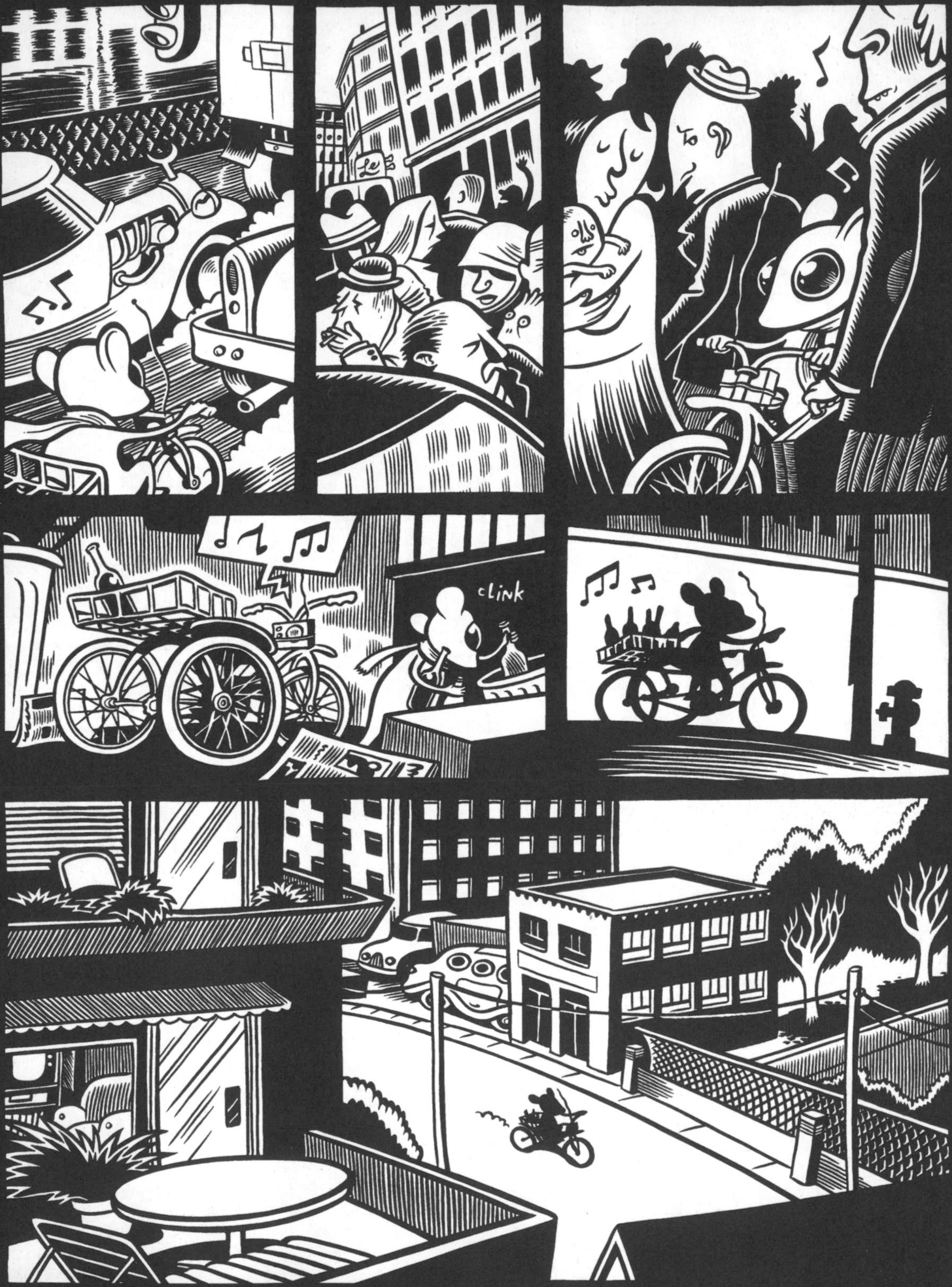
clink

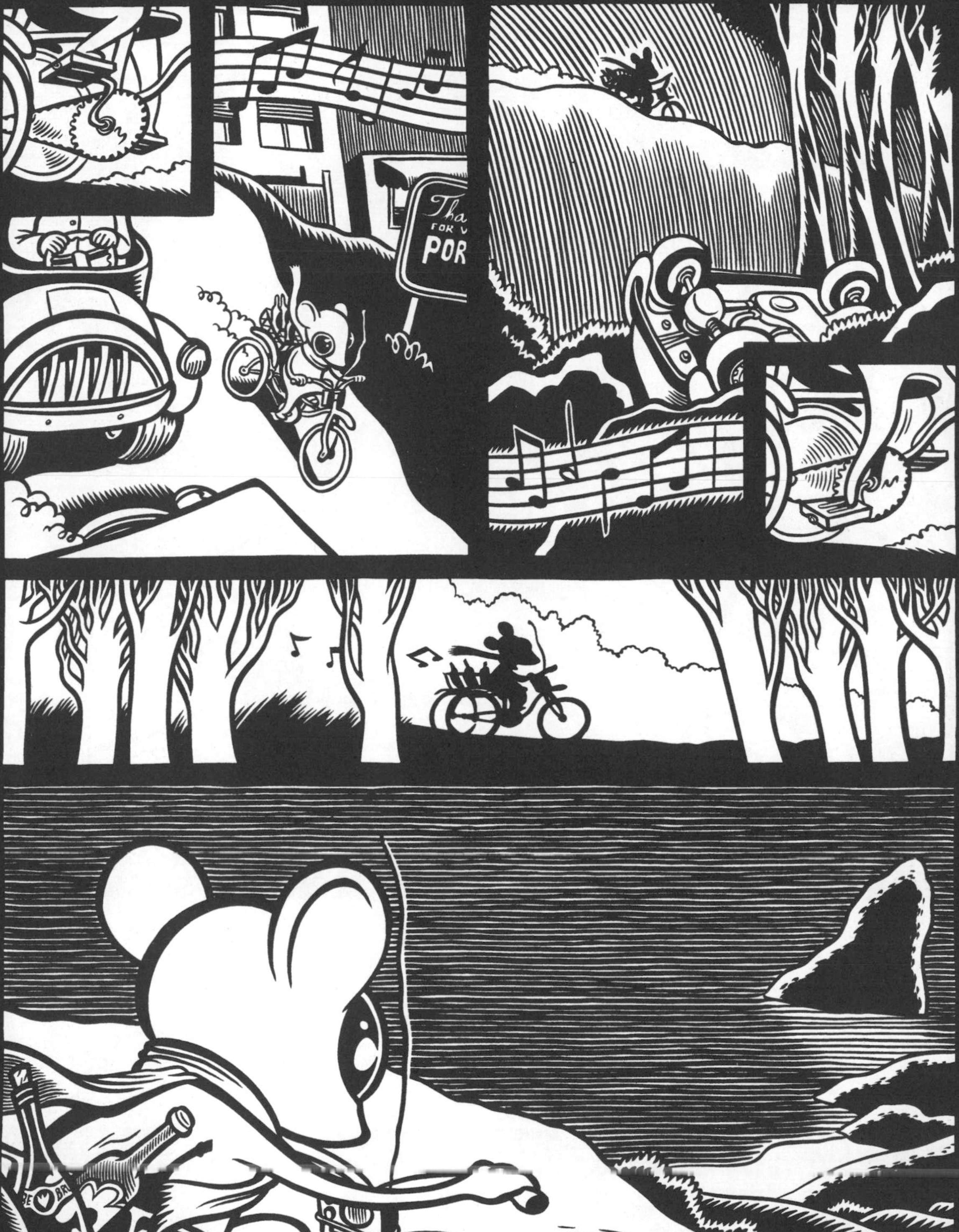

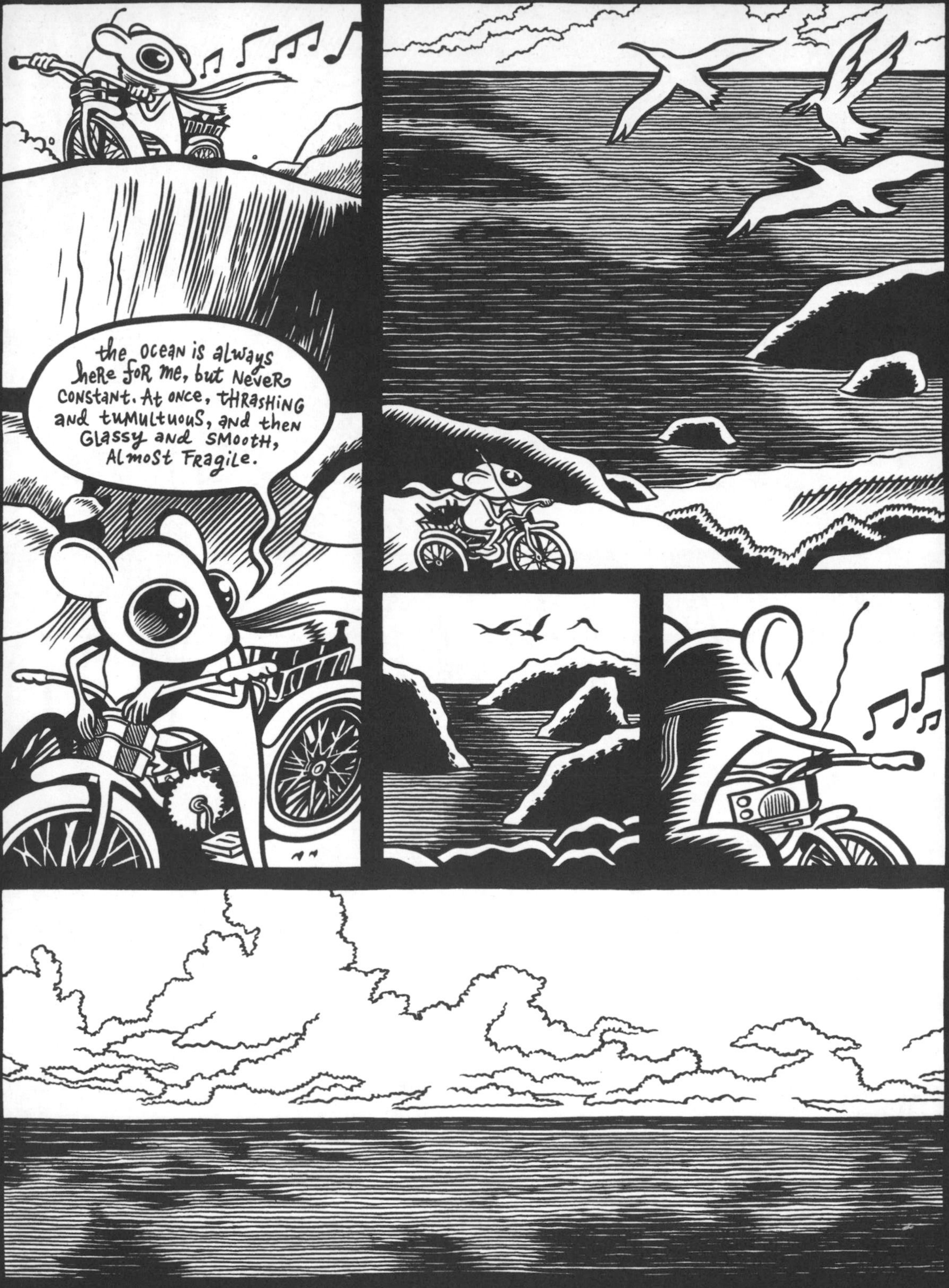
the ocean is always here for me, but never constant. At once, thrashing and tumultuous, and then glassy and smooth, almost fragile.

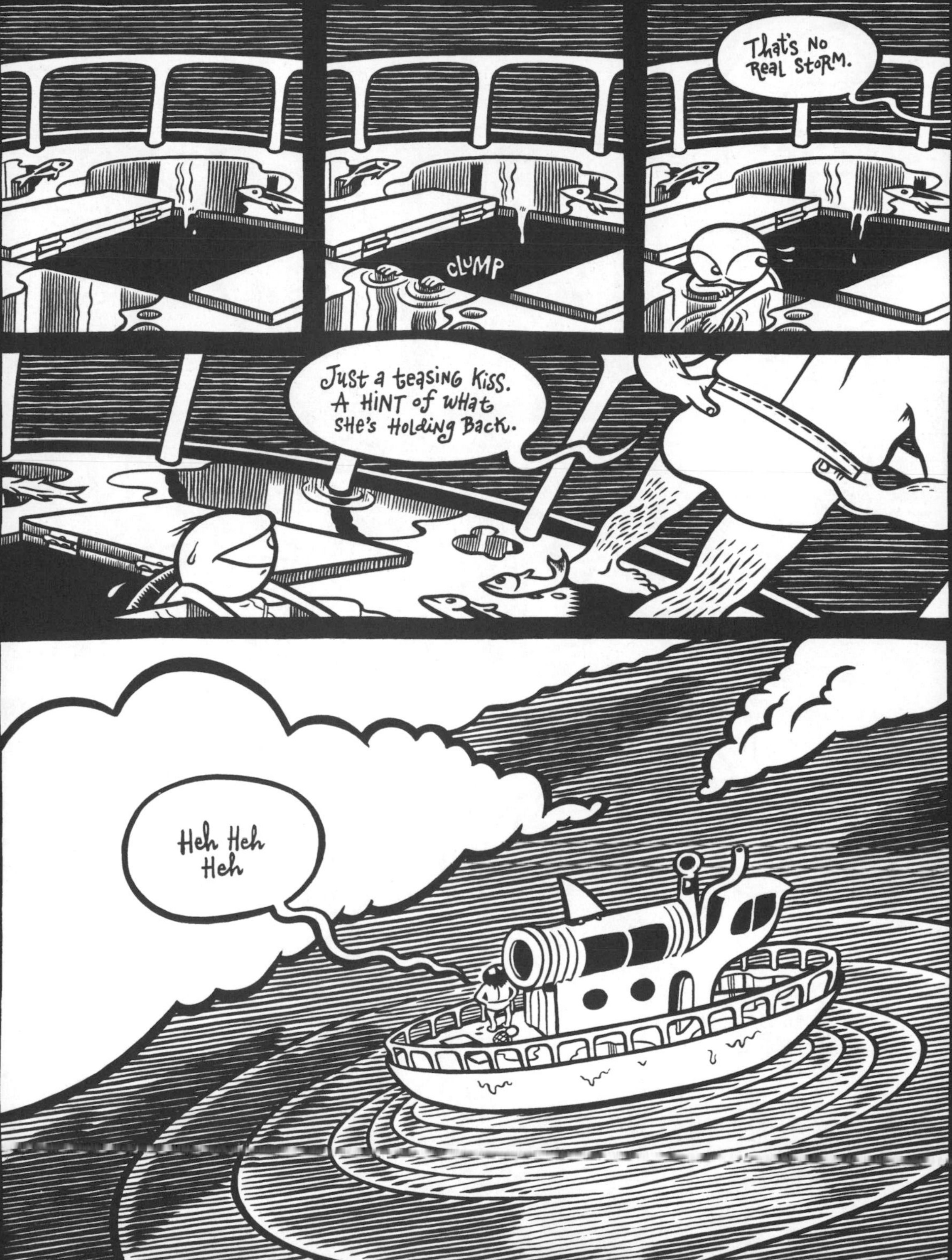
That's no real storm.
CLUMP
Just a teasing kiss. A hint of what she's holding back.
Heh Heh Heh

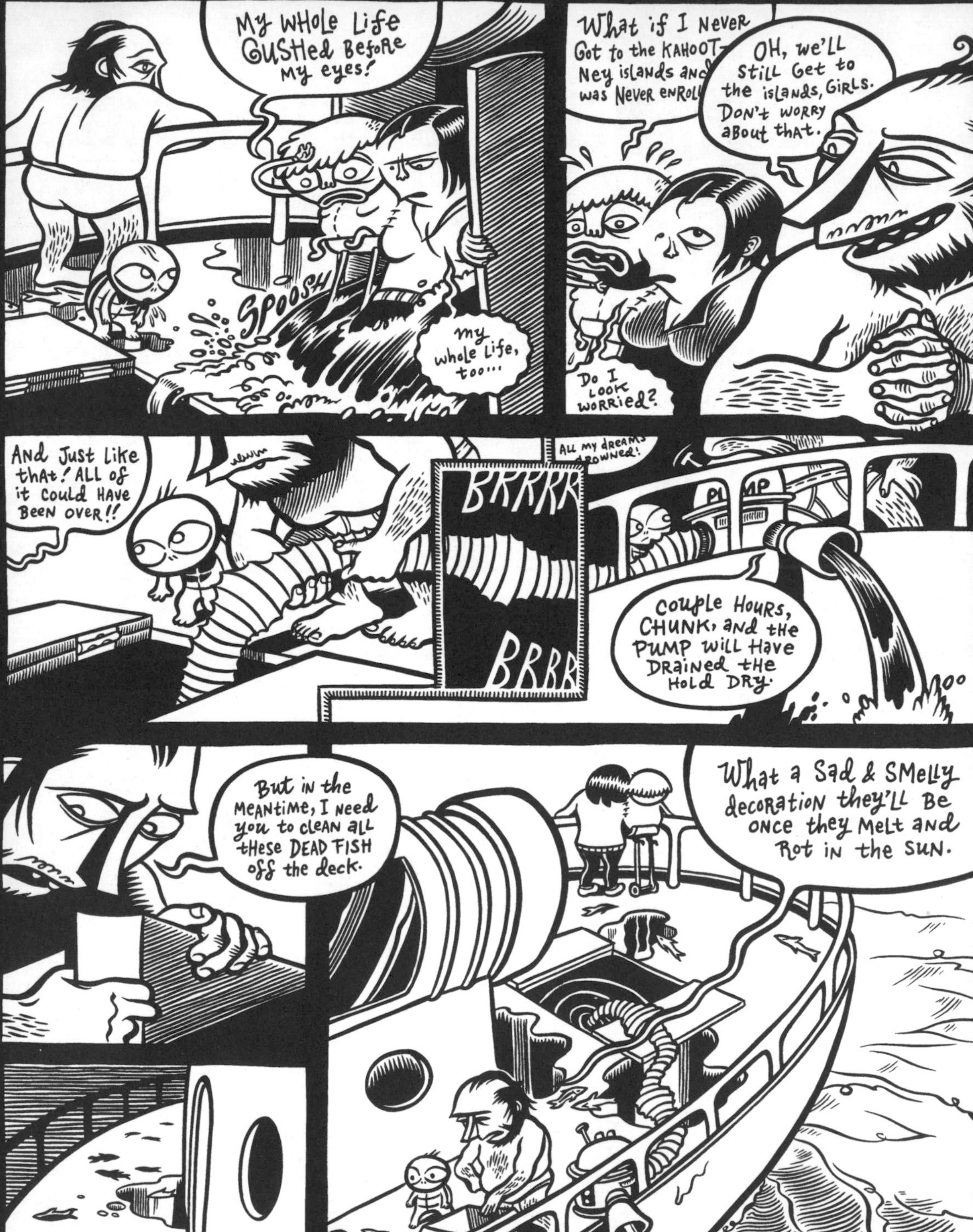
My WHOLE Life GUSHed BefoRe my eyes!
SPOOSH
my whole Life, too...
What if I Never Got to the KAHOOT-Ney islands and was Never enRoll
OH, we'LL still Get to the isLands, GiRLs. Don't worry about that.
Do I Look worried?
And Just like that! ALL of it could Have Been over!!
ALL my dreams drowned!
BRRRR
BRRR
PUMP
Couple Hours, CHUNK, and the PUMP will Have Drained the Hold Dry.
But in the Meantime, I need you to clean all these DEAD FISH off the deck.
What a Sad & SMelly decoration they'LL Be once they Melt and Rot in the SUN.

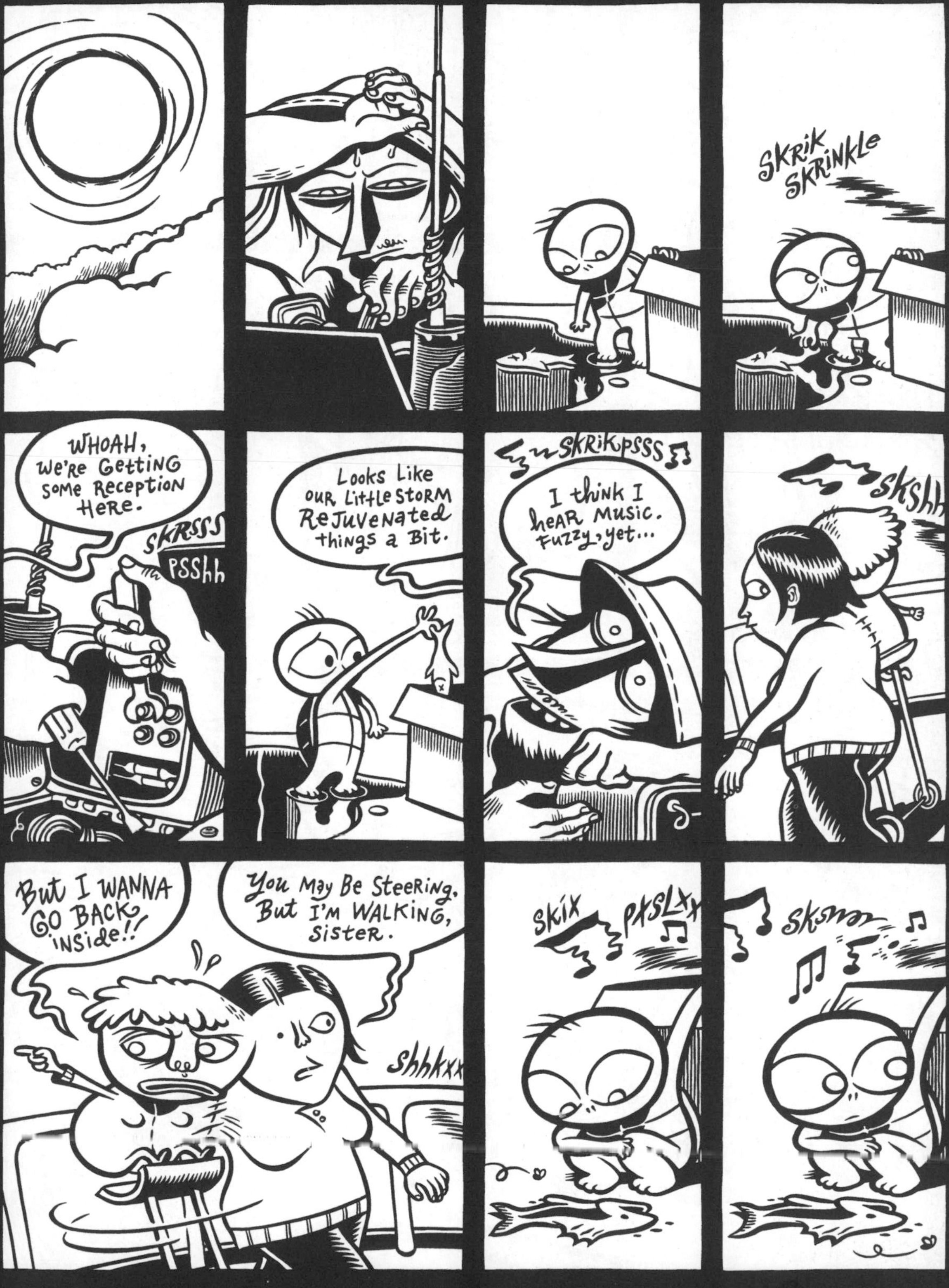
SKRIK
SKRINKLE
WHOAH, WE'RE GETTING SOME RECEPTION HERE.
SKRSSS
PSShh
Looks like our little STORM REJUVENATED things a bit.
SKRIKPSSS
I think I hear MUSIC. Fuzzy, yet...
SKShh
But I WANNA GO BACK inside!!
You May Be Steering. But I'M WALKING, Sister.
Shhkxx
SKIX
PXSLXX
SKSNER

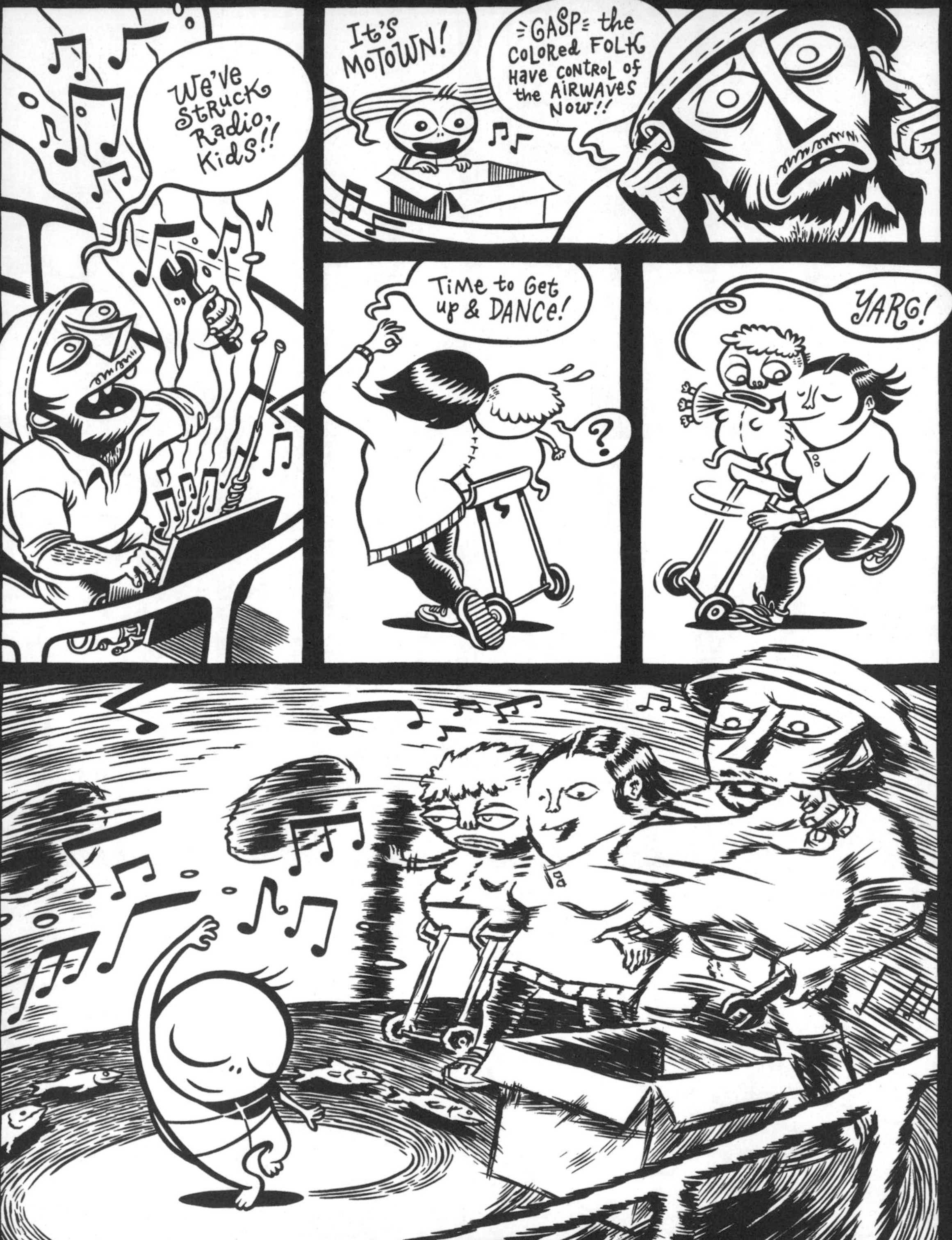
We've STRUCK Radio, KidS!!
It's MOTOWN!
GASP the COLORed FOLK Have CONTROL of the AIRWAVES NOW!!
TiMe to Get up & DANCe!
?
YARG!

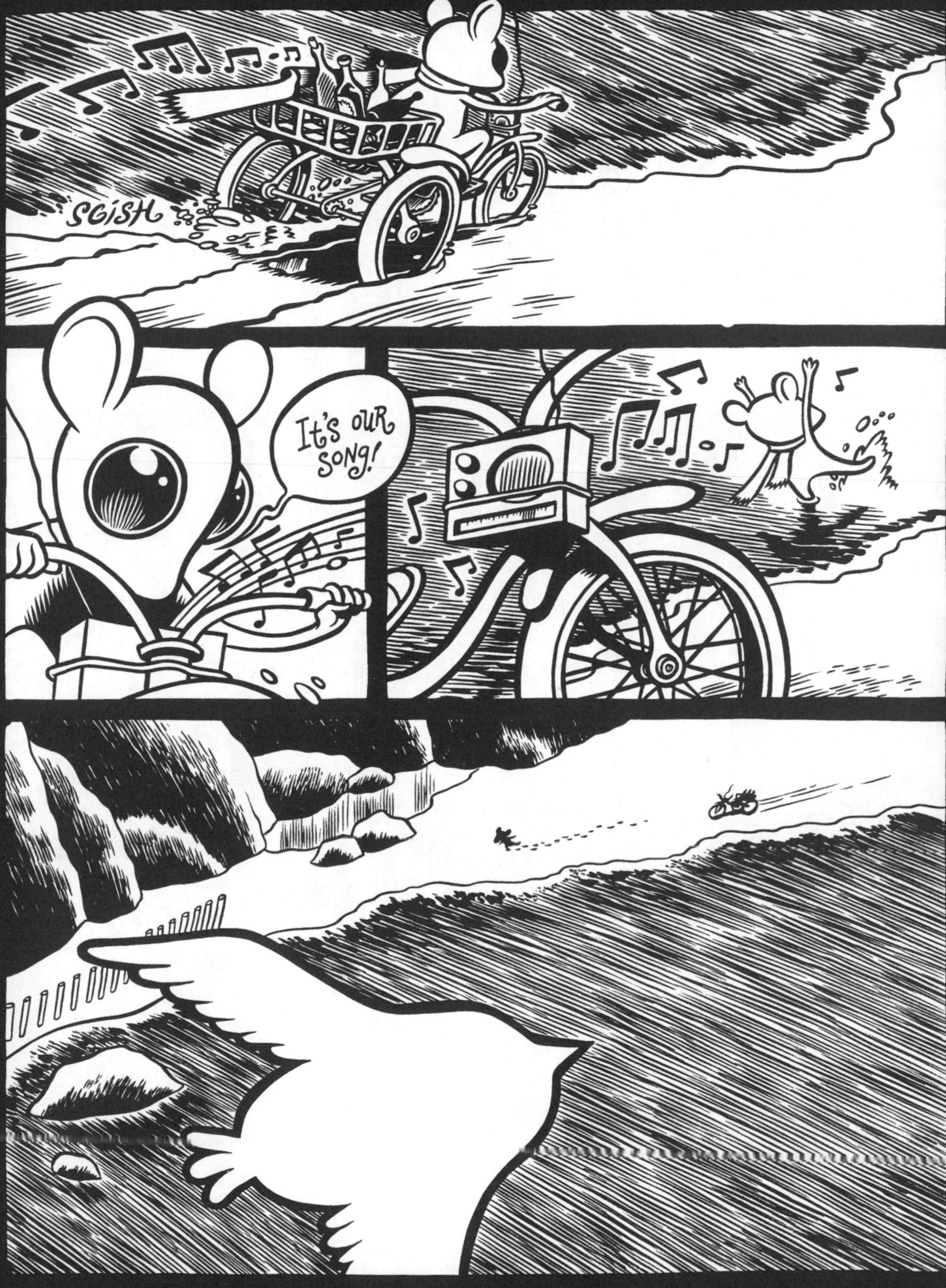
SQISH
It's OUR SONG!

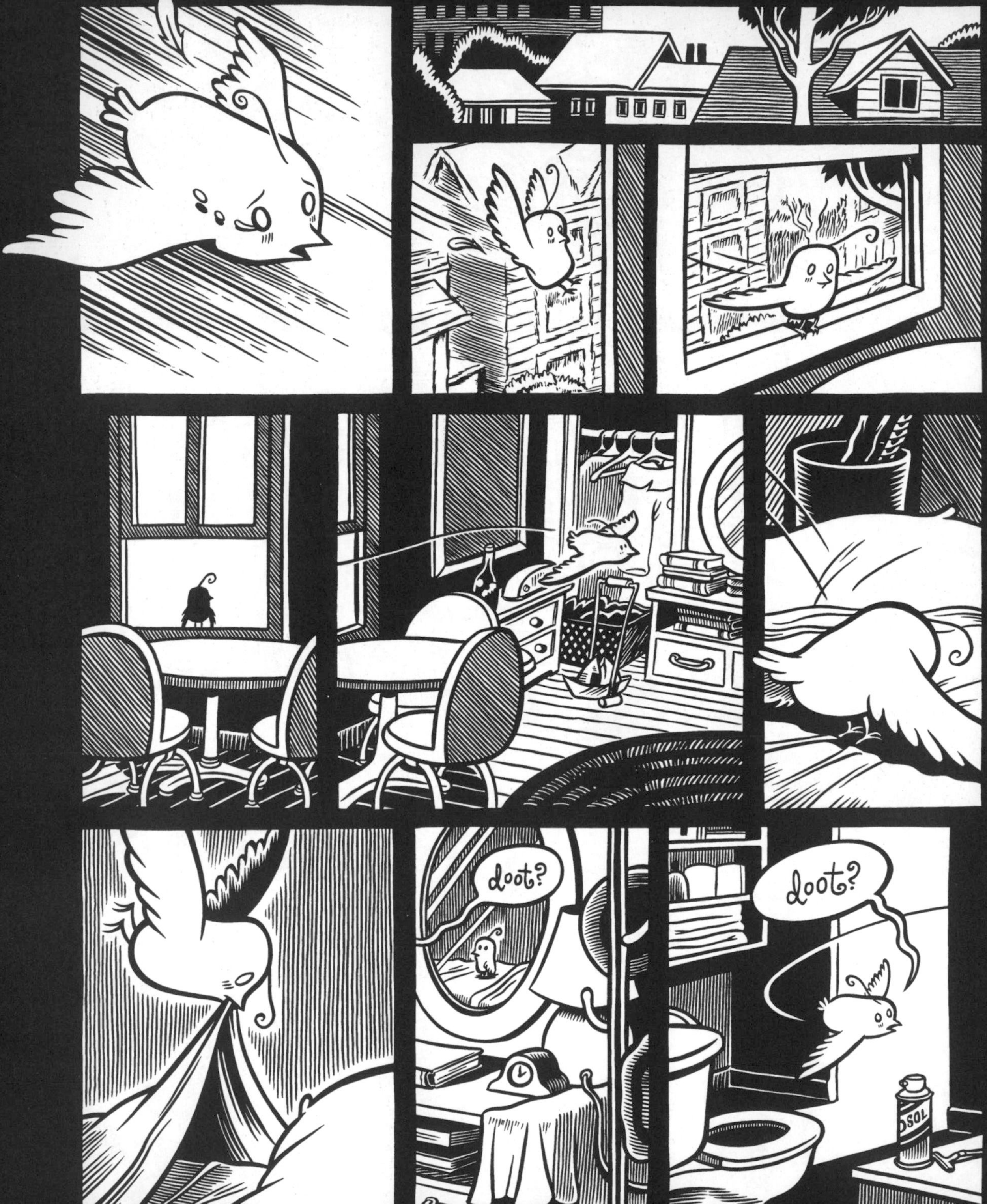
doot?
doot?
OSOL

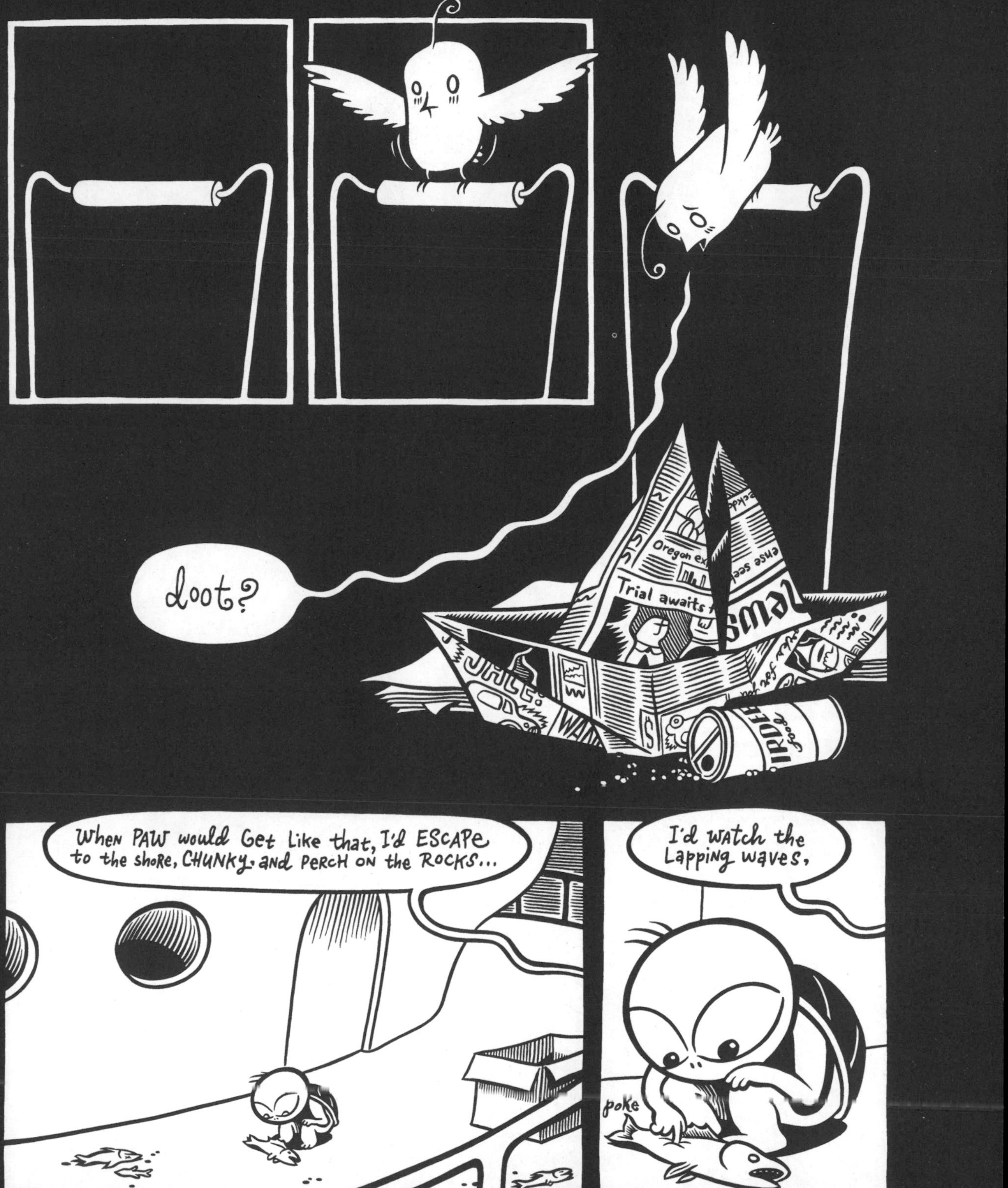
doot?
When PAW would Get Like that, I'd ESCAPE to the shore, CHUNKY, and PERCH ON the ROCKS...
I'd WATCH the Lapping waves,
poke

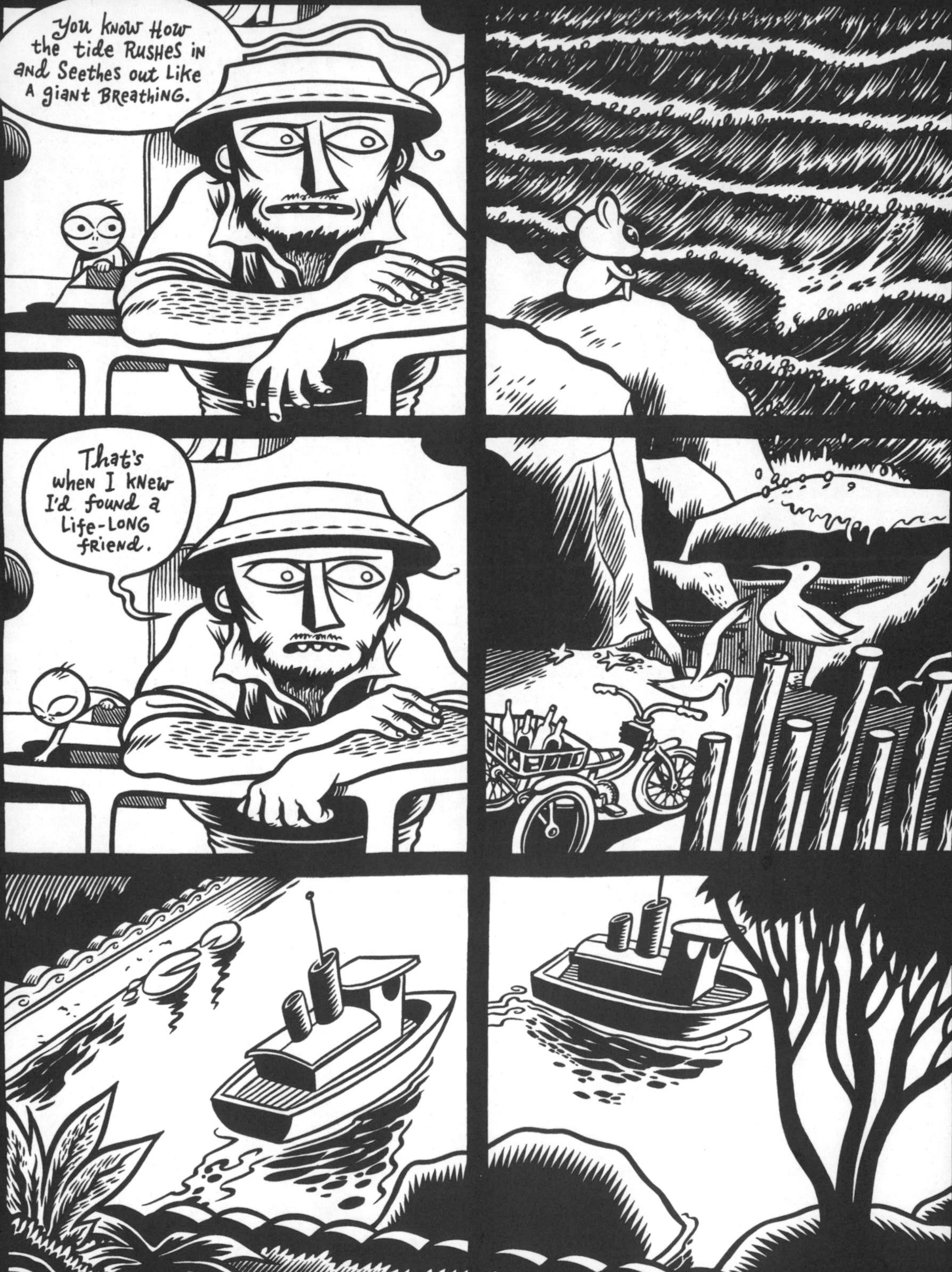
You know how the tide rushes in and seethes out like a giant breathing.
That's when I knew I'd found a life-long friend.

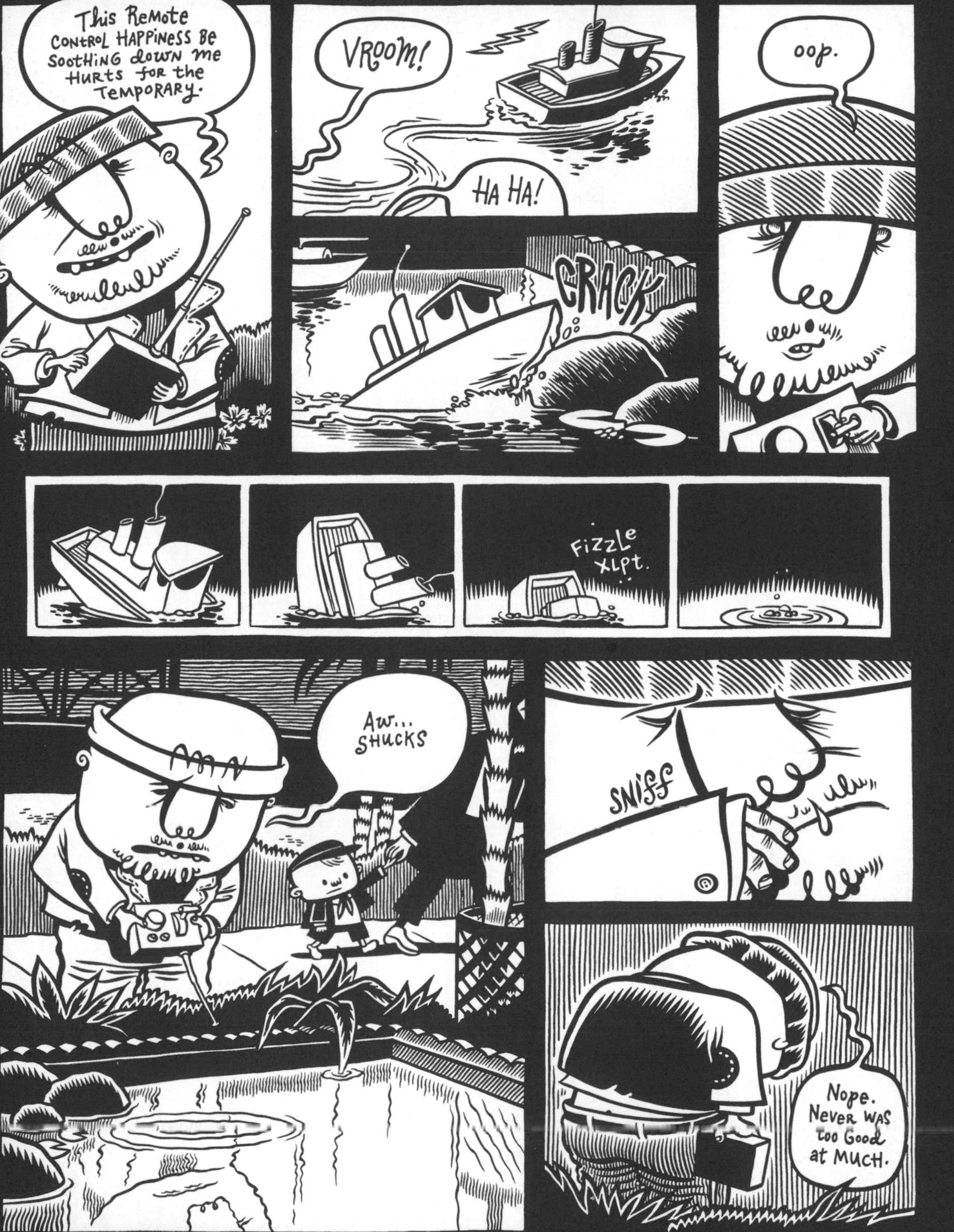

This Remote CONTROL HAPPINESS BE SOOTHING down me HURTS for the TEMPORARY.
VROOM!
HA HA!
oop.
CRACK
FIZZLE
XLPT.
AW... SHUCKS
SNIFF
Nope. NEVER WAS too Good at MUCH.

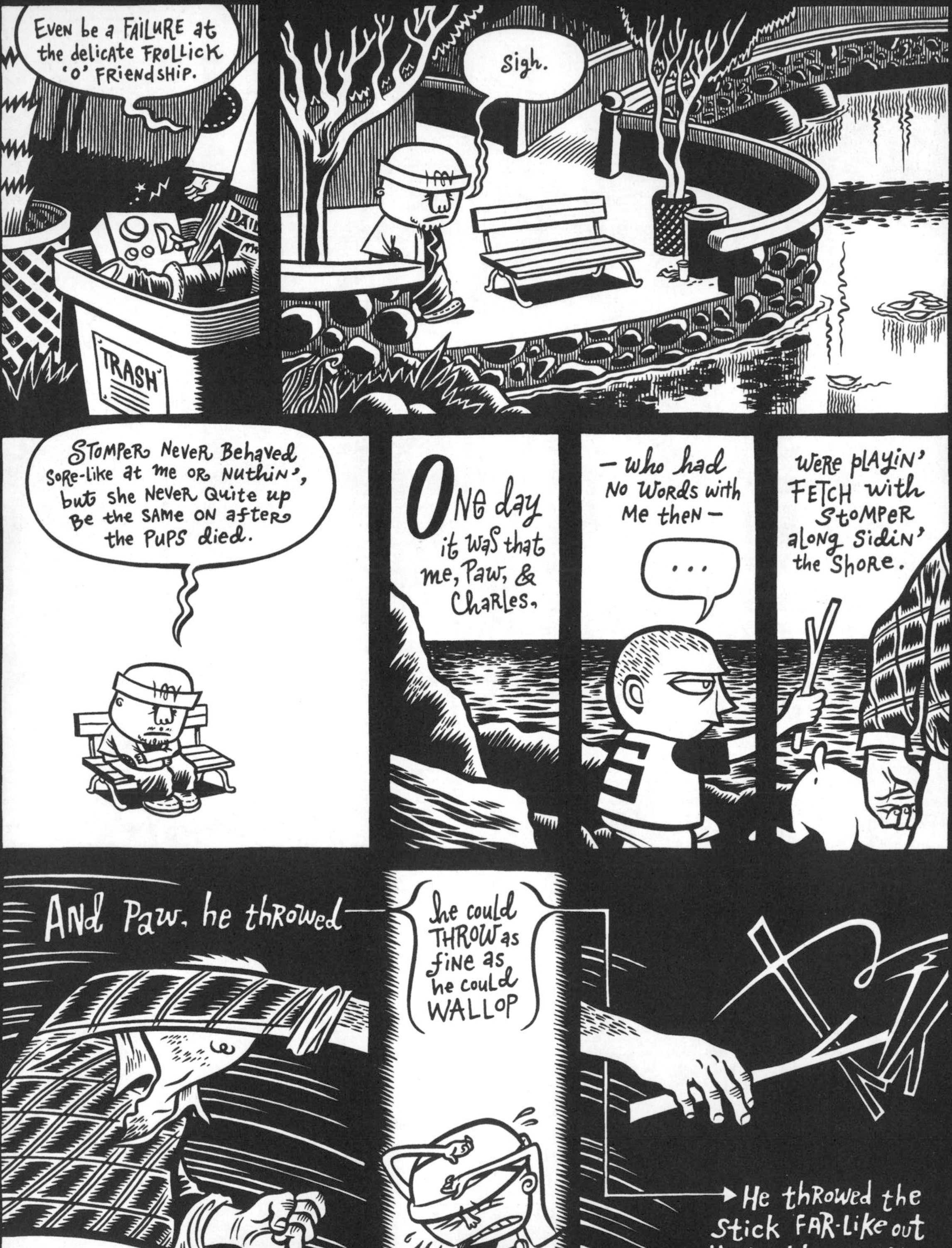

Even be a FAILURE at the delicate FROLLICK 'o' FRIENDSHIP.
TRASH
Sigh.
STOMPER NEVER Behaved SORE-like at me OR NUTHIN', but she NEVER Quite up Be the SAME ON after the PUPS died.
ONE day it was that me, Paw, & CharLes,
— who had No Words with Me then —
...
WERE PLAYIN' FETCH with STOMPER aLONG SidiN' the SHORE.
AND Paw, he throwed
he could THROW as fine as he could WALLOP
He throwed the stick FAR-Like out iNsto the oceaN.

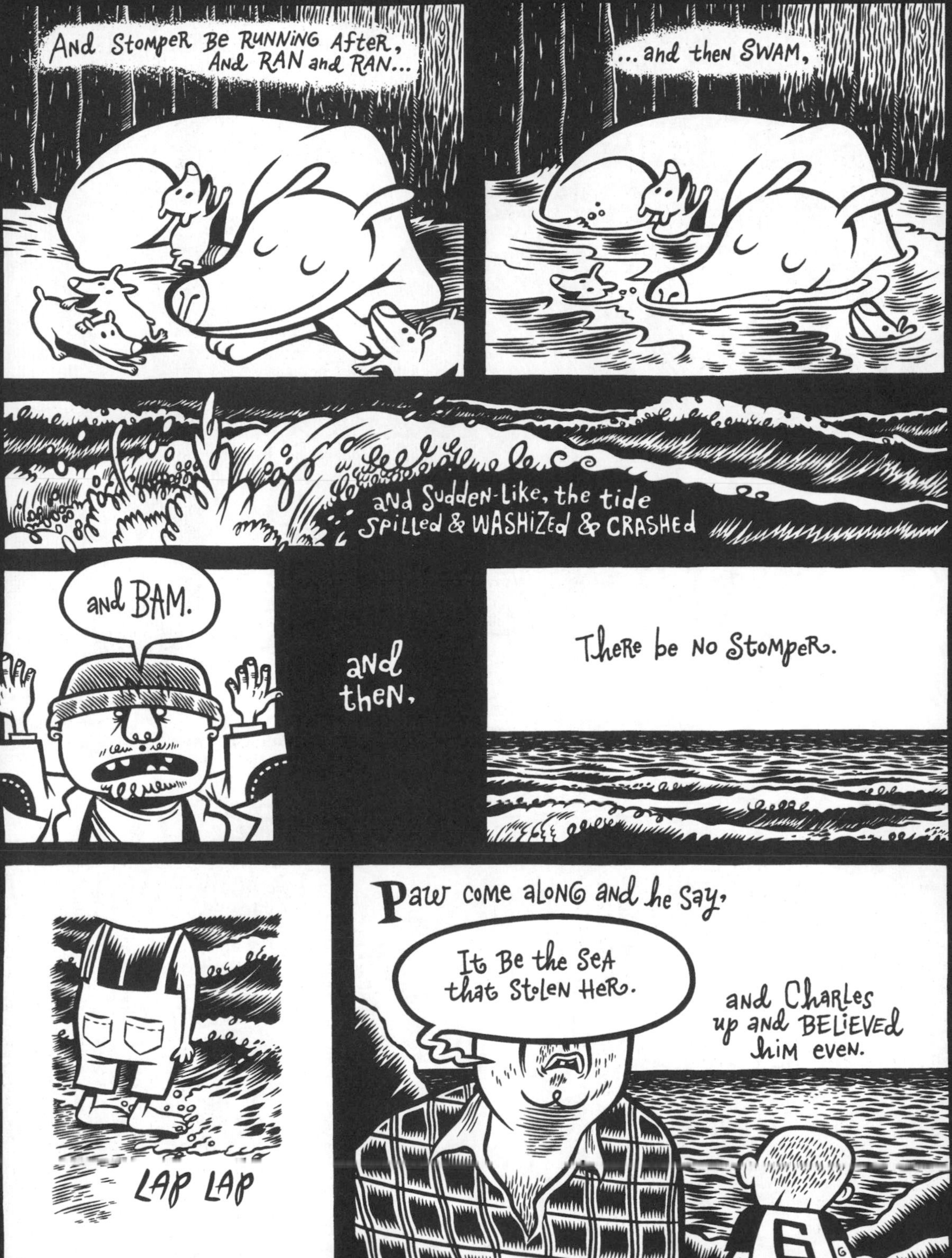

And Stomper Be Running After, And RAN and RAN...
...and then SWAM,
and Sudden-like, the tide spilled & WASHIZed & CRASHed
and BAM.
and then,
There be no Stomper.
LAP LAP
Paw come along and he say,
It Be the Sea that Stolen Her.
and Charles up and BELIEVED him even.
6

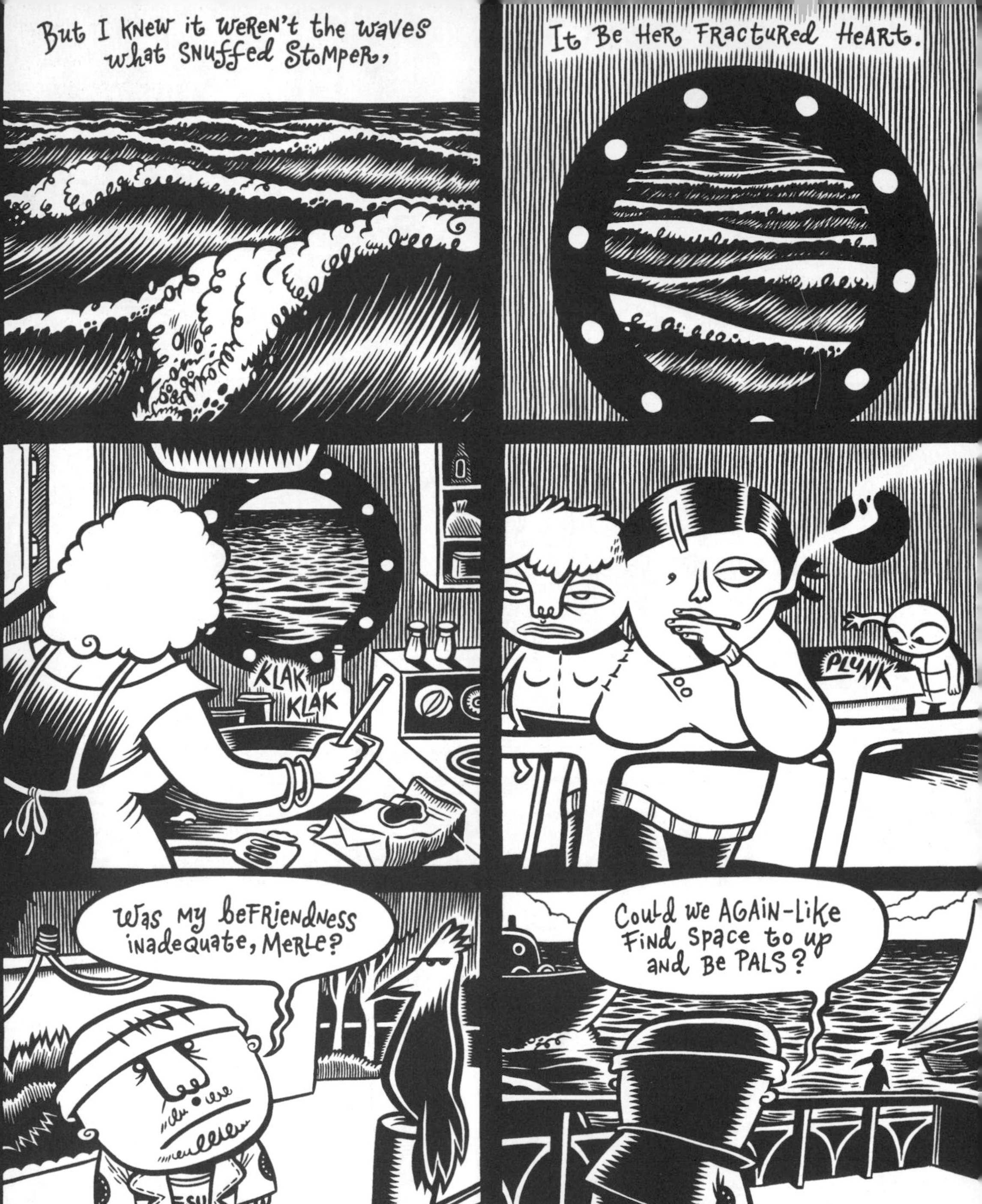
But I knew it weren't the waves what snuffed Stomper,
It be her fractured heart.
KLAK KLAK
PLUNK
Was my befriendness inadequate, Merle?
Could we AGAIN-like find space to up and be PALS?

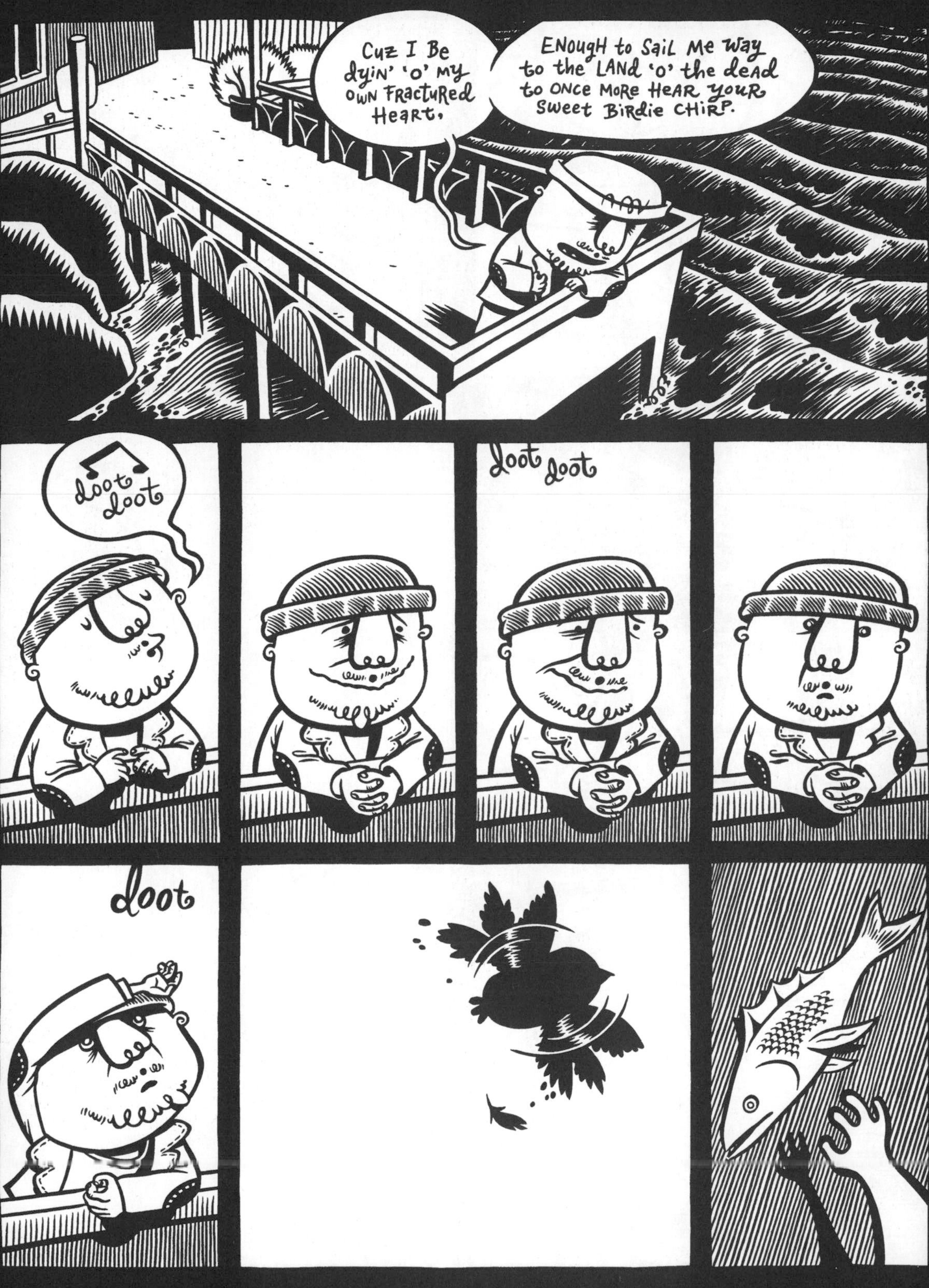
Cuz I Be dyin' 'o' my own Fractured Heart,
Enough to Sail Me way to the LAND 'o' the dead to once more hear your sweet Birdie Chirp.
doot doot
doot doot
doot

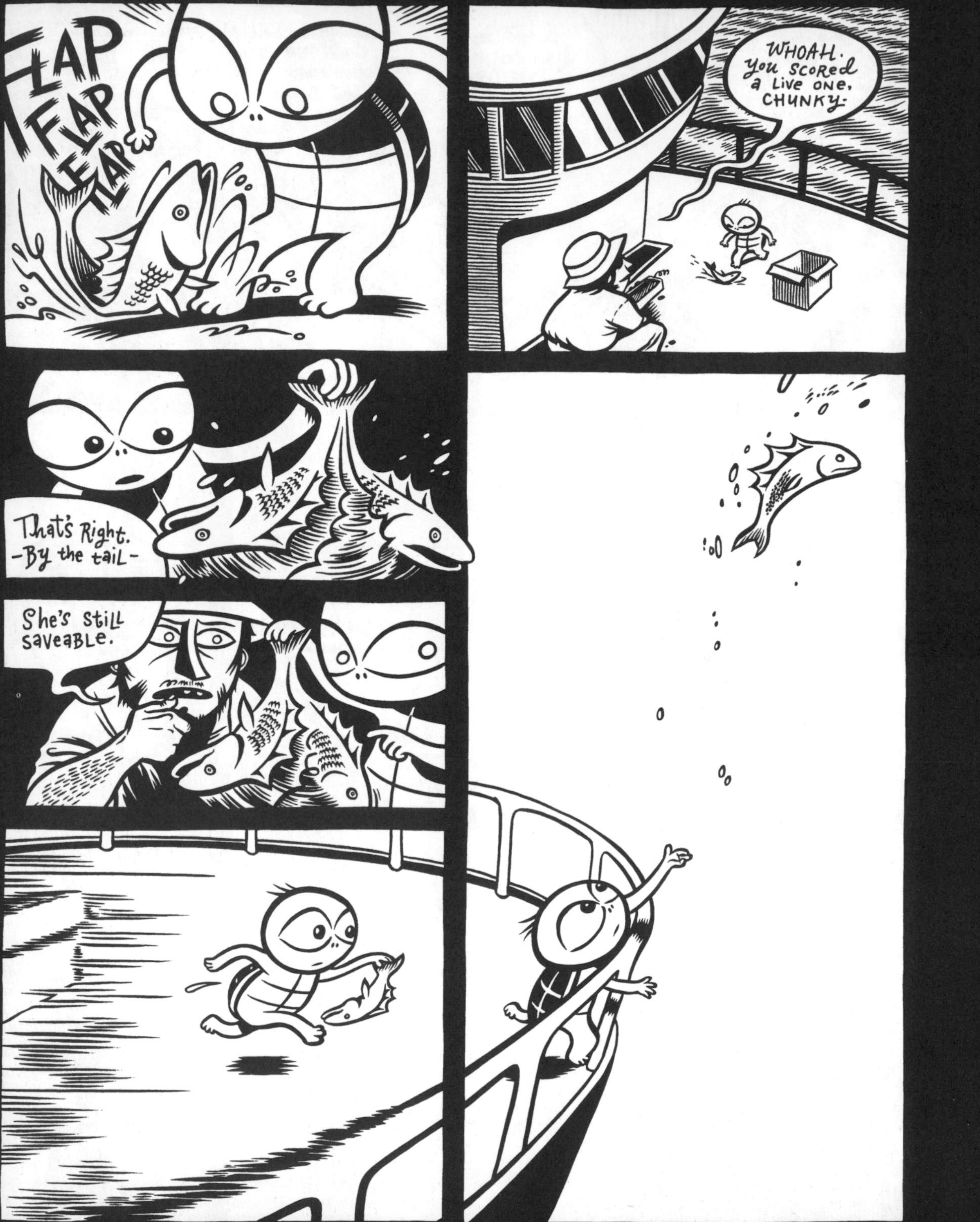
FLAP FLAP FLAP FLAP
WHOAH. You scored a live one, CHUNKY.
That's Right. -By the tail-
She's still saveable.

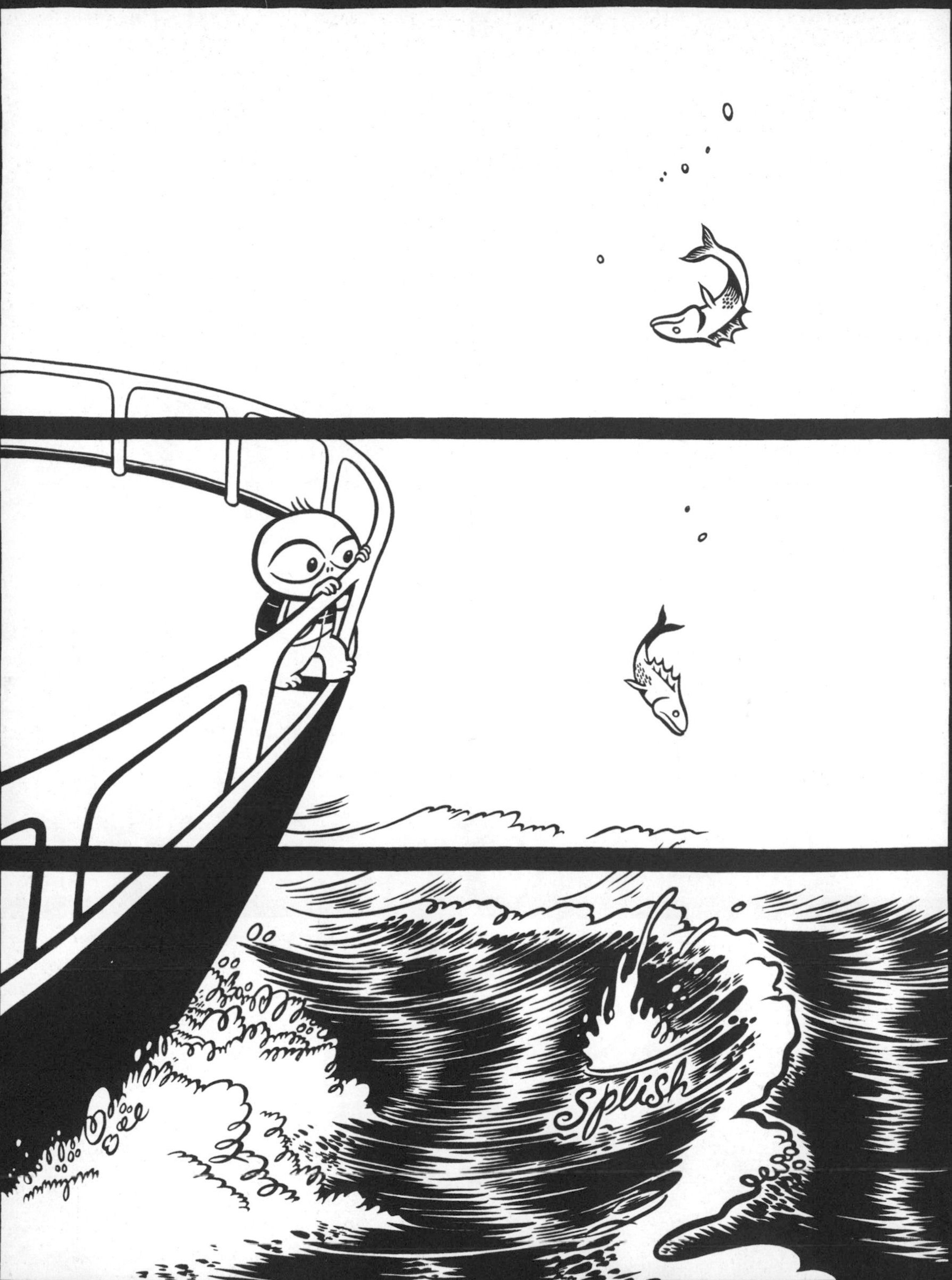
Splish

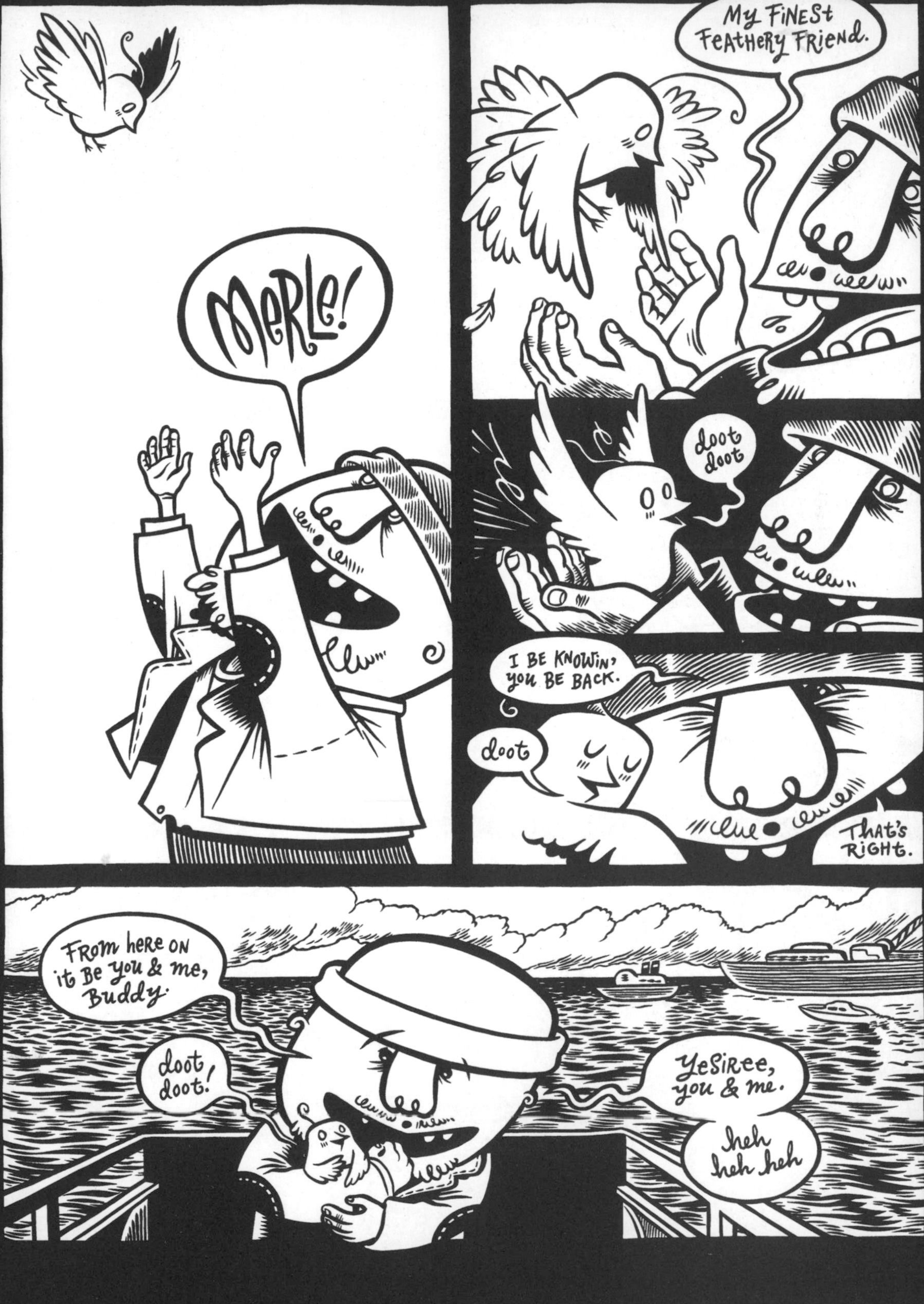

MERLE!
My FINEST FEATHERY FRIEND.
doot doot
I BE KNOWIN' YOU BE BACK.
doot
THAT'S RIGHT.
FROM here ON it Be you & me, Buddy.
doot, doot!
YeSiRee, you & me.
heh heh heh

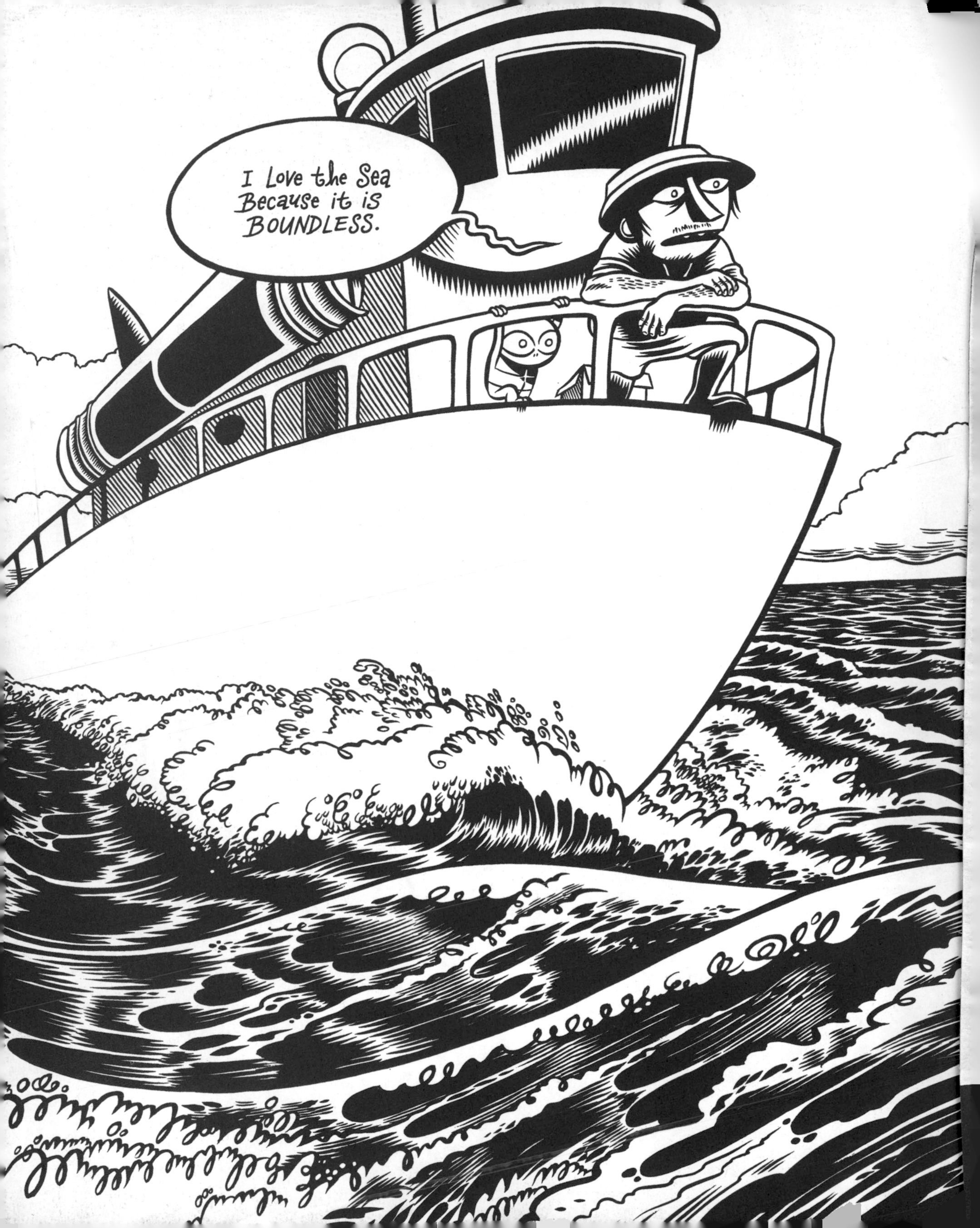
I Love the Sea Because it is BOUNDLESS.

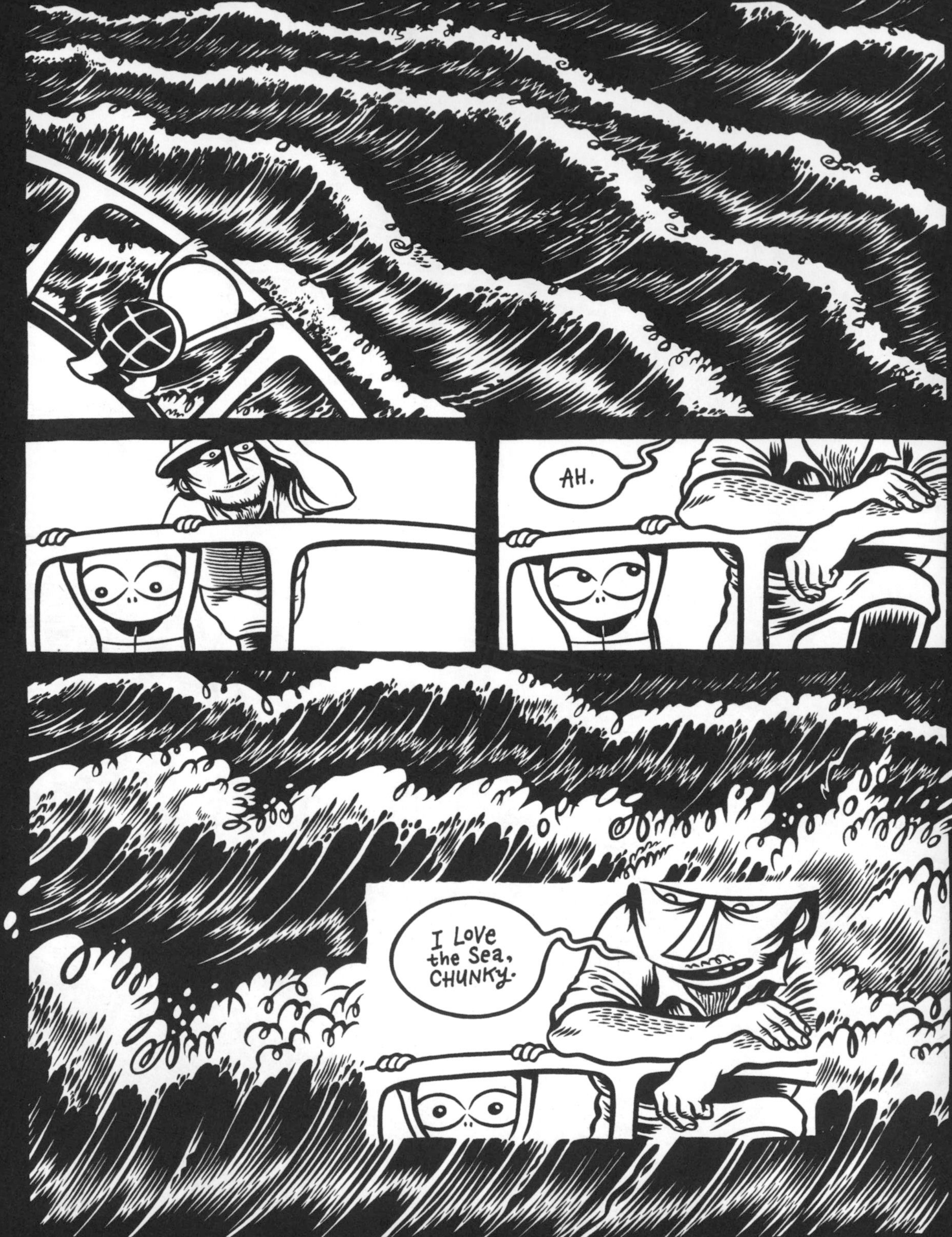
AH.
I LOVE the Sea, CHUNKY.

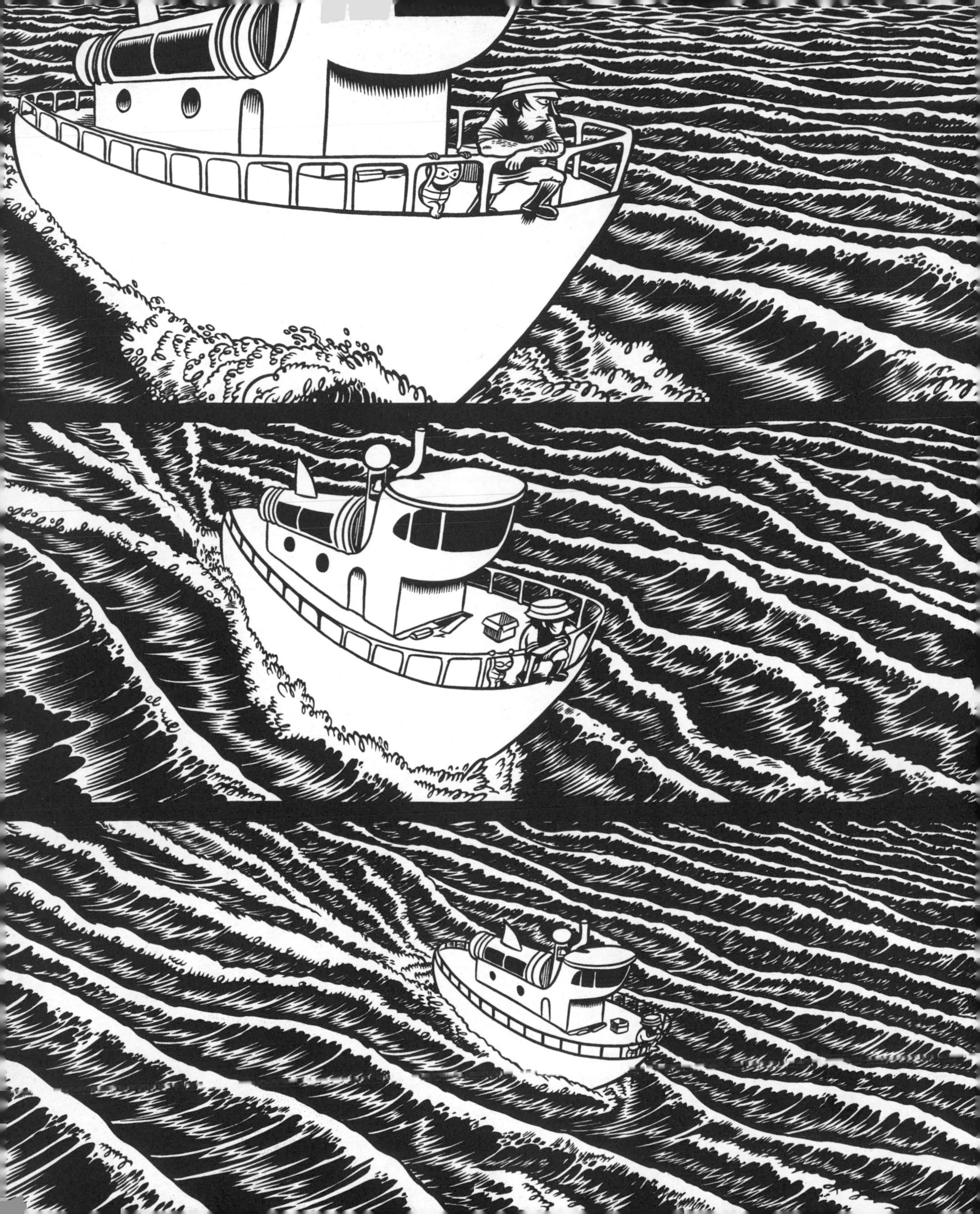

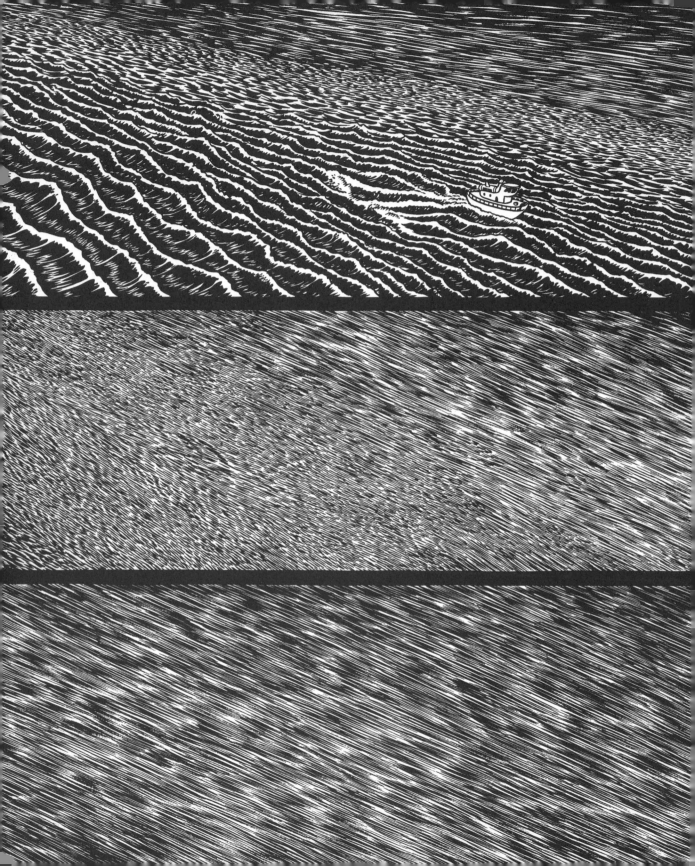

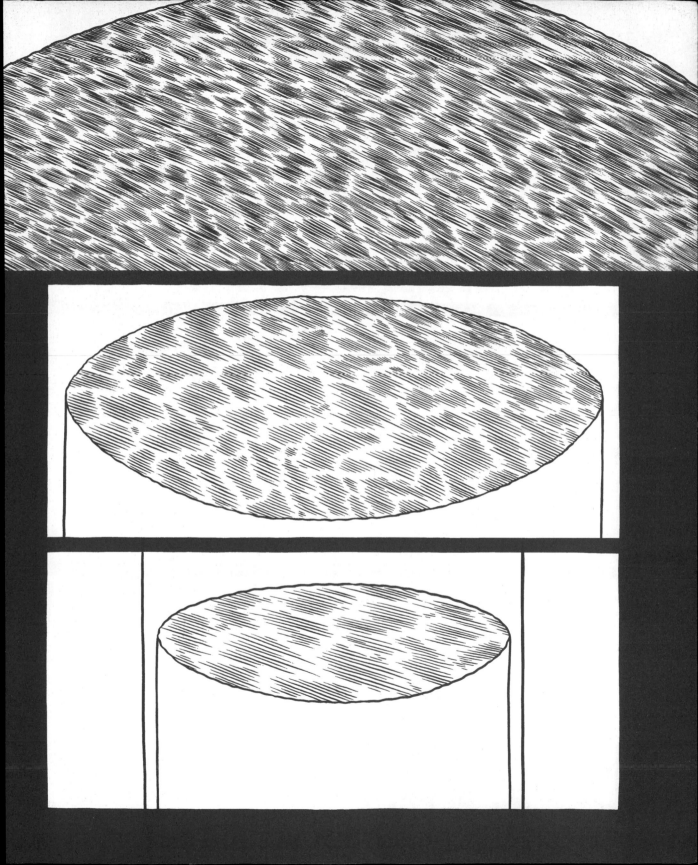

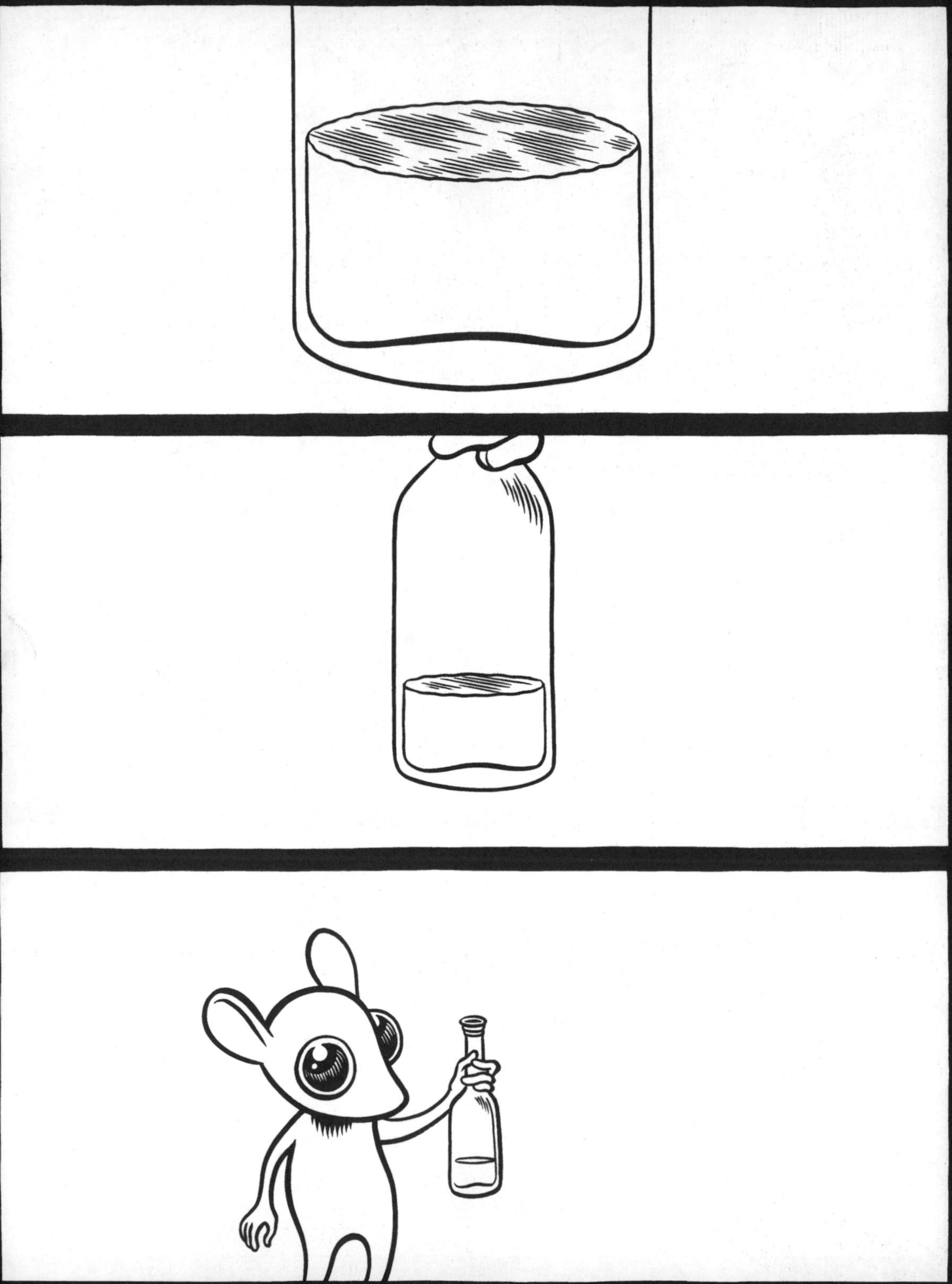

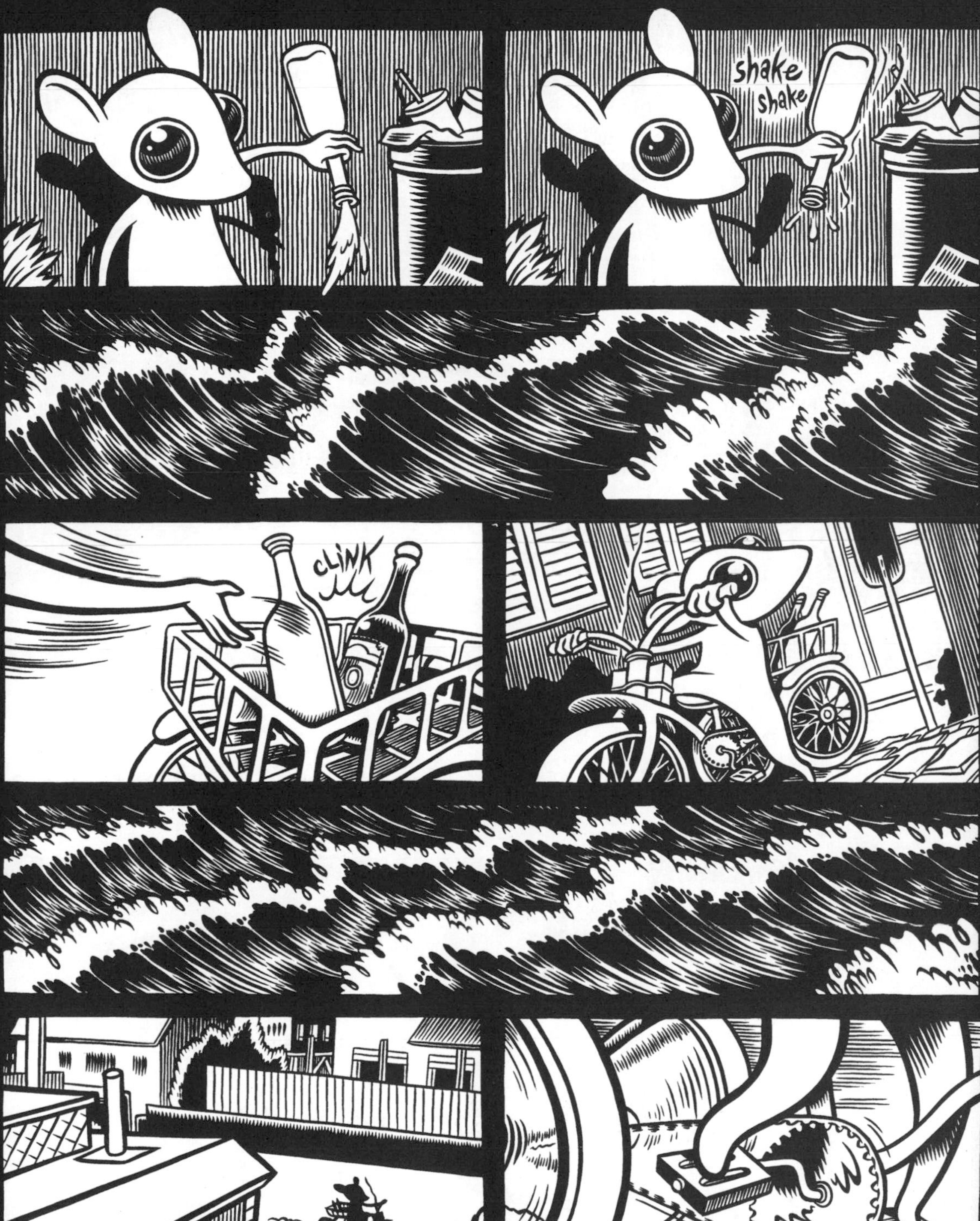
shake
shake
CLINK

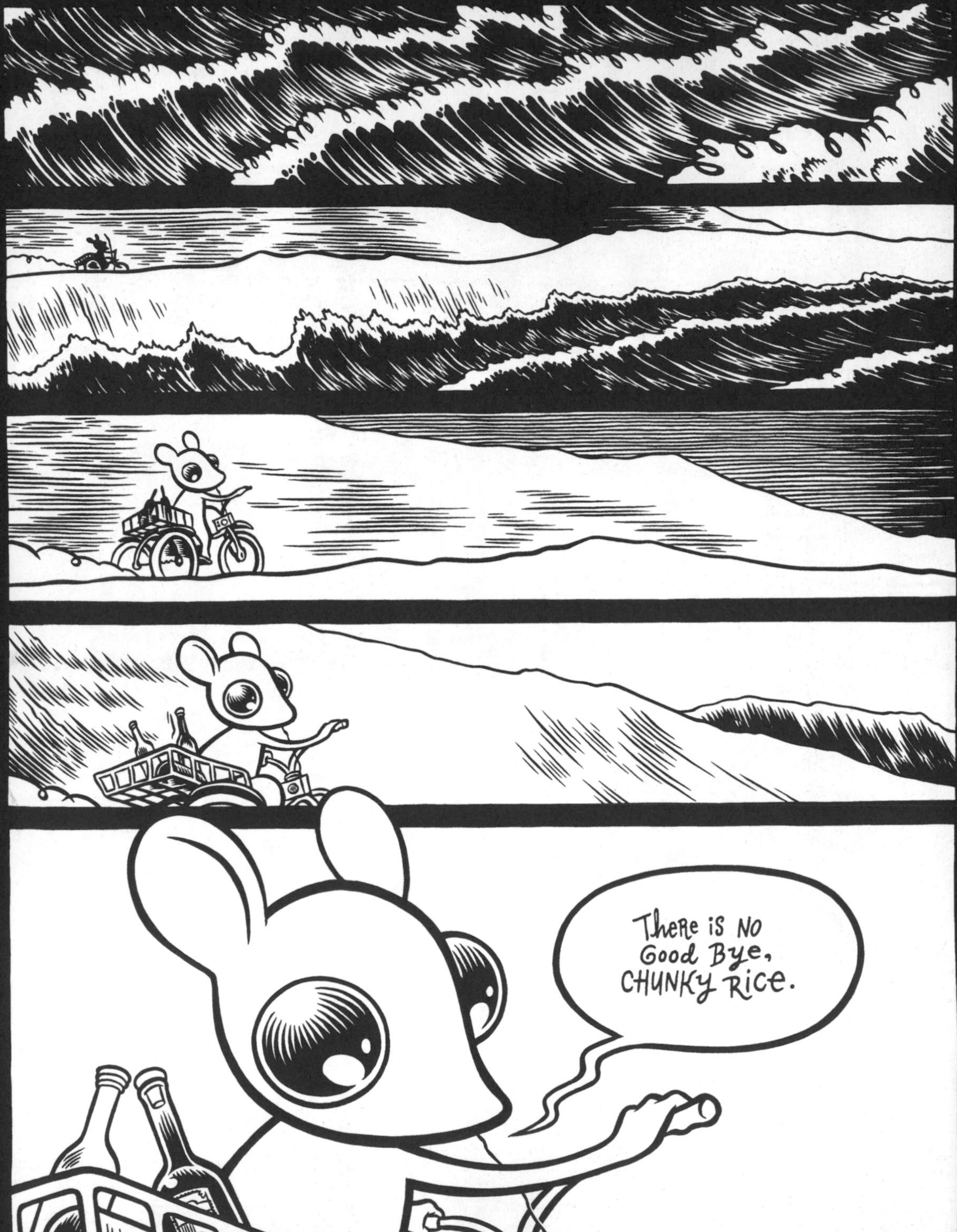
There is NO Good Bye, CHUNKY RICE.